New Edition

first certificate
expert

COURSEBOOK

Jan Bell • Roger Gower

Pearson Education Limited
Edinburgh Gate
Harlow
Essex CM20 2JE
England
and Associated Companies throughout the world.

www.pearsonELT.com/examsplace

© Pearson Education Limited 2005 and 2008

The right of Jan Bell and Roger Gower to be identified as authors of this Work has been asserted by them in accordance with the Copyright, Designs and Patents Act 1988.

First published 2003
New Edition published 2008
New Edition published 2012

ISBN: 978-1-4472-9231-4
Set in 10.5/13.5 Minion

Printed and boiund in Spain

Authors' Acknowledgements

With grateful thanks to Heather Jones, Bernie Hayden Fran Banks, Jacqui Robinson and Pietro Alongi for their work on the original edition; Ian Wood, Alison Ramsey and Alice Kasasian for their work on the second edition; and all the team at Longman.

Publishers' Acknowledgements

We are grateful to the following teachers whose input helped us to develop this material: Claudia Martin, Monica Sanin; Rita Zeinstejer (Argentina); John Bleasdale, Thomas Malvica, Nancy Stenson (Italy); Konrad Brzozowski, Aleksandra Gelner (Poland); Kamalakar Sirra, Ascension Villalba Varona (Spain); Rosita D'Lasselle (UK).

The publishers and authors would also like to thank the following for their feedback and comments during the development of the material:

Anne Alexander, Katerina Anastasaki, David Corkill, Rolf Donald, Marek Doskocz, Piotr Gralewski, Drew Hyde, Lucrecia Luque-Mortimer Nick Kenny, Jacky Newbrook, Nick Shaw, Arek Tkacz.

We are grateful to the following for permission to reproduce copyright material:

Atlantic Syndication for an extract adapted from "Plane Terror of the lifesaver at 35,000 ft" published in The Daily Mail 1st July 1997 copyright © Atlantic Syndication 1997; Emotions Greeting Cards for extracts adapted from HYPERLINK "http://www.emotionscards.com" www.emotionscards.com; EPA European Pressphoto Agency b.v. for a picture of a Mexican boy during hurricane Dean copyright © EPA 2007; Express Newspapers Plc for extract adapted from "The way we are" published in The Express Saturday Magazine on 19-25 September 1999; Guardian News & Media Ltd for an extract adapted from "Our lost childhood" by Lorna Martin published in The Observer 19th September 2006 and a screenshot from HYPERLINK "http://www.guardian.co.uk" www.guardian.co.uk 21st August 2007 copyright © The Guardian 2006, 2007; Independent News & Media Ltd for an extract adapted from "Me and my big mouth" by Andrew Buncombe published in The Independent 17th June 2006 copyright © The Independent 2006; Serena Mackesy for an extract adapted from "Straight from the horse's mouth" by Serena Mackesy published in The Independent 24th September 2000 copyright © Serena Mackesy; News International Syndication for extracts adapted from "Someone's got to do it" by Candida Crewe published in The Times 7th April 2001, "Teenager quids in as shop trips up over currency" by Helen Studd published in The Times 4th January 2002 and "Welcome to America" published on HYPERLINK "http://www.travel.timesonline.co.uk" www.travel.timesonline.co.uk 15th October 2006 copyright © NI Syndication, London 2001, 2002, 2006; Lewis Pugh and Plank PR for extracts about Lewis Pugh; and The Random House Group for an extract adapted from The Talented Mr Ripley by Patricia Highsmith published by William Heinemann. BBC Wildlife for an extract from "Tiritiri Matangi and Ulva Islands" by Tui De Roy in BBC Wildlife Travel Supplement April 2003 copyright © BBC Wildlife; Guardian News & Media Ltd for an extract adapted from "What's the big idea?" by Kate Mikhail published in OM Magazine 22nd September 2002 copyright © Guardian; A.M. Heath & Co Ltd for an extract from The Transit of Venus by Shirley Hazzard copyright © Shirley Hazzard 1998; Moving Mountains Trust for material adapted from HYPERLINK "http://www.movingmountains.org.uk/" www.movingmountains.org.uk; and Powell's Books for an extract adapted from an interview with Thomas Keller by Dave Welch.

In some instances we have been unable to trace the owners of copyright material and we would appreciate any information that would enable us to do so.

Photo Acknowledgements

The publisher would like to thank the following for their kind permission to reproduce their photographs:

(Key: b-bottom; c-centre; l-left; r-right; t-top)

Acestock.com: 135br; ©Age Concern England: 122bl; Alamy Images: Adrian Sherratt 11c, 93bl; Alex Segre 163bc; Ambient Images Inc 79c; apply pictures 31r; Blend Images 117tl; Bubbles Photolibrary 35; Dave Lidwell 18tr; Dave Porter 110; Digital Vision 140; Education Photos 31bc; Ian Shaw 9br, 31tc; Jenny Matthews 31l, 123; Joe Tree 73tc; John Powell 126; John Sturrock 23br; Juergen Henkelmann Photography 14b; LMR Group 26l; Marc Hill 9tr; Mark Lewis 51b; Photofusion Picture Library 133b; The Photolibrary Wales 32; uptheres 65l; Ardea: Ardea 47; Axiom Photographic Agency Ltd: Axiom/Tania Cagnoni 18l; BBC Photo Library: 118; BBC Worldwide Ltd : by Brian Bates & John Cleese,2000 67tc; by Susan Greenfield,2000 67bc; Camera Press Ltd: 39; Jamie Kingham 25; Photography by FOTOBLITZ/stills/GAMMA 91t; CartoonStock: Cornered / Mike Baldwin 124b; Corbis: 59r, 96, 121tl, 135tc, 163cr, 163tr, 171r, 172, 212r, 213tl; Adrian Williams/Zefa 105l; Ariel Skelley 135tl; Ashley Cooper 28; Cameron 79b; Carl & Ann Purcell 56r; Chuck Savage 16l; ©Corbis 33; Corbis 45tr; Dideon Mendel 131; Digital Art 65tr; Don Mason 11t; Eric Cahan 105cl; ESA/NASA/HANDOUT/epa 69; Franz-marc/Frei 87l; Hill Street Studios/Blend Images 149br; Jed Share and Kaoru 107bl; John Springer Collection 115br; Jon Feingersh/Blend Images 107tr; Katy Winn 81b; Kevin Dodge 149tr; Meeke/Zefa 107br; Michael Brennan 115bc; Mitchell Gerber 115tc; Neil Rabinowitz 26r; Patrik Giardino 11b; Pulp Photography 56l; Randy Faris 16bc; Reuters 82/1; Richard A. Cooke 157r; Rohit Dhingra 105r; Rune Hellestad 82/6; Sagel & Kranefeld/zefa 73br; Todd Davidson/Illustration Works 56c; Tony Demin 117tr; Demon Imaging: 212l, 221tl; Getty Images: 2006 CBS Worldwide Inc 82/4; 2006/Alexander Tamargo 83; 40tl, 50, 59cl, 59tl, 93br, 93tl, 93tr, 107tl, 121tr, 133t, 149bl, 149tc, 149tl, 163tl, 166, 171l, 211l, 220l, 221bl, 221br; AFP 53, 73tr, 92, 124; AFP/Stringer 58tr; Andreanna Seymore 16r; Andy Sacks 23bl; Carlos Lopez-Barillas 143r; Chien-Min Chung 161; Dave Hogan 13; Dave M. Benett 19, 81l; David Madison 223tr; Frederick M. Brown/Stringer 115tr; Gareth Cattermole 129t; Jeremy Walker 121b; Justin Sullivan 73tl; Macduff Everton 18br; Matt Cardy/Stringer 95; Michael Becker 81t; ML Harris 73cl; National Geographic 77b; Neil Emmerson 223br; Time & Life Pictures 152; Tobi Corney 23tr; Ronald Grant Archive: 164l; EL DESEO 91b; Universal Pictures/Dream Works 115tl; Guzelian Ltd: 151; Robert Harding World Imagery: 23tl, 37b, 37t, 40r, 59bl, 59c, 149cl; Harper Collins Publishers Ltd: by Steve Jones 67t; ©Honda: 213 (Honda); iStockphoto: Alex Slobodkin 73cr; Jaguar: 213 (Jaguar saloon), 213 (Jaguar); Jeep Crysler: 213 (Jeep); John Birdsall Photography: 221tr; Kobal Collection Ltd: 85; Lebrecht Music and Arts Photo Library: 210l; Memories Picture library: 139t; David Smith 139b; Nick Gordon: Nick Gordon 46; Oxfam: 122bc; Oxford Salter's: 98t; PA Photos: 213tr; Corrado Giambalro/AP 63; Penguin Books Ltd: 67b, 164r; Photodisc: 135bl; Pictor International: 40bl, 48; Popperfoto.com: 77t, 175t; PunchStock: 163tc; agefotostock 73bl; Blend Images, LLC 223bl; Corbis 128b; Getty Images 9l, 16tc; Image Source 223tl; Jupiter Images Corp. 58tl; Redferns Music Picture Library: 210r; Mike Prior 82/2; peter Noble 82/5; Renault: 213 (Renault); Retna Pictures Ltd: 82/3; James Quinton 115bl; Rex Features: 51tl, 65br, 87r, 163bl, 175b, 209r; Andrew MacColl 81r; Science and Society Picture Library: 70l, 70r; Science Photo Library Ltd: 148, 150; Shelter: 122tl; Sue Greenhill: 221cr; SuperStock: 135tr; TopFoto: 89b; Clive Barda/ArenaPal 89t; David Wimsett/uppa.co.uk 143l; Fujifotos/The Image Works 157l; Spectrum/HIP 79t; Volvo: 213 (Volvo); WWF-UK: reg charity no. 1081247. A company limited by guarantee no. 4016725. Panda symbol*1986 WWF World Wide Fund for Nature (formerly World Wildlife Fund).*WWF Registered trademark 122r

Picture Research by: Ann Thomson

The Publisher has made every effort but has been unsuccessful in locating the copyright owners of the following images. We would be grateful for any information that would allow us to update our records:

37 (inset), 45l, 49, 51tr, 138, 149cr, 163br, 167, 209l, 211r

Every effort has been made to trace the copyright holders and we apologise in advance for any unintentional omissions. We would be pleased to insert the appropriate acknowledgement in any subsequent edition of this publication.

Picture Research by: Ann Thomson

Illustrated by Juan Alvarez, Francis Blake, Sandy Nichols, Russ Wilms (from Three in a Box)

Cover design by Raven Design

Designed by Jackie Hill at 320 Design Ltd

Exam overview

► See page 178 for Exam reference

The Cambridge First Certificate in English has five papers. Each paper receives 20 per cent of the total marks and each has equal value. The pass mark is based on an overall mark (you do not need to pass every paper to pass the exam). There are three pass grades (A, B and C) and two fail grades (D and E). Normally, you need to get about 60 per cent to achieve a grade C.

Paper	Task type	Task description
Paper 1: Reading • 1 hour • Three parts • 30 reading comprehension questions in total	**Part 1:** multiple choice (8 questions). **Part 2:** gapped text (7 questions). **Part 3:** multiple matching (15 questions).	**Part 1:** answering four-option multiple-choice questions on a text. **Part 2:** completing a gapped text with sentences which have been removed and placed in jumbled order. **Part 3:** matching information to 4–6 different texts (or different parts of a text).
Paper 2: Writing • 1 hour 20 minutes • Two tasks (one compulsory, the other a choice from five options)	**Part 1:** letter or email (compulsory). **Part 2:** one writing task from a choice of five.	**Part 1:** using information provided to write a letter or email. (120–150 words) **Part 2:** carrying out a writing task, using appropriate format and style. (120–180 words) Questions 2–4 may include a letter, an article, an essay, a report, a review, a story. Question 5 is a two-option question based on the set books.
Paper 3: Use of English • 45 minutes • Four parts • 42 questions in total	**Part 1:** multiple-choice cloze (12 questions). **Part 2:** open cloze (12 questions). **Part 3:** word formation (10 questions). **Part 4:** key word transformation. (8 questions).	**Part 1:** choosing a word or phrase from four options to fill in gaps in a text. Vocabulary. **Part 2:** filling in gaps in a text with an appropriate word. Grammar. **Part 3:** changing the form of a given word to make it fit the gaps in a text. Vocabulary. **Part 4:** using a given word to complete a sentence so that it means the same as a previous sentence. Grammar and vocabulary.
Paper 4: Listening • Approximately 40 minutes • Four parts • 30 questions in total	**Part 1:** multiple choice (8 questions). **Part 2:** sentence completion (10 questions). **Part 3:** multiple matching (5 questions). **Part 4:** multiple-choice (7 questions).	**Part 1:** eight short unrelated extracts, each with a multiple-choice question with three options. **Part 2:** a longer text or monologue with sentence completion questions. **Part 3:** five short related monologues to match to a list of six options. **Part 4:** a longer text or monologue with three-option multiple-choice questions.
Paper 5: Speaking • Approximately 14 minutes • Four parts	**Part 1:** interview, giving personal information (3 minutes). **Part 2:** individual 'long turn', giving information and expressing opinions (1 minute each candidate). **Part 3:** collaborative task, exchanging information and ideas (3–4 minutes). **Part 4:** discussion, developing the topic from Part 3 (4 minutes).	**Part 1:** examiner asks each candidate questions about themselves. **Part 2:** each candidate, individually, compares and contrasts two photos, and comments briefly on the other candidate's photo. **Part 3:** each candidate works with a partner to discuss a task, using pictures or diagrams. **Part 4:** the examiner leads a discussion between the two candidates, developing the topic of Part 3.

Contents

Contents

First Certificate Examination: Top 20 Questions

1 How many marks are needed to pass the exam?
To pass the exam with a grade C, you need around 60 per cent of the total marks.

2 Do I have to pass each paper in order to pass the exam?
No. Each paper doesn't have a pass or fail mark. The final grade A, B, C, D or E is arrived at by adding the weighted marks from all the papers together.

3 Are marks deducted for wrong answers?
No. If you're not sure, make a guess, you may be right.

4 Am I allowed to use a dictionary?
No.

5 In Paper 1 (Reading), Part 3 has more questions, so is it more important?
No. The three parts are equally weighted. In Parts 1 and 2, each question = 2 marks, whereas in Part 3, each question = 1 mark.

6 In Paper 1 (Reading), how long should I take on each question?
This is up to you. You can do the tasks in any order. Knowing how to use your time well is a part of the test.

7 In Paper 2 (Writing), what happens if I don't use all the given information in Part 1?
You will lose marks. The examiners are looking for both the correct information and good language. So read the question, the input text and the handwritten notes very carefully.

8 In Paper 2 (Writing), how should I lay out the addresses?
Don't include addresses. If you do include them, the examiners will ignore them, as this is not part of the task.

9 In Paper 2 (Writing), what happens if I write too many or too few words?
The word count is given as a guide only. Don't waste time counting; the examiners don't, they are more interested in your English! It is unlikely that answers under 120 words will contain enough information/ideas to fulfil the task. Over-long answers are more likely to contain mistakes. Plan your time so that you write about the right amount and have time to check what you have written.

10 In Paper 3 (Use of English), what happens if I make a small mistake in a key word transformation?
There are 2 marks for each answer, so you could still get 1 mark even if there was a small error.

11 In Paper 3 (Use of English), Parts 2, 3 and 4, if I'm not sure, can I give two alternative answers?
If there are two answers, and one of them is wrong, no marks are given. So, it's better to decide which of your answers is best!

12 In Paper 3 (Use of English), Part 4, do contractions count as one word or two?
Two, e.g. *don't* = two words, *do* + *not*.

13 What happens if I misspell a word in Paper 3 (Use of English), Parts 2, 3 and 4?
All spelling must be correct in Paper 3.

14 What happens if I misspell a word in Paper 4 (Listening)?
As long as the word is recognisable, you will get a mark. Spelling is not tested in Paper 4.

15 How many times will I hear each recording in Paper 4?
Each text is played twice.

16 In Paper 4 (Listening), Part 2, do I have to use the words in the recording or other words?
The word(s) you need to write are heard in the recording and are heard in the same order as the questions.

17 In Paper 4 (Listening), Part 2, what happens if my answer is too long to fit on the answer sheet?
Most answers are single words, numbers or groups of 2–3 words. If you think the answer is longer, then it is probably the wrong answer. If you write information which is not the answer in addition to the answer, you will not get the mark, as you have not shown that you know exactly what the answer is.

18 In Paper 5 (Speaking), do I have to go with another student? Can I choose my partner?
You cannot be examined alone as the ability to discuss with another student is being tested in Part 3. In some centres you can choose your partner, in others not. You should ask the local organiser. Don't forget that in Parts 1, 2 and 4 of the test, you talk to the examiner, not to your partner.

19 Is it a good idea to prepare what you are going to say in Part 1?
It's a good idea to practise, but don't forget that the examiners give marks for natural communication in English. If you give a prepared speech which doesn't answer the examiner's question, you will lose marks.

20 What if my partner makes lots of mistakes, or doesn't talk in Part 3?
Don't worry. The examiners will help if necessary. Don't forget, you are not in competition with your partner. If you can help them, this will impress the examiners. Remember that Part 3 is about interaction, so you have to ask and answer questions as well as say what you think.

Lifestyles

Overview

- **Reading:** skimming and scanning
- **Language development 1:** present and past habits
- **Writing:** an informal email (Paper 2 Part 2)
- **Speaking:** comparing and contrasting photos (Paper 5 Part 2)
- **Listening:** skills: listening for gist and specific information
- **Language development 2:** comparatives and superlatives
- **Use of English 1:** key word transformations (Paper 3 Part 4)
- **Use of English 2:** multiple-choice cloze (Paper 3 Part 1)
- **Language development 3:** collocations: adjectives and nouns

Lead-in

- Look at the extract from the *Longman Exams Dictionary*. Mark the key points that define *lifestyle*.

> **life·style** /ˈlaɪfstaɪl/ *n* [C] the way a person or group of people lives, including the place they live in, the things they own, the kind of job they do, and the activities they enjoy: *Regular exercise is part of a **healthy lifestyle**.*

- The photos show typical aspects of a student's lifestyle in the UK. Which would you most/least enjoy? Why?

- Think of one adjective that describes your lifestyle best.

Family life

Reading

Before you read

Skimming

Scanning

1 Look at the title of the article opposite and the introduction. In what ways can parents be 'pushy'?

2 a Skim the article and match the subheadings 1–3 with each section. In section A, the main ideas have been underlined for you.
   1 They stay in too much.
   2 We expose our children to as many different activities as possible.
   3 Childhood should be a time to be free.

  b Underline the parts of sections B and C which contain the main ideas.

3 You are going to scan the text to answer the questions below.

  a Look at the example question. The highlighted words in section A of the text link to the key words in the question, which are also highlighted.

  b Answer questions 1–13. The key words are highlighted for you.

Which section or sections mention(s) the following?

- the importance of practising new skills if you want to improve | **0** | **A**
- the benefits to children of having a computer | **1**
- the practical difficulties of getting children to after-school activities | **2**
- parents enjoying 'fun time' with their children | **3** | **4**
- children feeling under pressure to succeed | **5**
- the dangers of children being expected to do something they don't want to | **6**
- the worry of letting children be independent | **7**
- limiting time spent playing computer games | **8** | **9**
- playing music for pleasure | **10**
- the difficulty of being a 'one parent family' | **11**
- parents' fear of technology | **12**
- competitive parents | **13**

---

  c Compare and justify your answers. Which words and phrases in the text link to the key words in the questions?
     EXAMPLE: Question 1: *good way to keep in touch… keep up her Spanish*

Vocabulary

4 Look at the underlined words and guess what they mean.

Discussion

5 Which family's lifestyle is most similar to/different from yours?

Our lost childhood?

Last week a group of teachers, authors and psychologists said video games and 'pushy parents' were robbing children of their happiest years. But is that true? Here we speak to three very different families.

A The Thomases

Do our children like to chill out in front of the TV or computer or with Nintendo games? Absolutely, if they are allowed to because they are just like all modern children all over the world. But there has to be a balance.

Parents need to invest time so that they can give their children the chance to try out as many different things as they can afford to. It's important that they don't push them into activities, though, just because they themselves wanted to be a footballer or a ballet dancer. That's damaging.

Both our boys play football, for a club and the school, so they train a couple of times a week and play at the weekend. Charlie also plays basketball and the drums. William learns the electric guitar and Laura sings and plays the guitar and does kickboxing classes. They also go to trampolining lessons. But we make it clear to them that if they want to do well at something they need to work hard and keep doing it over and over again until they get better at it.

There's only one evening when someone is not out, and that's Friday. It's spent eating pizzas and deciding on the logistics of how we are going to get each child to their different classes over the weekend.

B The Luckhursts

The best thing you can give your children is time. Proper time. Not a few snatched minutes here and there while you rush them off to ballet or violin lessons, but time spent playing with them, talking and listening to them. I encourage my kids to play the piano, but only to amuse themselves. They don't have a PlayStation but they watch a little TV.

These days children are packed off to all sorts of lessons at an ever younger age. They are expected to achieve more and more younger and younger, and are made to feel a failure if they don't reach the targets. I think the rivalry between parents at school is particularly sad – as if anyone cares whose child learns to ride a bike first, or learns to read before anyone else!

Childhood is the only time in your life when you can play and not have the worries that adults have. So why are we trying to rush it?

C The McGraths

We lived in Spain until three years ago and the children were constantly on the go there. You see more people doing things together as a family like going to the park and whenever they're not with their parents, children tend to be outside playing with each other.

Here in Britain, games consoles and the Internet have taken over from this. If my son had his way, he'd be on his Wii the minute he got home from school. For Natalie it's Internet chat-rooms. She loves them, and actually they're a good way for her to keep in touch with her friends in Spain, and keep up her Spanish at the same time.

I worry they're not playing out enough, but since I separated from my husband it's not easy to keep them constantly entertained and sometimes I'm happy for them to go on the computer because it gives me a break.

I'd like to send them to classes, but I can't afford it. The boys play football together on the field, and Natalie does cheerleading and goes to a youth club. I'd like her to go swimming but the nearest pool is a bus ride and a walk away, and I feel uneasy about letting her go off on her own.

I know we tend to complain that children don't play in the garden and go out on their bikes the way we did, but I doubt I'd have been riding bikes if we'd had the Internet. They are all computer literate and it's going to be fundamental to their lives, whereas maybe as adults we're scared of the world they're growing up in because we don't really understand it.

Language development 1
Situations and habits in the present

1 a Which person in the picture does each sentence describe?

1 She *lives* in a small house with her husband and children.
2 His children *are growing up* fast!
3 He*'ll sit and doze* in an armchair all evening.
4 She*'s always making* long calls on the phone.
5 He*'s staying* with the family at the moment.
6 She usually *goes out* in the evening.

b Match the meanings in the list a–f to the sentences in Exercise 1a. Look carefully at the context. Then complete the table below.

a a regular event
b an annoying or surprising habit
c characteristic behaviour
d a long-term situation
e a changing situation
f a temporary situation

2 a Complete the dialogues with appropriate verb forms from Exercise 1b.

1 A: .... *(you/live)* in a house or a flat?
   B: We .... *(live)* in a flat for now, but we .... *(look for)* a house.

2 A: Who .... *(you/get on)* best with in your family?
   B: My father. He .... *(tell)* us endless funny stories.

3 A: .... *(anyone/annoy)* you in your family?
   B: Yes, my brother. He .... *(always/take)* my CDs without asking me.

4 A: How often .... *(you/go out)*?
   B: I usually .... *(go out)* every night, but I .... *(study)* a lot at the moment, so I .... *(only/go out)* at weekends until my exams are finished.

5 A: .... *(you/like)* learning English?
   B: Yes, I do. It was difficult at first, but it .... *(get)* easier now.

b In pairs, ask each other the questions in Exercise 2a, and give answers which are true for you.

Form	Meaning	Examples
A Present continuous (two meanings)	1	....
	2	....
B Present continuous + *always*	....	....
C Present simple (two meanings)	1	....
	2	....
D *will* + infinitive	....	....

▶ Grammar reference page 187

State verbs

3 a Look at these sentences. Does each one describe a state (S) or an action (A)?

1 I don't understand.   S
2 Do you know Peter?   ....
3 We don't have a big house.   ....
4 Sorry, I'm having lunch.   ....

b Read the information in the box and complete it with the verbs from Exercise 3a.

> A Some verbs are not used in the continuous because they describe states, not actions, e.g. *believe, like, seem, want, own, ..., ...* .
>
> B Some verbs are not used in the continuous when they describe states, but can be used in the continuous when they describe actions, e.g. *look, appear, see, think, feel, ...* .

▶ Grammar reference page 187

4 Correct the mistakes in these sentences.

1 I'm having two brothers.
2 Jan has a shower – can you call back later?
3 I don't understand this word. What is it meaning?
4 Marina thinks about getting a car. Do you think it's a good idea?
5 We are not owning our house, we rent it.
6 The house look old, but it's quite modern inside.
7 What do you look at? Oh yes, I can see it now.
8 Phil sees a client at the moment. He won't be long.

Past habit

5 a Read the extract below by the singer Jamelia. Mark **two** past habits and **one** past state.

Early memories

When I was a child, we used to live in Birmingham. My mum used to take me to Black History lessons on Saturdays and they would teach us about Nelson Mandela.

b Answer the questions.

1 Did she go to Black History lessons once or many times?
2 Did they teach them about Nelson Mandela once or many times?
3 What verb forms are used to describe these past habits?
4 Underline the correct answer: *take/live* is a state verb. You can't use *would/used to* with a state verb.

c Complete the information in the box with *used to* or *would* or the past simple.

> A To talk about past habits, use ....
> (*My mum used to take me.*) or (*They ....*
> *teach us about Mandela.*).
>
> B To talk about past states, use ....
> (*We .... live in Birmingham.*).
>
> C The past simple can also be used for past habits and states. (*I .... in Birmingham.*
> *They .... us about Mandela.*)

▶ Grammar reference page 189

6 Complete the sentences using the correct form of the past simple, *would* or *used to* and the words in brackets. There may be more than one possibility.

1 Sorry I .... (**forget**) to write to you last week.

2 I .... (**live**) in France when I was a child. We .... (**have**) two beautiful cats.

3 When I was younger, my family ....
(**always/go**) to the beach in summer. We ....
(**have**) some great beach parties!

4 My father .... (**be**) a businessman. Often he .... (**work**) six or seven days a week, until he .... (**retire**) in 1995.

7 a Complete these sentences about yourself.

1 My … is always … .
2 I used to live … , but now I … in … .
3 At school I would often … .

b Now compare your experiences with other students.

8 Match the sentence halves from an informal letter.

1 I'm writing to tell you
2 I live in Poznan,
3 I live in a flat with
4 We don't look like each other,
5 When I'm not surfing the Internet,
6 When I was a child,

a but we have very similar personalities.
b we used to visit your country every summer.
c something about myself.
d I like going to clubs with my friends.
e a city in the west of Poland.
f my parents and my brother.

Writing Informal email (Paper 2 Part 2)

Lead-in

1 Discuss these questions.

1 Who do you write informal emails to?

2 What kind of things would you write in an email to a new pen friend?

Understand the task

2 Read the task below and answer the question.

What is the PURPOSE of the email?

a to ask for information b to give information c to entertain the reader

> You have been given the email address of an English-speaking person who is looking for a contact in your country. Write an email about you and your family, and suggest meeting at some time in the future.
>
> Write your **email** in **120–180** words in an appropriate style.

Plan your email

3 a What information do you need to include in the email? Make a list.

EXAMPLE: job, hobbies …

b Copy and complete the paragraph plan with the information you have listed.

Paragraph 1: Why you are writing.

Paragraph 2: About you.

Paragraphs 3/4: About your family.

Paragraph 5: Suggesting meeting.

Language and content

4 a These extracts from a student's email are inappropriate. Rewrite them using informal language from the table on page 13.

1 It would be a pleasure to become acquainted with you.

2 I am an inhabitant of a small town in Spain.

3 We have a very good relationship.

4 At the next opportunity to write, I will despatch a photograph of us all.

5 When I was a child, it was customary for us to spend our vacations by the sea.

6 She has a similar appearance to me. However, she can seem rather talkative.

7 I understand you are in search of a pen friend.

8 Does the possibility ever arise for you to visit my country?

9 The reason for my writing is that …

10 I should like to take this opportunity to inform you of my family situation.

Giving a reason for writing	*Just a short note to let you know … .* *I thought I'd drop you a line because … .* *I'm writing because … .* *I hear you're looking for a pen friend.*	Lifestyles	*We like to … .* *We would always go on holiday … .* *I often used to … .*
Introducing yourself	*My name's … .* *I live in … .*	Talking about the future	*Do you ever get the chance to …?* *It would be great to meet you sometime.* *Next time I write, I'll send a photo.*
Talking about people	*Let me tell you about my family.* *He likes … .* *She looks like me, but she can be a bit … .* *We get on (well) … .*		

b Look at these statements giving advice about informal emails. Do you think they are *True* or *False?*

1 Use a personal, conversational style.
2 Avoid simple words.
3 Avoid phrasal verbs.
4 Avoid direct questions to the reader.
5 Use short simple sentences.
6 Use contractions.

c Find examples in the table above to justify your answers.

d Which of the expressions below would be appropriate to open and close the email? Which ones would not be appropriate, and why?

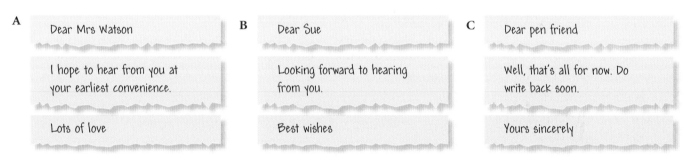

A
Dear Mrs Watson

I hope to hear from you at your earliest convenience.

Lots of love

B
Dear Sue

Looking forward to hearing from you.

Best wishes

C
Dear pen friend

Well, that's all for now. Do write back soon.

Yours sincerely

Write your email

5 Now write your email, using some of the language above. You must answer all parts of the question. Do not include any postal addresses. Write your answer in 120–180 words.

Check and improve your email

6 Edit your work using this list. Check your:
- paragraph plan (Have you included all the points?)
- use of present and past tenses
- use of time expressions
- style
- spelling
- number of words.

Note: There is a full checklist in the Writing reference.

▶ Writing reference page 199

LANGUAGE SPOT: sentence word order

Put these groups of words in the correct order to make sentences.
1 very well always English I speak don't
2 always my mother and father on Fridays fish eat
3 having great right now in Paris my sister's time a
4 usually her all gave help her friends a lot of
5 in bed music would my grandmother listen to always
6 at the party very much everyone themselves enjoyed
7 you I'll next week an email send on Tuesday
8 as soon as write please back can you

Speaking   (Paper 5 Part 2)

Vocabulary: special occasions

1   **Match the photos A–D with these special occasions.**

1   a birthday party   2   a graduation ceremony   3   a wedding

2   **a**   **Match the verbs in A with the nouns in B. In some cases, there may be more than one possibility.**

A

take   cut   blow out   propose   unwrap   walk down   send out blow up   make   be given   exchange   rent

B

balloons   a certificate   the candles   photos   invitations   rings a marquee   a toast   the cake   the aisle   the presents   a speech

   b   **Match each phrase with one of the photos above and say**

- how it links to the special occasion.
- if there are other special occasions where you do this.

3   **a**   **Match these words and phrases with the definitions.**

honeymoon   registry office   reception   the best man   witnesses anniversary   bridesmaid

1   a place where people get married ....
2   a person who helps the bride ....
3   the person who helps the groom ....
4   the people who watch, and sign the marriage certificate at a wedding ....
5   the formal party after a wedding ....
6   a holiday after the wedding ....
7   exactly a year or number of years after the wedding ....

   b   **Mark the stressed syllable(s) on each of the words/phrases in the box.**

4 These are interview extracts. Choose the correct alternative and complete the gaps with one of the words or phrases in Exercises 2 and 3.

1 ALEX: Did you *go/get* married in a church or did you have a civil wedding in a .... ?

PETER: When we first *got/were* engaged Tania wanted a white wedding with lots of .... to look after her but later she wanted something less formal.

ALEX: Where did you hold the .... ?

PETER: At my parents' house. Everyone had a good time eating and drinking until we disappeared off on our ....

2 LINDA: Why did you decide to *hold/break up* such a small wedding reception?

IVANA: Because we haven't got much money and we didn't want to make a big fuss.

LINDA: Did you .... formal invitations to all your *guests/visitors?*

IVANA: No, no, it was all very casual. Nobody was expected to *dress up/dress down.*

5 Think of a special occasion that you celebrate in your country (e.g. wedding, baby being born, coming of age, passing exams, leaving a job) and a special day (e.g. New Year's Day, Mother's Day, Valentine's Day, a coronation). Tell each other how you celebrate both occasions. What similarities/differences are there?

Comparing and contrasting photos

6 **a** You are going to talk for one minute about two of the photos. Choose two that you would like to compare, and make notes about them under these headings:

- similarities between the two photos
- differences between the two photos
- what you would like/dislike about each celebration
- which celebration you would prefer to be at and why.

Speaking strategy

If you have to speak for an extended period such as a minute, divide the time into smaller sections and think about what to say in each section. Don't try to say everything at once!

b 🎧 Listen to someone talking about two of the photos and answer the questions.

1 Which two photos is she talking about?
2 Which celebration would she prefer to be at, and why?

c 🎧 Listen again and tick (✓) the expressions she uses from the table below.

Similarities	*Both of … are … .*	*Neither of them … .*
	They both seem to be … .	*In this one … and this one … .*
Differences	*One thing which is different in this one … .*	*This one is … , whereas … is … .*
	The main difference between … and … is … .	
Likes, dislikes, preferences	*I would like … , but … .*	*Although … , I'd like … , because … .*
	I wouldn't mind … but on the other hand … .	*I think I'd prefer … , as … .*

▶ Functions reference page 215

d Take turns to speak for a minute about the two photos you have chosen. Use your notes and expressions from the table.

Discussion

7 Think of a memorable celebration you've taken part in. Who took part and what happened? How would you describe the occasion (e.g. moving, funny, exhilarating)? Give reasons.

Listening

Before you listen

Listening strategy

Before you listen, think about the topic and try to predict some of the language you will hear.

1 **Discuss these questions.**

1 What are the most common reasons for people moving abroad to live in another country?

2 What do you think the advantages and disadvantages of living in the countries in the photos would be?

3 What words or phrases do you associate with each of the photos?

Listening for gist

Listening strategy

You can get a general idea of a topic without understanding every word. Just concentrate on key words and main points, rather than the details.

2 **You are going to hear three different people talking about living abroad.**

1 🎧 Listen and match each speaker (1–3) to one of the photos (A–C). Which words and expressions helped you to decide?

2 Why did each of the speakers first go abroad to these countries?

a study

b work

c holiday

Listening for specific information

Listening strategy

You often need to listen for specific pieces of information. The words you need to hear will often be similar to, but not exactly the same as, the words in the questions.

3 🎧 **Listen again and say which speaker says each of these things. There is one extra letter which you do not need to use. Mark the most important words in each statement first (the first one has been done for you).**

A **Mealtimes** are **important** in this country.

B People have been very kind to me.

C The cost of living is lower than at home.

D The climate isn't at all as I'd imagined.

E I don't feel I really belong anywhere.

F I sometimes feel a bit isolated.

G I wish I'd got more into the culture.

Speaker 1 ☐☐
Speaker 2 ☐☐
Speaker 3 ☐☐

Discussion

4 **Discuss how you would feel about living in another country. Talk about:**

• which countries you have visited or lived in, and how you felt about them.

• which countries you would like to live in, and why.

• what you missed/would miss most about your own country.

Language development 2
Comparatives and superlatives

1 a Correct the mistakes in these students' sentences.

1   Burns Night celebrates the birth of the poet Robert Burns. It is one of most important nights in Scotland.
2   For many Scots, Burns supper is the most good event of the year.
3   Usually more late it gets, more noisy it gets.
4   The speech before the toast was funnyiest I have heard.
5   The music was more loud that last year.
6   The celebration was more lively one I've ever been to.
7   Outside it was just as chilly than last year.
8   Next year I'll leave more early. I couldn't get hold of a taxi.

b   Check your answers in the Grammar reference on page 185.

c   Complete the text with comparative or superlative forms of the words in brackets.

The Mexican holiday Cinco de Mayo (5 May), which remembers the Mexican defeat of the French army in 1862, is celebrated **(1)**.............. (*enthusiastically*) in the state of Puebla than in other parts of Mexico. It is not **(2)**.............. (*popular*) holiday in Mexico. In fact, it is celebrated **(3)**.............. (*widely*) by Mexicans in the USA than in Mexico, and the holiday is **(4)**.............. (*well-known*) in the USA than Mexican Independence Day. In recent years, Cinco de Mayo has become **(5)**.............. (*big*) than ever and is promoted as a celebration of Mexican culture, food and music. Participation is now **(6)**.............. (*wide*) than before, and non-Mexican Americans are **(7)**.............. (*enthusiastic*) about it as Mexicans. In California, the **(8)**.............. (*lively*) and **(9)**.............. (*sensational*) parties take place in Los Angeles. Celebrations have become **(10)**.............. (*commercialised*) in recent years, but Cinco de Mayo is still a great festival.

Modifying adjectives and adverbs

A   To express a big difference:
- *far/a lot/(very) much* + comparative
  He is **far better** than the other singers in the band. (~~very better~~)
  The food is **a lot nicer** in this café. (~~very nicer~~)
  The festival is (**very**) **much more popular** this year (~~very more popular~~)
- *by far/easily* + superlative
  He is **by far the best** singer in the band.
  The festival is **easily the most popular** in the country.
- *not nearly as … as*
  This party is **not nearly as good as** last year's.
  This is **not nearly as** good **a** party **as** last year's.

B   To express a small difference:
- *slightly/a bit/a little* + comparative
  The music is (only) **slightly better** than before.
  The concert was **a bit/a little better** than I expected.
- *just about* + superlative
  It was **just about the longest** carnival procession ever.
- *nearly/not quite as … as*
  The first show was **nearly as good as** the second one.
  The weather **isn't quite as hot as** it was last time.

2   Look at the information in the box above and complete the sentences with comparative or superlative forms.

1   Fiesta Broadway in Los Angeles is .... (*by far/large*) Cinco de Mayo celebration in the USA.
2   This year it was .... (*much/crowded*) than it was last year.
3   This year's parade was .... (*not quite/long*) as last time.
4   The costumes were .... (*a lot/colourful*) than before.
5   The food is .... (*far/spicy*) than I remembered.
6   I tried .... (*easily/mild*) dish, and it made my mouth burn!
7   And I'm sure I was .... (*just about/bad*) dancer there.

3 a   Choose one of these topics and write four sentences about it. Compare:
- three types of dance you know (e.g. salsa, tango, ballet – *fast/slow, easy/hard, cheap/expensive…?*)
- three types of music (e.g. rap, jazz, opera – *interesting/boring, noisy/quiet…?*)
- three types of food (e.g. Italian, French, Chinese – *spicy/mild, light/heavy, tasty/bland…?*)

b   Discuss your ideas. Give reasons for your opinions.

Use of English 1   (Paper 3 Part 4)

Key word transformations

▶ page 180

Task strategy

- Read both sentences carefully.
- Identify what is missing from the second sentence.
- Identify what kind of word the key word is (noun, verb, etc.) and what structure it could be used with.
- Look at the words before and after the gap to see what kind of structure could fit.
- Write 2–5 words without changing the key word. (contractions = two words)
- Read your sentence to check that it makes sense and is correct.
- Make a guess if necessary.

HELP

➤ **Question 1**
Do you need an active or passive form?

➤ **Question 2**
Be careful! Do you need an article?

➤ **Question 3**
You need a phrasal verb.

1 a Look at the examples and follow the instructions in the task strategy box.
EXAMPLE: Peter is a lot older than Martin.
as
Martin is .... Peter.
EXAMPLE: The only person Jane didn't like was her boss.
apart
Jane liked everyone .... her boss.

What area of grammar is focussed on in the first example?
a modifying adverbs   **b** comparison of adjectives

What area of vocabulary is focussed on in the second example?'
a preposition phrases   **b** phrasal verbs

b Do the first half of the task below. Use the Help clues if necessary.
Complete the second sentence so that it has a similar meaning to the first sentence, using the word given. **Do not change the word given.** You must use between two and five words, including the word given. Write only the missing words.

1 Fewer people read Carlton's books these days.
widely
Carlton's books .... these days.

2 Lucy doesn't swim nearly as well as Kate.
swimmer
Kate is .... Lucy.

3 He was offered some work but he wasn't able to accept it because he was too busy.
turned
He was offered some work but he .... because he was too busy.

4 Rap music isn't nearly as popular as it was ten years ago.
less
Rap music is .... it was ten years ago.

2 Now do the second half of the task. This time there are no Help clues.

5 I find studying more difficult as I become older.
is
I find it .... as I become older.

6 My brother never asks when he borrows my things.
always
My brother is .... asking.

7 I've always found learning languages easy.
good
I've always .... learning languages.

8 Traffic today doesn't move much faster than 100 years ago.
little
One hundred years ago, traffic moved .... than today.

3 Answer the questions about the task.
1 Which questions test:
- vocabulary?   • comparative or superlative structures?
- tense forms?

2 Which of the questions did you find the most difficult and why? Which of these areas of language do you need more practice in?

Use of English 2 (Paper 3 Part 1)

Lead-in

1 Look at the picture. What hospitality customs do you have in your country?

Multiple-choice cloze

▶ page 179

Task strategy

- Read the title and whole text quickly, ignoring the spaces.
- Read the text again. Try to guess what kind of word fits each space.
- Choose which answer A–D fits the grammar and meaning.
- If you aren't sure, cross out answers which you know are incorrect.
- Read the text again to check.

2 a Read the title and text quickly and answer the questions. (Ignore the spaces at this stage.)
  1 What did servants do for travellers in ancient times?
  2 What might be given to a guest in Japan?
  3 Why might guests eat too much in a foreign country?

b Do the task. Follow the task strategy and use the Help clues if necessary.
Read the text below and decide which answer **A**, **B**, **C** or **D** best fits each space. There is an example at the beginning (**0**).
  0 A hoped **B** considered **C** expected **D** intended

HOSPITALITY

Hospitality – looking after visitors – is universal, but in different cultures hosts are (**0**) ..C.. to receive guests in different ways.

In much of the ancient (**1**) ...., it was the custom to provide passing travellers with food and water, and (**2**) .... after them well. Indeed in some regions, if visitors were in the middle of a long (**3**) ...., servants would wash their feet.

Today, some old customs have (**4**) .... In a traditional Japanese household, if a guest admires a (**5**) .... object in the house, the host will give it to the guest straightaway. And it is still (**6**) .... in parts of Russia to greet guests with bread and salt on a special cloth. The guest is (**7**) .... to kiss them and hand them back to the host. Sometimes the guest breaks (**8**) .... a small piece of bread, dips it in the salt and eats it.

In some countries, when (**9**) .... guests arrive from abroad they may feel they have been given a particularly (**10**) .... meal. But this is probably because the host politely (**11**) .... offering more food and drink, and the guest is too embarrassed to (**12**) .... anything down.

HELP

➤ **Question 1**
Which word can mean *civilisation*?

➤ **Question 2**
Which phrasal verb means *care for*?

➤ **Question 6**
Which word means *customary*?

➤ **Question 10**
Which word might express a feeling in your stomach?

➤ **Question 12**
Which phrasal verb means *refuse*?

		A	B	C	D
1		A globe	B earth	C world	D planet
2		A look	B name	C take	D go
3		A day	B travel	C term	D journey
4		A supported	B survived	C preserved	D existed
5		A usual	B precise	C distinct	D particular
6		A typical	B everyday	C ordinary	D average
7		A needed	B wanted	C required	D desired
8		A off	B down	C out	D in
9		A strange	B foreign	C alien	D unfamiliar
10		A strong	B dense	C wide	D heavy
11		A keeps on	B takes up	C comes off	D puts in
12		A slow	B turn	C keep	D take

c Answer the questions about the task.
  1 Did you guess any words before looking at the options?
  2 Which questions test:
    - the correct word from a set with similar meanings?
    - phrasal verbs?
    - adjective + noun combinations?

d Make a note in your vocabulary book of any expressions, phrasal verbs or adjective + noun combinations you want to remember.

Language development 3
Collocations: adjectives and nouns

> Look at this adjective + noun collocation from the
> Use of English text on page 21:
> *a **heavy** meal*   *a ~~strong~~ meal*
> but:
> *a **strong** drink*   *a ~~heavy~~ drink*
> When you learn an adjective, note which nouns it
> collocates with.
>
> **(LOOK)** **Find five more adjective + noun collocations
> in the Use of English text on page 21.**

1 Complete the diagram with nouns from the dictionary
extract below.

> **sour** *adj* **1** having a sharp acid taste that stings your tongue
> like the taste of a lemon: *sour apples* **2** milk or other food
> that is sour is not fresh: *In warm weather, milk can go sour.*
> **3** unfriendly or looking bad-tempered: *Rob gave me a sour
> look.* **4 sour grapes** the attitude of someone who pretends
> to dislike something they really want

2 a Match the nouns in the list below to these adjectives.

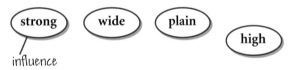

influence

> heels possibility English variety
> number influence grin speed feelings
> choice argument clothes gap

b Complete these sentences with one of the
adjective + noun combinations from Exercise 2a.

1 My grandparents have .... on the
subject of hospitality.
2 Can you give me directions to your house in
.... so that I can understand them?
3 Dan's face broke into a .... when I
invited him in.
4 Everyone drives at such a ....
today – it's so dangerous.
5 Four different types of tea – what a ....!
6 In more traditional cultures, grandparents
have a .... on children.
7 Please take your shoes off in the gym. ....
.... can damage the floor.
8 If you call Toni, there's a .... that he'll
invite you to visit him.

Phrasal verbs with *up* and *down*

3 Look at these two sentences with the phrasal verb
pick up. Which one has an obvious meaning, and
which one an idiomatic meaning?
1 I *picked up* a cup that was lying on the floor.
2 She *picked* me *up* at the hotel and took me to the
party.

4 a In these sentences the meaning is fairly obvious.
Complete the sentences with *up* or *down.*
1 The dinner won't cook if you don't turn the heat
....
2 We can't afford a big party – we need to keep
costs ....
3 The old bus station has gone – they've pulled it
....
4 When you see someone's glass is empty, go and
fill it ....
5 He settled .... on the sofa to read his book.
6 The town's getting bigger – they've put ....
a lot of new houses.

b Some of these phrasal verbs have an idiomatic
meaning. Match the sentence halves to make the
most likely sentences. Use a dictionary if necessary.

1 Please tidy up   a the apartment and sell
                              it for a big profit.
2 I never turn down   b your best friend by
                              breaking a promise.
3 Remember to   c the time of the next
  wrap up   train on the website.
4 She took down   d the mess as soon as
                              possible.
5 Look up   e the presents before
                              going to the party.
6 They put up   f the offer of a lift home.
7 Never let down   g the decorations from
                              the wall.
8 He decided to do up   h a tent in the garden.

c Match the phrasal verbs in Exercise 4b to these
near synonyms.
a decorate   e refuse
b look for information f put in special paper
c fail someone   g remove
d erect   h make neat and organised

5 Make a note of the phrasal verbs you want to
remember in your vocabulary book. Write the
<u>whole</u> sentence and mark the phrasal verb.

6 Discuss these questions.
1 Who tidies up in your house?
2 Has a friend ever let you down? What happened?
3 How often do you look up a word in English?

MODULE 2
Earning a living

Overview

- **Reading:** skills: skimming, reading for detail
- **Language development 1:** past simple and present perfect tenses
- **Writing:** formal letter of application (Paper 2 Part 2)
- **Speaking:** discussion: giving opinions, agreeing and disagreeing (Paper 5 Parts 3 and 4)
- **Listening:** skills: listening for gist and opinions
- **Use of English 1:** open cloze (Paper 3 Part 2)
- **Language development 2:** articles; *some/any*; *something/anything*
- **Use of English 2:** word formation (Paper 3 Part 3)
- **Language development 3:** forming adjectives; phrasal verbs: education

Lead-in

- Which of the jobs in the photos do you think are most/least difficult demanding or interesting?
- Some people 'work to live', and others 'live to work'. Which do you do? What about other people you know?

Reading

Before you read

1 Look at the photograph of three men who set up a business together.
  1 What do you think their business is?
  2 What might the problems be with setting up this kind of business?

Skimming

2 Skim the text and match sections 1–5 to these subheadings (a–e).
  a A recipe for financial success
  b Overcoming the problems
  c A force for good in the world
  d It's now or never
  e Investing in people

> **Reading strategy**
>
> The first and last paragraph of a text (introduction and conclusion) and the first or last sentence of the other paragraphs (topic sentence) usually contain the main ideas. Use them to get a general understanding of the text.

3 a Read the uncompleted sentences 1–6 below. Don't look at the options A–C yet. Look at the text and mark the relevant parts.

Reading for detail

  b Now choose the answer A, B or C which you think fits best according to the text. The first one has been done for you. The highlighted words show how the answer was found.

> **Reading strategy**
>
> To understand the details in a text, read it slowly and carefully. You may need to read parts of the text more than once.

  1 The three friends gave up their 'real jobs' because they
    A had always dreamed of setting up a fruit drinks business.
    B had realised that one of their business ideas might be a success.
    C had decided their 'real jobs' did not allow them to live healthy lives.

  2 Innocent's main obstacle to selling their smoothies was
    A deciding how to package the drink.
    B getting someone to put their money into the business.
    C solving the problem of how to keep the drinks fresh for longer.

  3 The expression *messing about with them* suggests they didn't
    A change what was in the drinks.
    B worry about which bottles the drinks were in.
    C check how long the drinks were kept in the shops.

Vocabulary: deducing meaning

  4 The business has become very successful because
    A the partners concentrate on what they do well.
    B the product changes according to what the buyers want.
    C the company has benefited from the partners' experience in advertising.

  5 Employees are motivated to work for Innocent because they
    A are paid more than people in similar jobs.
    B appreciate working for a prize-winning company.
    C feel they are important to the success of the organisation.

  6 Innocent is a successful company because
    A it has not allowed itself to become too big.
    B it is much admired for its underlying philosophy.
    C its drinks are helping many children to be healthier.

4 a Look at the underlined words and guess what they mean. If you don't know the meanings, follow the reading strategy and try to work them out.

These men are Innocent!

1 _____

Back in 1998, three 26-year-olds, Adam Balon, Richard Reed and Jon Wright, made up their minds that it was time they either left their well-paid jobs in management consultancy and advertising and went into business together or stopped talking about it. What kind of business they wanted to set up they weren't quite sure but it was something they had been discussing ever since they were at university together. Deciding that the way forward was to make it easier for busy people to be healthy, the trio bought some fruit and made smoothies, which they then tested on people at a small jazz festival in London. 'We put up a large sign asking, "Should we quit our jobs to make these smoothies?" and put out one bin saying "Yes" and another saying "No." The Yes bin filled up immediately with empty bottles and the next day they resigned from their jobs.

2 _____

However, launching Innocent smoothies did not happen overnight. Experts in the food industry told them that their product was too expensive, its shelf life was too short, and without the use of <u>additives</u> their idea wouldn't work. Even more worryingly, the numerous banks they approached were not too keen on financing them and it wasn't until their savings were about to run out that a wealthy businessman took a leap of faith and invested in the business. Ignoring most of the advice they'd been given, Innocent then went on to create a range of drinks made from 100% fresh fruit and nothing else. Careful production and high-tech packaging gave the drinks the longest possible shelf life, but they stuck to their beliefs by not 'messing about with them' at all. The next step was to persuade local shops to <u>stock</u> their product, which they delivered personally in their grass covered minibus.

3 _____

Their airy office in London – affectionately known as 'Fruit Towers' – is open plan, the 'grass' floors, table football games, beanbags, and casually dressed trendy young staff representing the fresh feeling Innocent is trying to create. But alongside all this <u>quirkiness</u> (call them and you are greeted with a cheerful 'Hello, banana phone!') is an impressive business. New recipes created in the high-tech kitchen are tried out on the people in the surrounding office buildings, although new product ideas, however fashionable, are rejected if they are too far from their main focus (making a natural, healthy, great-tasting drink). Their confidence that a quality product will sell itself appears to have paid off; despite <u>minimal</u> advertising, Innocent currently sells around a million drinks a week, turnover is around £75m and they now have a 61% market share of the smoothies industry.

4 _____

Aside from the greenery, one of the first things you notice about 'Fruit Towers' is how happy everyone there seems to be. Convinced that success relies on the well-being and happiness of the people who work there, the three partners were determined to put the focus on making their employees feel valued. So as well as financial <u>incentives</u> like company shares, healthcare, and extra bonuses, the staff are motivated by personalised 'outside work' treats such as snowboarding trips, scholarships to enable them to pursue outside interests and studies, and a wide choice of social and sporting activities. Innocent employees are positive, motivated and proud of where they work, which is why the company has won numerous awards including Guardian Employer of the Year in 2005 and top place in the Sunday Times Best Small Companies to work for list.

5 _____

Wright, Balon and Reed had firm ideas from the very beginning about the kind of company they wanted to run. 'If we call it Innocent we have a responsibility to be innocent, and as we expand the more innocent we become,' says Reed. The enormously popular company works only with companies who have sound ethical and environmental standards, invests 10% of their profits in the countries from which they buy their fruit, encourages recycling and gives away drinks to the homeless. At only 33, Reed is even acting as an advisor to the government on getting children to eat healthily. Innocent's approach is well-timed. Just as its drinks appeal to cash-rich, time-poor <u>workaholics</u>, its approach to business is attractive to those who are disillusioned with the big multi-national corporations who are making vast profits while contributing to the destruction of our planet.

Language development 1
Past simple and present perfect

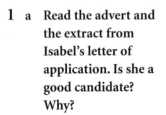

Summer Camp Jobs
IN CALIFORNIA

- Spanish-Speaking Counselors required.
- Good English essential.
- Must be fun-loving, patient and concerned for the welfare of young people.

1 a Read the advert and the extract from Isabel's letter of application. Is she a good candidate? Why?

My first language is Spanish. However, I have often been to California to visit my American friends and I have learned a lot of English over the years. Last year I spent two months on an internship program in San Francisco. Although I haven't worked at a summer camp before, two years ago I helped at a children's charity here in Peru for a month.

Spelling note:
program (American English);
programme (British English)

b Underline examples of the past simple and circle examples of the present perfect simple in Isabel's letter.

c Answer these questions.
Do we know exactly when she:
- visited friends in the USA?
- learned English?
- was on an internship program?
- helped at a children's charity?

d Complete this box with examples from Isabel's letter.

> **A** The present perfect simple expresses **experience; actions and situations at an unspecified time** in the past.
> EXAMPLES:
> 1 ....
> 2 ....
> 3 ....
>
> **B** The past simple expresses **actions at a specified time** in the past.
> EXAMPLES:
> 1 ....
> 2 ....

▶ Grammar reference page 188

2 a Complete these extracts from a job interview. Use the correct form of the past simple or the present perfect simple.
1 A: (*you/live abroad?*) ....
   B: (*Yes*) ....
   A: (*Where/live?*) ....
   B: In Dublin.
   A: (*When/go there?*) ....
   B: In 2002.
2 A: (*you/work in an office?*) ....
   B: (*No*) ....
3 A: (*you/ever go to/the USA?*) ....
   B: (*Yes*) ....
   A: (*When/go there?*) ....
   B: Last year.
   A: (*Why/go there?*) ....
   B: To study English.
4 A: (*you/use English in your work before?*)
   ....
   B: (*No*) ....

b Ask each other the questions in Exercise 2a, and give answers which are true for you.

Present perfect simple and continuous

3 a Read the next part of Isabel's letter.

> I have lived in Lima since 2006. I have been studying for a degree in education for two years and I have just taken my second-year exams, though I haven't had the results yet. Recently, I have been taking part in a series of workshops on children's games, which I find very interesting.

b Underline examples of the present perfect simple and circle examples of the continuous in Isabel's letter.

c Answer these questions.
1 Does Isabel live in Lima now?
2 Is she still studying for a degree?
3 Which is more permanent, 1 or 2?
4 Has she finished her exams?
5 Has she finished taking part in the workshops?

d Complete the box with examples from Isabel's letter.

> A The present perfect simple expresses more **permanent** actions or states which started in the past and continue to the present.
> EXAMPLE: ....
> B The present perfect continuous expresses more **temporary** actions or situations which started in the past and continue to the present.
> EXAMPLE: ....
> C The present perfect simple expresses **recent finished actions** including repeated actions.
> EXAMPLE: ....
> D The present perfect continuous expresses **recent longer activities**, which may not be finished.
> EXAMPLE: ....

▶ Grammar reference page 188

e Look at the box and complete the phrases with *for* or *since*.

for or *since*?

Use *for* with a period of time, and *since* with a point in time:
for two years *since* 1990

1 .... ages
2 .... my birthday
3 .... a long time
4 .... six o'clock
5 .... half an hour
6 .... I was born

4 Tick (✓) the correct sentences. Correct the wrong ones.
1 Sorry we're late. We've been sitting in traffic.
2 I've been having some good news. I've got the job!
3 Marta's been taking exams all week. She's exhausted.
4 I've read that book. Do you want it back?
5 Emma's been falling over and hurt her knee.
6 The lift isn't working so we've used the stairs all day.

5 a Complete the extract from a letter with the correct form of the verbs in brackets: past simple, present perfect simple or continuous.

> I (1)...................... (be) here for two months now and (2)...................... (not write) to you yet. Sorry! I hope you (3)...................... (not wait) for a letter. I (4)...................... (work) a lot and I (5)...................... (not have) much free time. At first I (6)...................... (feel) a bit lonely, but recently I (7)...................... (make) some friends. I (8)...................... (try) to find somewhere to live for weeks and I think I (9)...................... (find) a flat at last. Up to now I (10)...................... (stay) with a colleague.

b Complete these sentences about yourself.
1 I've written … .
2 I've never … .
3 I've … since … .
4 I've been …ing … this year.
5 I haven't … this month.

6 Find and correct the eight mistakes in this piece of writing.

> I have been born in Peru 26 years ago and I've lived here all my life. I am married for two years but we don't have any children yet. I've been working in a bank since four years and I enjoy it a lot. In my spare time I'm trying to improve my English – I've had private lessons since six months. I also love reading. Last year I have tried to read a novel in English. I go to the mountains for my holidays during six years because I love walking. I've also gone to Brazil two years ago to stay with some friends.

Writing   Formal letter (Paper 2 Part 2)

Lead-in

1   Look at the different types of letter in the list. Which ones would be formal, and which informal?
   a   introducing yourself to a pen friend
   b   asking for information from a friend
   c   applying to go to university
   d   asking for information from a bank
   e   applying for a job
   f   giving news to your family

Understand the task

2   Read the task below and answer the questions.
   1   WHO are you writing to?
   2   What is the PURPOSE of your letter?
   3   What INFORMATION will you include in your letter? (Read the question carefully.)
   4   What EFFECT do you want to have on the reader? (How do you want them to feel about you?)

You see this advertisement in a student newspaper. You are interested in applying for the job.

Beach lifeguard assistant wanted

Are you a strong swimmer?
Do you know about first aid?
Do you enjoy working with people?
Then you might be the person for us!

We are looking for someone in August to assist our lifeguards, provide supervision during beach activities and observe swimmers. Lifeguard qualification and experience desirable but not essential as training will be given.

If you are interested, write to the Lifeguard Manager saying why think you are the right person.

Good hourly rates.

Write your **letter** of application in 120–180 words in an appropriate style. Do not write any postal addresses.

Plan your letter

3   a   Tick (✓) the points you should include in each paragraph.
      Paragraph 1: Reason for writing
      • Your name   • Where you heard about the job

      Paragraph 2: About you:
      • Age   • Where you are from   • Where you live
      • Number of brothers and sisters   • Education
      • Training/qualifications   • Work experience   • Hobbies
      • Appearance   • What kind of person you are

      Paragraph 3: Your reason for applying
      • Present job   • What you hate about your present job
      • Why you are suitable for the job

      Paragraph 4: Conclusion
      • When you are available for interview
      • Names and addresses of two people who can recommend you

   b   Make notes about yourself for each paragraph.

Language and content

4 a Look at this extract from a student's letter. Which sentences are appropriately formal, and which are too informal?

1 I noticed the lifeguard job in the student magazine and I want to have a go.
2 I am 20 years old and I live in Holland.
3 I'm studying at uni right now and I am pretty good at PE.
4 I've never done this kind of stuff before but I'm a great swimmer.
5 I suppose you could say I really like working with different people.
6 The job would give me valuable work experience during the summer holidays.
7 I'd do the job really well — you don't have to worry about that.
8 I'll drop in for a chat.
9 I hope you'll have a good think about it and give me the job.
10 I look forward to hearing from you in the near future.

b Rewrite the inappropriate sentences in a more formal style. Use phrases from the table below.

Saying why you're writing	*I would like to apply for the position of ... which I saw advertised ... .* *One of my reasons for applying is ... .*	Talking about the job	*I feel I would be suitable for the job ... .* *I think I would be a suitable candidate for ... because ... .* *The job would give me the opportunity to ... (get further work experience during the summer).*
Talking about yourself	*I am ... years old and I ... .* *At present I am ...(working for/a student at) ... .* *I am a good (swimmer).* *I regret I have had no experience of ... (this kind of work).* *For the last (two) years I have been ... (studying/working) ... .* *When I was at ... I ... .* *I very much enjoy ... (working with people/travelling).*	Offers	*I would be happy/free/able to (attend an interview/provide references).* *I am available to attend an interview ... .*
		Concluding	*I hope you will consider my application.* *I look forward to hearing from you in the near future.*

c Which of these words or phrases could you use to open and close the letter?

Dear Sue   Dear Sir or Madam   Hi!   Dear Ms Smith   Hello
Regards   Yours faithfully   Yours   Yours sincerely   Yours truly

Write your letter

5 Now write your letter, using the ideas and some of the language above. Do not write any postal addresses. Write your answer in 120–180 words.

Check and improve your letter

6 Edit your work using this list. Check your:
- paragraph plan (Have you included all the points?)
- use of the past simple and the present perfect
- style
- number of words.

Note: There is a full checklist in the Writing reference.

▶ Writing reference page 200

A learning experience

Speaking
Paper 5 Parts 3 and 4

Vocabulary: education

1 **Discuss these questions.**

In your country:

1 at what age do you go to different types of school - nursery, primary and secondary? At what age do you go to college or university?

2 what is the school-leaving age?

3 how have schools changed over the years?

2 **Which of the picture(s) opposite do you associate with these? Match each of these with one or more of the pictures.**

> higher education playgroup undergraduate uniform tutorial
> playground lecturer curriculum head teacher homework
> continuous assessment degree strict discipline exams

3 **Discuss these questions.**

1 Which of these subjects have you studied? At what age did you study them? Which would you like to study?

> mathematics history engineering science sociology drama
> philosophy languages economics

2 What is a person called who specialises in the subject? Which is the stressed syllable in the word?

3 These are three common subjects: *PE, ICT, DT*. In which do you study a) design b) keep fit c) computing?

4 Which subjects are/were you good at? Which do/did you enjoy most?

5 Which ones are the most/least useful in future life?

4 **Complete the sentences with one of these verbs in the correct form.**

> skip attend revise re-sit do apply get study fail pass pay

1 'I hated maths at school. I didn't do any of the homework, never ………… attention to the teacher and …………. classes whenever I could. Of course, the first time round I ……….. my exams and had to ……… them the following year. The second time round I ………. , which I was really pleased about. It really boosted my confidence and I decided to ………. to one of the better universities. To my amazement, I got in and I'm there now – studying maths!'

2 'Marc's very bright. He always ………. very well when he was at school. I'm sure he'll ……… a good degree, even though he doesn't ………….. very hard. Of course, he hardly ever …………. lectures or ………… the things we've done. I sometimes resent the fact he's so clever!'

5 **What sort of pupil are/were you? What are/were the good and bad things about the schools you go/went to?**

Discussion 1

Speaking strategy

In a discussion, it's important to give your opinion, but also to ask for other people's opinions and respond to them.

6 a Which three of these things do you think are the most important in a school for children under 11? Tick (✓) them. Which one do you think is the least important?

- lots of equipment (e.g. computers, laboratories)
- highly-qualified teachers
- good exam results
- individual attention
- beautiful buildings
- small classes
- (not) having a uniform
- being near home
- clubs after school
- good sports facilities

b 🎧 Listen to two people discussing the list above. What do they think are the most and least important factors? Why?

c 🎧 Listen again and complete the expressions they use in the table below.

Giving opinions	.... , ... me, one of the most important .... is ... .
	I just .... it matters ... .
	The .... important factor for me is ... .
Strong agreement	That's ....
	So do I.
	I agree ....
	Neither do I.
	I think ... .
	I couldn't ....
Tentative agreement	I .... so.
Disagreement	I agree .... to a .... , although ... .
	Yes, but what about ...?
	Do you ....?
	But don't you agree that ...?
	Actually, I think it's ....

▶ Functions reference page 215

d Work in pairs or groups. Discuss the list in Exercise 6a. Try to agree on either the most or the least important thing in the list.

Discussion 2

7 a Look at the statements and decide whether you agree with them.
1 Schooldays are the happiest days of your life.
2 We can learn more from computers than from teachers.
3 Schools don't prepare children for 'the real world'.
4 Life experience is more useful than college or university.

b Discuss the statements and give reasons for your opinions.

Listening

Before you listen

1 a You will hear a radio discussion in which two students are talking about their first few weeks in higher education. First discuss these questions:

1 How does being at college/university differ from being at school?

2 What are the advantages and disadvantages of continuing your education rather than getting a job?

b Look at the listening task below. Read the questions but not the options A–C. Mark the main points (the first two have been done for you). What do you think the answers might be?

2 🎧 Listen to Leanne and Harry. Did they say what you predicted in 1b?

Listening for gist

Listening for opinions

3 a 🎧 Listen again. For questions 1–5, choose the best answer A, B or C.

1 What **advice** does Leanne give about **getting to know people** in the first weeks at university?
A Join lots of sports clubs.
B Try not to judge people on first impressions.
C Make friends with people studying the same subject as you.

2 What does Harry **regret about his first two weeks** at college?
A not going out enough
B not doing more work
C not saving his money

3 Leanne was able to manage financially at university by
A living at home.
B getting a part-time job.
C finding ways of economising.

4 What is Harry's view on attending lectures?
A Don't bother going.
B You should make detailed notes.
C They are useful as an introduction to the subject.

5 What do they both find difficult about working without supervision?
A motivating yourself
B not getting distracted
C understanding the task

b Compare and give reasons for your answers.

Discussion

4 Discuss the questions below.

1 What advice would you give to school-leavers starting higher education?

2 What do you think is the best way to get to know new people?

Vocabulary: collocation

5 Match the verbs from Column A with the words or expressions they went with in the interview. There may be more than one possibility.

A		B	
1	go	a	costs
2	make	b	advantage of something
3	join	c	time (on something)
4	take	d	to lectures
5	cut	e	around (a subject)
6	read	f	a club
7	waste	g	wrong
		h	friends
		i	the most of something

Use of English 1 (Paper 3 Part 2)

Lead-in

1 Look at the photo of Albert Einstein. What do you know about him?

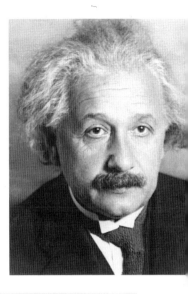

Open cloze

▶ page 179

2 a **Read the text quickly and answer the questions. (Ignore the spaces at this stage.)**

1 In what field is Einstein famous?

2 What problems did he have as a student?

3 How did he get time to develop his ideas?

Task strategy

- Read the title and text quickly for a general understanding. Ignore the spaces.
- Decide what type of word is missing in each space – a noun, an article, a verb?
- Put only one word in each space and do not use contractions (*isn't*, *doesn't*, etc.).
- Always write something.
- Read the text again and check your answers make sense and are correctly spelt.

HELP

In this text some, but not all, of the gaps require *a/the* or a determiner (e.g. *all, both, most*, etc.) of some kind.

➤ **Question 1**
Choose between *a* and *the*. Think about the difference.

➤ **Question 2**
Choose a determiner that combines with *nearly*.

➤ **Question 4**
Which words can be used to add one negative statement to another?

➤ **Question 7**
Choose a word which expresses contrast (e.g. *however, although, nevertheless, despite*)

➤ **Question 10**
Remember what is said about these subjects earlier!

➤ **Question 12**
Definite or indefinite article?

---

b **Do the task. Follow the task strategy and use the Help clues if necessary.**

Read the text below and think of the word which best fits each space. Use only one word in each space. There is an example at the beginning (0).

ALBERT EINSTEIN (1879–1955)

Albert Einstein is **(0)** _one_ of the best-known scientists of the twentieth century. Yet he was not **(1)**............ particularly good student. At school in Munich, he got reasonable grades in nearly **(2)**............ subjects, and was outstanding in mathematics and physics, but he disliked doing **(3)**............ he was told. He didn't like exams and **(4)**............ did he like attending classes, so he left school early.

(5)............ failing the entrance exam, Einstein was eventually admitted to **(6)**............ Swiss Federal Institute of Technology in Zurich in 1896. **(7)**............ he did fairly well as a student in Zurich, after graduation he was unable to get a job in a university, mainly **(8)**............ he was thought to be extremely lazy. Instead, he worked in **(9)**............ secondary school, where he taught mathematics and physics, **(10)**............ of which he was good at.

Some two years later, in 1902, Einstein got a job at the Swiss patent office in Bern. In 1905, his special theory of relativity **(11)**............ published – one of the greatest intellectual achievements in **(12)**............ history of human thought.

c **Answer the questions about the task.**

1 Which questions test:
  - articles and determiners?
  - connecting expressions?

2 Which one of these is also tested:
  - present perfect?
  - passives?
  - pronouns?

3 Which questions did you find difficult and why?

Discussion

3 **Was your school career similar to Einstein's? In what way was it different?**

Language development 2
Articles

A   *a/an*: before singular, countable nouns
- The first time we refer to something:
  A man went into a café to ask for directions.
- With jobs:
  She's an airline pilot.

B   *the*
- To refer to something already known:
  The man had seen the café from his car.
- In certain expressions:
  I play the piano.
  Are you going to the cinema tonight?
- Before most seas, oceans, rivers, groups of islands/mountains, deserts, and nationalities:
  The Pacific Ocean
  The British can be very reserved.
- When there is only one of something:
  The United Nations are meeting in New York.
  The sun rises very early in summer.

C   *No article*
- When talking about something in general:
  Schools are too big nowadays.
- Before subjects of study:
  I study physics.
- Before most countries, continents, towns and streets:
  I live in France.
- In certain expressions, e.g.:
  at home, in summer/winter

LOOK Find examples of articles in the Use of English text on page 33 and match them to the uses above.

▶ Grammar reference page 182

1 a   Correct these students' sentences.

1   The best course was the one I did on the economics. The teacher was very good and I made a good progress.

2   Nina's studying the German at evening classes in the London.

3   My brother is 19. He's at the university in the Africa and wants to become English teacher because it would give him good opportunity to travel.

4   When we were in Japan we noticed that most Japanese students work harder than the American students I met in USA.

5   I go to college by the train. Unfortunately, the train is often late.

b   Complete the following text with the best form for each space – a, an, the or Ø (no article).

When **(1)**............. students in England were asked by **(2)**............. national newspaper what kind of **(3)**............. college they would like to go to, they agreed that one of **(4)**............. most important things was **(5)**............. location of **(6)**............. college and **(7)**............. other was **(8)**............. state of **(9)**............. buildings. **(10)**............. majority said they wanted **(11)**............. light, well-decorated college with **(12)**............. comfortable seats in the lecture rooms. They also wanted **(13)**............. college with **(14)**............. flexible timetable where they could spend **(15)**............. time on what they enjoy and where learning **(16)**............. new skills was fun and exciting. Interestingly, no one said they didn't want to go to **(17)**............. college at all.

some/any; something/anything

A   *some/any (of)*
*I got **some** good grades in my exams.* (countable)
*The teacher gave me **some** good advice.* (uncountable)
***Some** (of the) grades were outstanding.* (= a limited number)
***Some of them** were excellent.* (*of* before pronouns)
*Were **any** of them bad?* (it doesn't matter which ones)
*It was **some** weeks/time before the exam results came out.* (a large number/amount of)
*Take **any** books you want.* (it doesn't matter which ones)
*Tell me if you have **any** problems.* (they may not exist)

B   *something/anything*
*I want to give you **something** to read.* (positive) (*a thing*)
*I don't want to give you **anything**.* (negative) (*a thing*)
*Have you got **anything** for me?* (I don't know if you have.)
*Have you got **something** for me?* (I hope/think you have.)
*There's **hardly anything** left to eat.* (= almost nothing)
*Have you seen **anything** interesting lately?*
(*something/anything* + adjective)

2   Read this extract from a student's email to her parents and mark the correct word in each pair.

It's been quite **(1)** some / any time since I've been in touch. Sorry about that. There never seems to be **(2)** some / any time to do **(3)** something / anything these days – except work of course. Anyway, I've decided to have **(4)** some / an time off in the next few weeks. I'm not promising **(5)** something / anything definite but I'm hoping to get home for at least a couple of days. But I'll need **(6)** some / any money for the train fare – I've got **(7)** any / hardly any left in the bank until my next cheque comes through. Could you lend me **(8)** some / any? I'll be able to get **(9)** some / any work in a restaurant in the holidays, so I'll pay you back then. Apart from that, what I'd like to do more than **(10)** something / anything else when I get home is just relax

Use of English 2 (Paper 3 Part 3)

Lead-in

1 Discuss these questions.

1 Have you got a good memory? What kind of things do you forget?
2 What techniques do you use to help you remember things?

Word formation ▶ page 179

Task strategy

- Read the title and whole text first for general understanding. Ignore the spaces.
- Read each sentence. What kind of word is needed in each space – a noun, adjective, adverb or verb?
- Change the form of each word on the right to fit the space.
- Read the whole text again. Check it makes sense.
- Check your spelling. (It must be correct.)

HELP

Some words might need a prefix or a suffix and some might be negative.

➤ **Question 1**
  Choose from these negative prefixes: *un-, in-, dis-, non-*
➤ **Question 2**
  Choose from these adjective suffixes to change this verb into an adjective: *-ish, -less, -ate*
➤ **Question 3**
  Choose from these suffixes to change this noun into an adjective: *-able, -less, -ful, -est*
➤ **Question 5**
  Is this an adjective or an adverb?
➤ **Question 7**
  Past participles can be used as adjectives when they come before the noun.
➤ **Question 10**
  Choose from these suffixes: *-ible, -ic, -ive, -ful*

2 a Read the title and text quickly and answer the questions. (Ignore the spaces at this stage.)

1 What can be stressful for students at exam time?
2 What suggestions are there for improving the memory?

b Do the task. Follow the task strategy and use the Help clues if necessary.
Read the text below. Use the word given in capitals at the end of some of the lines to form a word that fits in the space in the same line. There is an example at the beginning (0).

Remembering for exams

It's **(0)** ..frustrating..for everybody not to be able to   **FRUSTRATE**
remember things but having a bad memory can be a
particular **(1)** .... for students at exam time.   **ADVANTAGE**
Anyway, I did a search on the Internet and found
(2) .... ideas for improving your memory but one   **COUNT**
idea I thought particularly **(3)** .... was that we   **HELP**
should try and use all our senses when given
(4) .... to learn. So, for example, instead of reading   **INFORM**
(5) ...., we should record the material and then   **SILENT**
listen to it. Apparently, the **(6)** .... of speaking and   **COMBINE**
listening helps reinforce the **(7)** .... text. Another   **WRITE**
theory, which some people might find **(8)** ...., is that   **LIKELY**
there is a greater **(9)** .... of our memorising   **POSSIBLE**
something successfully if we do it when the house is
(10) ...., and preferably just before bedtime.   **PEACE**

c Answer the questions about the task.

1 Are there any answers you would like to check in a dictionary?
2 Which answers required:
  • nouns
  • adjectives
  • adverbs?
3 Which answers required a suffix?
4 Which answers required a negative prefix?
5 Which questions did you find difficult and why?

Discussion

3 Do you agree with the ideas in the text? How do you revise?

35

Language development 3
Forming adjectives

A Suffixes
1 Sometimes we add a suffix to form an adjective:
suit (verb) > *suitable* (adjective)
health (noun) > *healthy* (adjective)
2 Sometimes the stem has to change:
decide (verb) > *decisive* (adjective)
beauty (noun) > *beautiful* (adjective)

B Sometimes we make internal changes:
freeze (verb/noun) > *frozen* (adjective)
heat (verb/noun) > *hot* (adjective)

C We can add a prefix to change the meaning of an adjective:
regular > *irregular*; *honest* > *dishonest* (opposite)
national > *international* (between)

▶ Grammar reference page 183

1 a Complete each sentence with the word in brackets and one of the suffixes in the list.
-ible -ful -less -ic -al -ous -ate -ly -ish -y

1 That boy is naughty but he's .... (*harm*).
2 It's .... (*nature*) for a child to be like that sometimes.
3 Despite his illness, Paul made the .... (*courage*) decision to sit his exams.
4 Beth often behaves in a very silly and .... (*child*) way.
5 Our teacher gave us some .... (*help*) suggestions about studying.
6 Mr Turner has always been .... (*passion*) about science.
7 Please clean any .... (*dirt*) equipment after you have done the experiment.
8 The sports teacher at my old school was .... (*horror*)!
9 There have been .... (*drama*) changes in the education system.
10 I like my music teacher as she's very .... (*live*).

b Answer these questions about yourself.
1 Have you ever been *irresponsible*? What happened?
2 Do you think everybody is *dishonest* on occasions?
3 Is your handwriting the most *illegible* in the class?

Phrasal verbs: education

2 a Match the phrasal verbs in italics in the sentences to the definitions a–j below.
1 The Principal *handed in* his resignation.
2 The students *turned up* late for class.
3 The teacher *got* her ideas *across* very well.
4 We *worked out* the answers very easily.
5 He *stayed on* at university another year.
6 I *got down to* work as soon as I arrived.
7 A taxi *picked* them *up* and took them to college.
8 She *kept up with* the other students.
9 We *carried out* a survey on staff attitudes.
10 He *went over* the exercise with his students.

a arrived
b collected
c managed to understand
d stayed level with
e performed
f examined
g gave to a person in charge
h communicated
i started
j remained

b Complete these sentences with the phrasal verbs from Exercise 3a in the correct form.
1 Haven't your notes .... yet? Perhaps they're in your coat.
2 Are you .... after class tonight or going home?
3 Who's going to .... that experiment?
4 It's time I .... marking the papers.
5 .... your answers carefully.
6 I haven't .... my homework yet. It's still in my bag.
7 I can't .... all the latest technology.
8 Come and .... your old coursework from my office.
9 He didn't really .... his meaning .... to the students.
10 We're trying to .... the best way to meet students' needs.

The world around us

Overview

- **Reading:** gapped text (Paper 1 Part 2)
- **Language development 1:** adjectives and adverbs
- **Writing:** email (Paper 2 Part 1)
- **Speaking:** individual long turn (Paper 5 Part 2)
- **Listening skills:** listening for specific information
- **Use of English 1:** open cloze (Paper 3 Part 2)
- **Language development 2:** -ing forms and infinitives
- **Use of English 2:** multiple-choice cloze (Paper 3 Part 1)
- **Language development 3:** nouns and adjectives: the weather

The Galapagos Islands, home of the land iguana

Red Square, Moscow

Lead-in

- The places in the photos are both World Heritage sites. Why do you think they were chosen?
- Why is it important to preserve our natural and cultural heritage?

Our cultural heritage

Reading (Paper 1 Part 2)

Before you read

1 How much do you already know about the history of London?

Skimming and scanning
▶ Reading strategy
Module 1A page 10, Module 2A page 24

2 Skim and scan the text. (Ignore the gaps at this stage.) Find the answers to the questions in 1.

Gapped text
▶ page 178

3 You are going to read an article about the history of London. Seven sentences have been removed from the article. Choose from the sentences A–H the one which fits each gap (1–7). There is one extra sentence which you do not need to use. The first one is done for you.

Task strategy

- Read the whole of the base text and example sentence carefully.
- Read the text before and after each gap. Predict the missing information.
- Look for a sentence in the box that fits the topic.
- Look for grammatical links (e.g. pronouns); lexical links (e.g. synonyms).
- If you're not sure, go to the next gap.
- Read the text again with your answers, to check it makes sense.

a Look at the example. The highlighted word show why D fits.
- *Yet it has had more than its fair share of misfortunes* refers back to *21ˢᵗ century Britain is an exciting place to be.*
- *this invasion*, in the sentence after the gap refers back to *the Roman occupation in AD43.*

b Do the task. Follow the task strategy. For gaps 2 and 3, the links have been highlighted for you.

A Unfortunately, this new period of wealth was hard hit by a global economic crisis shortly followed by another attack on the city, in which much of London was ruined.

B Diseases such as cholera were common and the dumping of waste in the Thames meant that the period became known as 'The Great Stink'.

C During his reign the River Thames became the focal point of London, as the navy was expanded and ships were sent out to explore the world.

D Yet it has had more than its fair share of misfortunes throughout its long history, going back to the Roman occupation in AD43.

E These dreams suffered a huge blow when, 18 years later, a rebellion was launched against the invaders and Londinium was burnt to the ground in the first of many disastrous fires.

F This meant that the dogs and cats who could have caught many of the disease-carrying rats were severely reduced and as a result around 100,000 people are estimated to have died in this disaster.

G But the city's location on the Thames was far too good for its decline to continue.

H In fact, many of the streets in the city were named after the particular trade which was practised there.

c Compare and justify your answers. What links helped you?

Discussion

4 Discuss these questions.
1 What were the 'highs' and 'lows' of London's history? What were the high and low points of your country's capital city?
2 Which city in the world do you think has had the most interesting history?

Vocabulary: near synonyms

5 Find words or phrases in the text that are near synonyms of:
1 progressive (para 1)   5 destroy (para 4)
2 adding (para 1)   6 disaster (para 5)
3 discouraged (para 2)   7 horrible smell (para 6)
4 cleanliness (para 3)   8 get bigger (para 7)

A COLOURFUL HERITAGE

21st century London is an exciting place to be. Dubbed 'swinging London' in the 1960s, the city has been at the forefront of fashion, popular music, cutting edge art and dance ever since. Around 12 million tourists a year visit the city to experience its culture, history and lively nightlife and preparations for the 2012 Olympic Games are currently injecting new energy into the East End.
1 _____D_____

Prior to this invasion there were no significant settlements in the area of forests and marshes which was to become known as Londinium. By developing it as an important trading centre for goods brought up the River Thames by boat, the Romans hoped to establish the city as the future capital of England . **2** _____.

Not to be put off, the new rulers quickly defeated Boudicca and her followers and went on to rebuild the city, building a wall around it to protect it from further attacks . However, the Roman Empire crumbled in the 5th century, and once more the power and influence of London took a downward turn .

3 _____ Trade soon began to expand again until in the 9th century the Danish Vikings attacked the city and burnt it to the ground once more. For the next hundred years it is a confused tale of Anglo-Saxon, Danish and Norman kings invading and controlling the city. The crowning of the Norman King, William the Conqueror at Westminster Abbey in 1066 marked the beginning of the Middle Ages in London, and a more settled era. Within the original Roman walls the city continued to grow but since the houses were made of wood and plaster and crowded tightly together, fire was a continual hazard and hygiene so poor that when the Black Death swept through Europe in the 14th century it killed nearly a half of London's inhabitants.

A new London was born in the 16th century when Henry VIII made himself Head of the Church in England, giving away much of the land previously owned by the church for private development. **4** _____
It was also the period of the first theatres, including the recently rebuilt Globe Theatre, made famous by Shakespeare's plays. By the 16th century there were about 200,000 people living in London. Unfortunately, the following century was to be dominated by two disasters which again would wipe out much of the population and devastate most of the city itself.

London was no stranger to the plague, but a fatal variety brought over by rats on trading ships caused panic. While those who could escaped the city, sufferers were locked in their houses along with their families, and orders were given for all household pets to be killed. **5** _____
Although the next calamity, the Great Fire, only took eight lives and put an end to the plague, it burnt down four fifths of the city. It was during this period that Sir Christopher Wren designed and built many of the well-known London churches seen today, including St Paul's Cathedral.

The Industrial Revolution saw the population explode to six million in a hundred years as Victorian London became the centre of trade and of a large powerful Empire. The early part of the 19th century was the golden age of steam, as railways connected different parts of Britain to its capital and the first ever underground railway was built. Much of today's London is Victorian – the most famous building being the Houses of Parliament, rebuilt in 1834. However, despite all this economic expansion living conditions amongst the poor were dreadful. **6** _____. Charles Dickens vividly describes the London of that time in his novels as poor, dirty and crime-ridden.

The boundaries of the City spread outward in the 20th century, as the population continued to snowball. A spate of luxury hotels and department stores such as the Ritz and Harrods sprang up, the first of their kind.
7 _____. This time it was bombs rather than fire which caused the devastation; the post-war period saw massive rebuilding and also heavy immigration from countries of the old British Empire, which was to change the character of the city yet again.

Language development 1

Adjectives and adverbs

1 a Look at the photos in this extract from a magazine. Which of the sites do you recognise?

b Read the text. What do these sites have in common? (Don't worry about the words in italics at this stage.)

2 a In the context of the article, which of the words in italics are adjectives and which are adverbs? Write them in the correct place in the table.

Adjectives	Adverbs
natural	

b Answer these questions.

1 Most adverbs end in -*ly*. What exceptions are there in the text?
2 Which adjective in the text ends in -*ly*?
3 Some adverbs have two forms, depending on the meaning. What example is there of this?

c Check your answers in the Grammar reference on pages 183–184.

3 a Mark the correct word in each pair.

1 Usually it's *easy / easily* to know when you're looking at a World Heritage site.
2 Chartres Cathedral is *incredible / incredibly* well-preserved.
3 Our guide round the Summer Palace in Beijing spoke too *fast / quick*.
4 The Kremlin is a *classic / classically* Heritage site.
5 When we got to Glasgow it was very *late / lately* in the afternoon and it was snowing *hard / hardly*.
6 Some Heritage sites are quite *surprising / surprisingly*. For example, the city of Brasilia was *imaginative / imaginatively* created from nothing in 1956.

b Which place(s) in your country would you nominate as a Heritage site?

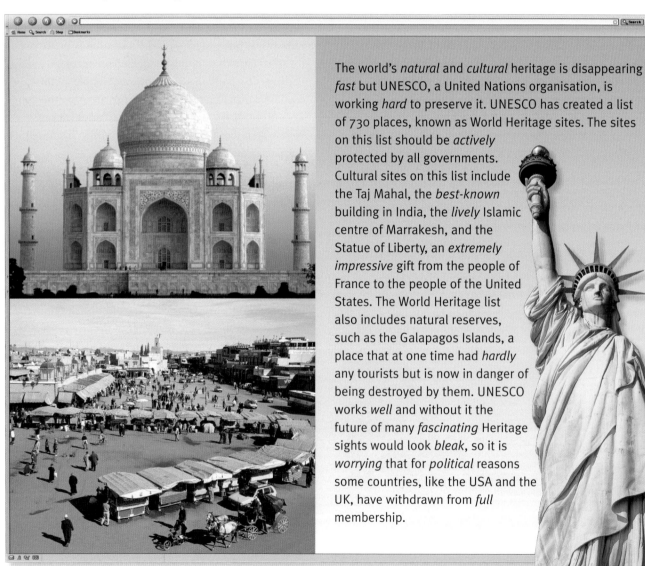

The world's *natural* and *cultural* heritage is disappearing *fast* but UNESCO, a United Nations organisation, is working *hard* to preserve it. UNESCO has created a list of 730 places, known as World Heritage sites. The sites on this list should be *actively* protected by all governments. Cultural sites on this list include the Taj Mahal, the *best-known* building in India, the *lively* Islamic centre of Marrakesh, and the Statue of Liberty, an *extremely impressive* gift from the people of France to the people of the United States. The World Heritage list also includes natural reserves, such as the Galapagos Islands, a place that at one time had *hardly* any tourists but is now in danger of being destroyed by them. UNESCO works *well* and without it the future of many *fascinating* Heritage sights would look *bleak*, so it is *worrying* that for *political* reasons some countries, like the USA and the UK, have withdrawn from *full* membership.

Adverbs of degree

A To make adjectives and other adverbs stronger.
- *extremely/very/really/remarkably*
  The castle is **really/remarkably** popular.
  It's a/an **very/extremely** popular attraction.

B To make adjectives and adverbs less strong.
- *rather/fairly/pretty* (positive and negative adjectives)
  The city wall is **rather/fairly/pretty** long.
  My town is **rather/fairly/pretty** small.
  It's **rather a/a rather/a fairly/a pretty small** town.
  (~~fairly a, pretty a~~)
  It's **a fairly/a pretty small** town.

- *a bit/a little* (negative adjectives only)
  London's **a bit/a little** expensive.
  London's **a bit of an** expensive city. (before a noun phrase)

- *quite*
  The palace is **quite** interesting.
  It's **quite an** interesting palace.
  (~~a quite~~ interesting castle)

C To emphasise ungradable adjectives.
- *absolutely*
  The temperatures were **absolutely** freezing.
  (~~very freezing, a bit freezing~~)
  There's an *absolutely* gorgeous view from the top.
  (~~very gorgeous~~).

▶ Grammar reference page 184

4 Read the information about adverbs in the box and decide which answer A, B, C or D best fits each space.
1 It was a .... simple idea.
   A bit   B little   C quite   D remarkably
2 Karl's got .... a fast car.
   A pretty   B very   C quite   D extremely
3 Everybody thinks he is .... crazy.
   A a little   B a little of   C a bit of   D quite a
4 Goya's paintings are .... well-known.
   A a bit   B absolutely   C very   D rather a
5 This is .... an important day.
   A fairly   B rather   C extremely   D pretty
6 Your new dress looks very ....
   A gorgeous B wonderful C marvellous D beautiful
7 The weather was .... wonderful.
   A very   B absolutely   C extremely D remarkably

5 Use the adjectives in the list below, and adverbs of degree, to talk about:
- a place you have visited
- a person you know well
- a good film or book.

| dull | interesting | lively | fantastic |

6 Correct these students' sentences.

1 It's easy to find my house. There's a very huge statue on the other side of the road.

2 The park is really lovely, and the new theatre is very fantastic.

3 You don't need to be smart dressed. People dress casually here in summer.

4 Builders are working very hardly to restore the Town Hall before the President's visit next month.

5 It's a fairly lively town, which I like, but the streets are sometimes bit noisy at night.

Writing   Email (Paper 2 Part 1)

Lead-in   **1** **Discuss these questions.**
  1   Which city would you most like to spend a weekend in? Why?
  2   What can a tourist see and do in your home town?

Understand the task   **2** **Read the task below and answer the questions.**
  1   WHO are you writing to?
  2   What is the PURPOSE of your email?
  3   How many pieces of INFORMATION should you include in your email?
  4   What STYLE are you going to use? (Remember who you are writing to.)

An old friend, Sue Brown, has written to you saying she would like to come and visit your home town. She has asked you a list of questions.

Read the beginning of Sue's email and your notes, which answer her questions. Then write an email to her, recommending the city as a place to visit and suggesting she should come and stay with you.

I'm going to a conference at that big Conference Centre on the coast on the 18 July so I thought I might come down and stay the night and then have a weekend with Tom in your home town. It'd be really helpful if you could tell me:

• how to get to your home town from the Conference Centre ← *Hourly train connections.*

• about a good hotel ← *Stay with me.*

• what we can see there ← *Lovely park. Medieval castle.*

• what kind of clothes we will need ← *Usually very hot weather in July. Shorts. T-shirts.*

Write an **email** in **120–150** words. You must use grammatically correct sentences with accurate spelling and punctuation in a style appropriate for the situation.

Plan your email   **3** **a** How many paragraphs will you have?

  b This is an example of a paragraph plan for the email. What points would you include in each paragraph? Make notes. The first and last paragraph are done for you.

  Paragraph 1: Reacting to Sue's email: Glad you're coming.
     Inviting her to stay: You can stay at my house.

  Paragraph 2: Travel instructions: ...

  Paragraph 3: Places to go: 1 ...
                 2 ...

  Paragraph 4: Clothes: ...

  Paragraph 5: Conclusion: More questions (phone?) Look forward to ...

Language and content

4 a Which paragraph would be more appropriate to begin the email? Why?

> **A** Thank you very much for your email of 10 July. I was delighted to hear about your visit to my home town. I am writing to invite you to stay with me at my house.

> **B** It was great to hear from you and I'm thrilled you're coming to visit me. I hope you'll stay with me – I've got loads of room to put you up now I've unpacked!

b Can you find any specific examples of formal and informal language in A and B above?

c Complete some of the expressions in the table for the email.

Getting there	*It's about … away by train. You can easily get here by … . It probably only takes … .*
Suggesting things to do	*I hope you will … .* *You really must … ./You absolutely have to … .* *You could go to the … .* *How do you fancy …?* *What/How about …?*
Suggesting what to bring	*It'd probably be a good idea … . Don't bother … .*

d Which sentence in each of the pairs below would be most appropriate in the last paragraph of the letter?

> **1**
> **A** Why don't you give me a ring when you get here?
> **B** May I suggest that you telephone me upon arrival?

> **2**
> **A** I look forward to meeting you.
> **B** I'm really looking forward to seeing you again.

> **3**
> **A** If you need further information please don't hesitate to contact me.
> **B** Let me know if there's anything else you'd like to know.

e How will you close the letter? (e.g. *Cheers, Love, Yours sincerely*)

Write your email

5 Now write your email using the ideas and some of the language above. You must include the most important information. Do not write any postal addresses. Write your answer in 120–150 words.

Check and improve your email

▶ Writing reference page 197–198

6 When you edit your email, what things will you check? Refer to the checklist in the Writing reference.

LANGUAGE SPOT: punctuation
Write this paragraph with appropriate capital letters and punctuation.

chester itself is a very pretty town it dates back to roman times so there are a lot of fascinating ruins and lovely architecture which im sure will interest you the roman amphitheatre is well worth a visit with its guides dressed up as roman soldiers there is also a cathedral and a church and there are red sandstone walls all round the town it takes about an hour and a half to walk around them but its a lovely walk henry james the american writer wrote about how much he loved the walls youll also find a river in chester where you can go for a boat trip or have a picnic if you have time to go shopping there are lots of wonderful shops

Speaking (Paper 5 Part 2)

Vocabulary: animals

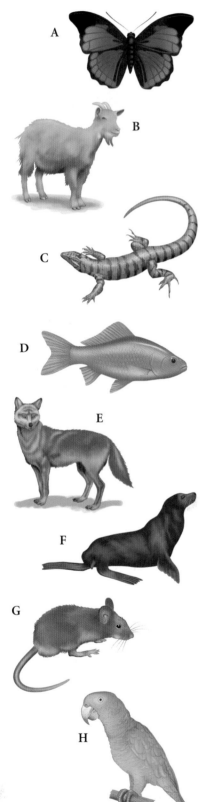

A

B

C

D

E

F

G

H

1 a **What are the names of these animals? Which have an irregular spelling in the plural?**

b **Which of them might you find in these places? (Name one only for each place.)**
- a farm   • the forest
- the jungle   • the house

Where might you find each of the others?

c **Name one which is an example of the following. (Some might be in more than one category.)**
- an insect   • a sea animal
- a rodent   • a domestic pet
- a reptile

d **Give an example of one which has:**

a tail, wings, claws, whiskers, a beak, hooves, fur, fins

e **Which of these animals:**
- squeaks? • howls? • screeches?

2 **Check in a dictionary you know the meaning and the pronunciation of the animals in the box and divide them into the categories below. (Some may go in more than one category.)**

Domestic pets   Farm animals   Wild animals   Birds   Insects

> sheep moose guinea pig pigeon bear whale tortoise giraffe
> penguin beaver bee leopard beetle bull rabbit ant shark
> mosquito squirrel vulture hamster calf dolphin

3 **Think of an example of an animal which:**
- bites   • hibernates
- pecks   • builds a nest
- stings   • is in danger of becoming extinct
- scratches

4 a **Which animals do you associate with these adjectives? You can choose from the animals in the box or any other animals you know.**

aggressive   elegant   proud   fierce   cunning   agile   affectionate
useful   intelligent

> jaguar donkey snake fox crocodile lion dog tiger cat

b **Use the adjectives above and any other adjectives you know to compare these animals.**

5 **Which animals:**
- a do you like most?
- b have you kept as a pet?
- c have a personality which is similar to yours?

6 Look at the photos. What jobs do they illustrate?

Comparing and contrasting photos

7 Answer these questions.
1 What do the photos have in common?
They both show … .
2 What is different about them?
In the one on the left … ,
whereas in the other one … .

Sample answer

8 **a** 🎧 Listen to the examiner and complete her instructions.
EXAMINER: I'd like you to compare and contrast these photographs and say what you think ....

b 🎧 Listen to a student doing the task and answer the questions.
1 Did he mention the same similarities and differences as you?
2 Did he use the same language to compare and contrast?

c 🎧 Listen again and tick (✓) the expressions he uses for giving a personal opinion.

> *Personally, I … .*
> *I'm not really very interested in … .*
> *It's very hard to say, but … .*
> *If I had to choose … .*

▶ Functions reference page 215

d Which two words didn't the student know? How did he explain them?

Individual long turn

▶ page 181

Task strategy
- Listen carefully to the instructions.
- Say what is similar and different about the photos. Don't just describe each one.
- Give your personal opinion in the second part of the task.

9 Work in pairs. Follow the task strategy.
STUDENT A: Compare and contrast the photos above and say what you think is difficult about these jobs.
STUDENT B: Compare and contrast the photos on page 209 and say why you think dogs are useful for this kind of work.

10 Did you:
- compare and contrast the pictures?
- give your personal reaction?
- speak for a full minute?

Discussion

11 What other jobs involve working with animals? Which ones would you most/least like to do? Why?

Listening

Before you listen

▶ Listening strategy
Module 1B page 18, Module 2B page 32

1 a You will hear an interview with Nick Gordon (in the photo above), who spent ten years in the rainforest. What do you think his job is? What do you think he liked and disliked about being in the rainforest?

  b 🎧 Listen to the first part of the interview and check your guesses.

Listening for specific information

Listening strategy

Read the questions first so you know what you need to listen for.

2 a Decide what kind of information is missing in Exercise 2b.
  EXAMPLE: *Question 1 – a time*

  b 🎧 You will now hear the rest of the interview with Nick Gordon. For questions 1–10, complete the sentences. Listen to the recording twice.

  1 Nick says that he first saw a jaguar at .... in the morning.

  2 The jaguar's coat was a mixture of .... and .... in colour.

  3 Nick was disappointed at not getting a .... of his first jaguar.

  4 Most male jaguars have a territory of .... in size.

  5 The fact that jaguars move around so much and so .... makes it easy to miss them.

  6 On a trip in search of jaguars, Nick was once given a very large .... to eat.

  7 Nick says that forest people have a feeling of .... for the jaguar.

  8 To help them study jaguars, researchers have fixed .... on to some they have caught.

  9 In some areas, jaguars are killed by .... because they are seen as a threat.

  10 The health of jaguars may be in danger due to contact with animals such as .... and ....

  c Compare and discuss your answers.
  1 How many words did you write in each gap?
  2 Were the words you needed on the recording?

Use of English 1 (Paper 3 Part 2)

Lead-in

1 a Do you think the following statements are *True* or *False*?

1 Cats don't see colours as clearly as people do.
2 A dog's sense of smell is much better than a person's.
3 Elephants have long memories.
4 Crickets can tell us the temperature.
5 Cows lie down before a storm.

b Check your answers on page 209.

Open cloze ▶ page 179

▶ Task strategy Module 2B page 33

2 a Read the title of the text below. What connection do you think it has with animals?

b Read the text quickly and answer the questions. (Ignore the spaces at this stage.)

1 How do some animals change their behaviour before an earthquake?
2 What use have the Chinese made of animals?
3 How can the animals' behaviour be explained scientifically?

c Do the task. Follow the task strategy on page 33 and use the Help clues if necessary.

Read the text below and think of the word which best fits each space. Use only one word in each space. There is an example at the beginning (0).

HELP

➤ **Question 1**
This question tests tenses. Which tense is correct here?

➤ **Question 7**
This is another question testing tenses. Were the animals restless before the reports were made or at the same time?

➤ **Question 9**
This city has been mentioned before. Which article is used to show this?

➤ **Question 13**
Which word is correct here, *It* or *There*?

PREDICTING EARTHQUAKES

It has long **(0)** ..been.. known that animals, birds and insects behave differently before an earthquake. People **(1)**............. seen fish jump out of water on to dry land, and mice appear dazed before quakes, allowing **(2)**............. to be caught easily.

In December 1974, Chinese scientists began **(3)**............. receive reports of snakes coming out of hibernation and freezing to death on the cold ground. This was followed **(4)**............. a series of minor tremors at the end of the month. The following month they received even **(5)**.............. reports of strange animal behaviour in the city of Haicheng. Many **(6)**............. these concerned cattle and horses which **(7)**............. become restless and were **(8)**............. frightened to enter buildings. As a result, city leaders evacuated **(9)**............. entire city. Soon after, a major earthquake struck; the city leaders had succeeded **(10)**.............. saving countless lives.

(11)............. then China has suffered a number of major quakes, which they were not as prepared **(12)**.............. Nevertheless, the Chinese have demonstrated that earthquakes do not always strike without warning.

(13)............. is a fact that some animals are very sensitive to sound, temperature, touch, light and even magnetic fields. Therefore, they may be able to detect the seismic activity **(14)**............. comes before an earthquake. It would **(15)**............. a pity to ignore the signs.

d Which questions in the task test:
• articles? • auxiliary verbs? • verb + verb patterns? • verb + preposition?

Language development 2
-*ing* forms and infinitives

A After a main verb we can use:
- an -*ing* form: *I like walking. I heard a man shouting.*
- a *to*-infinitive: *I wanted **to see** her.*
- an infinitive (without *to*): *Let me **help**!*
*That **makes** me **feel** better. Did anyone **see** John leave?*

B The -*ing* form is used after prepositions.
*I'm thinking **of getting** a new job.*
*Nadia is keen **on learning** new things.*

C The -*ing* form can also be used in some fixed expressions.
*The family **spent** a lot of **time arguing**.*
*It's always **worth asking** for a discount.*

D The infinitive can be used after:
- some adjectives: *She's **eager to learn**.*
- some nouns: *It was **my decision to leave**.*

(LOOK) at the Use of English text on page 47 and find examples of the structures above.

▶ Grammar reference pages 194–195

1 a Discuss these questions.
1 What causes a solar eclipse?
2 Have you ever seen a solar eclipse?

b Look at the notes made by a journalist about a solar eclipse. Put the verbs in brackets in the correct form.

Many creatures wanted (1)............... (*settle*) down to sleep.
Other animals, like owls, had problems (2)............... (*sleep*) and woke up.
I saw a bat suddenly (3)............... (*fly*) out of a tree.
I couldn't help (4)............... (*notice*) a strange, cold breeze.
Scientists were interested in (5)............... (*solve*) the mysteries of the sun.
Spectators saw the sky gradually (6)............... (*go*) dark. I regretted (7)............... (*not, bring*) a video camera. The experience was awesome – it made us (8)............... (*feel*) very small.
I found it hard (9)............... (*talk*) for a few minutes.
A lot of people made the decision (10)............... (*not, drive*) during the eclipse.

2 a The verbs *stop, try, remember* can be followed by -*ing* or a *to*-infinitive. Look at the sentence pairs below. What is the difference in meaning?
1 a He remembered to wear protective glasses.
  b He remembered wearing protective glasses.
2 a She tried using a camcorder to record the event.
  b She tried to use a camcorder to record the event.
3 a He stopped to look at the bright lights.
  b He stopped looking at the bright lights.

b Mark the correct form of the verb in each pair.
1 He stopped at the shop *to buy / buying* a pint of milk.
2 I tried *to get / getting* eggs but they didn't have any.
3 Lucy stopped *to drink / drinking* coffee ages ago.
4 Please remember *to post / posting* the letter.
5 I remember *to call / calling* Mike yesterday.
6 Try *to add / adding* some salt. It might taste better.

3 a Look at the photo. Have you heard of this natural phenomenon?

b Read about a couple's trip to see the Northern Lights. Then complete the spaces in the text. Use *to, on, from, for, of* or *in* and put the verb in brackets in the correct form.

Northern Lights in the skies above Scotland

The possibility (1)............... (*see*) the Northern Lights was Laura's main reason for visiting the Shetland Islands. She had been looking forward (2)............... (*go*) there for ages. I was more interested (3)............... (*get*) some rest and fresh air. When we arrived, Laura had a headache, so I insisted (4)............... (*put up*) the tent myself. She apologised (5)............... (*not, help*) and decided (6)............... (*go*) for a walk. I didn't object (7)............... (*her, go*) as I'm not very keen (8)............... (*walk*) and I thought it might help her headache. And anyway, I can rarely prevent (9)............... (*her, do*) what she wants to do! Soon, it got very dark. I decided to look for Laura. I was afraid (10)............... (*get lost*), but I needn't have worried – suddenly there were curtains of red, green and white light everywhere. It was the Northern Lights.

4 a Complete these sentences about yourself.
1 When I'm on holiday, I enjoy … .
2 My greatest ambition in life is … .
3 The country I'd most like … (visit) is … .

b Compare your answers with other students.

Use of English 2 (Paper 3 Part 1)

Lead-in

1 Read the title of the text below and look at the photo. Have you heard of Groundhog Day?

Multiple-choice cloze

▶ page 179

▶ Task strategy Module 1B page 21

2 a Read the title and text quickly and answer the questions. (Ignore the spaces at this stage.)
   1 What happens on Groundhog Day?
   2 Why has it become better-known in recent years?

b Do the task. Follow the task strategy on page 18 and use the Help clues if necessary.
   Read the text below and decide which answer **A**, **B**, **C** or **D** best fits each space. There is an example at the beginning (0).
   0 **A** eager **B** enthusiastic **C** optimistic **D** interesting

GROUNDHOG DAY

According to an (0)......d...... US popular tradition, the groundhog, a small furry animal, (1)............... of its winter sleep on 2 February. If the sky is (2)..............., he sees his shadow. This means there's going to be six more weeks of (3)............... weather and he returns to his hole. If the day is cloudy and he can't see his shadow, it means there will be an (4)............... spring and he stays above ground. Each year reporters (5)............... in Punxsutawney at dawn and a large (6)............... of cameras are focused on the burrow of a groundhog named Punxsutawney Phil. Is spring just around the (7)...............? That's what they want Phil to tell them. Or is it going to be a long, (8)............... winter with a risk of more (9)............... snow? Groundhog Day has become more popular in recent years, mainly because of the 1993 Hollywood film of the same (10)..............., which made Punxsutawney famous and (11)............... Phil into a major celebrity. The following February, over 30,000 people (12)............... in Punxsutawney, Pennsylvania for Phil's big day. Unfortunately, (13)............... the large crowds were hoping (14)............... a prediction of good weather, Phil saw his shadow and returned to his hole, so everyone knew that winter was going to (15)............... for a few more weeks.

...xsutawney Phil

HELP

➤ **Question 3**
Only one of these adjectives can combine with *weather* to mean *bad*.

➤ **Question 6**
Remember that cameras are countable.

➤ **Question 9**
Only one of these adjectives can combine with *snow*. The others combine with *fog* or *wind*.

	A	B	C	D
1	gets out	comes out	gets up	comes up
2	calm	apparent	clear	fair
3	low	severe	ill	rude
4	advanced	ahead	early	immature
5	gather	group	crowd	combine
6	quantity	number	total	sum
7	street	turn	bend	corner
8	stiff	hard	solid	forceful
9	strong	dense	heavy	warm
10	name	title	label	term
11	got	became	took	turned
12	turned up	called off	came on	looked over
13	despite	although	still	otherwise
14	for	to	by	on
15	exist	rest	last	hold

c Which questions test:
   • words that go together?
   • the correct word from a set with similar meanings?
   • fixed expressions?
   • phrasal verbs?
   • linking words?

d Which adjective + noun combinations in the text link to either weather or the seasons? Make a note of the words you want to remember in your vocabulary book.

Language development 3
Nouns and adjectives: the weather

1 **Discuss these questions.**
1 What's the weather like in your country at different times of the year?
2 What kind of weather do you like best?

2 a **Write the nouns below in the appropriate place in the table. Use a dictionary if necessary.**

breeze   drizzle   hail   shower   snow   gust
hurricane   thunder   gale   lightning   downpour

Rain	Wind	Storm

b **Read these statements about extreme weather. Mark the correct word in each pair.**

FASCINATING
WEATHER FACTS

1 When *thunder* / *lightning* strikes the earth, its temperature is hotter than the surface of the sun.

2 In the Antarctic, *gales* / *gusts* of wind can reach speeds of over 320 kilometres per hour.

3 In some parts of the world, *hail* / *drizzle* can damage crops and kill animals.

4 *Hurricanes* / *Downpours* are whirling storms that can create giant waves up to eight metres high.

5 Snow and hail are both frozen water, but *snow* / *hail* doesn't fall in thunderstorms.

3 a **Match the adjectives in A with the nouns in B. There may be more than one possibility.**

A		B	
1	torrential	a	breeze
2	tropical	b	shower
3	gentle	c	downpour
4	heavy	d	thunder
5	high	e	rain
6	light	f	wind
7	loud	g	storm
8	strong		
9	hard		
10	pouring		
11	chilly		

b **Which adjective in Exercise 3a best completes each sentence? There may be more than one possibility.**
1 Because of the .... winds, all flights have been cancelled.
2 We're soaked. We got caught in a .... shower.
3 We sat in the garden and enjoyed the .... spring breeze.
4 The storm's nearly over. The thunder's not as .... as it was.
5 The rain's quite .... Let's stay indoors.
6 The wind always turns a little .... in autumn.
7 In the tropics you usually get .... rain during a storm.

4 a **Weather adjectives can also be used to describe people or things. Match the adjectives in A with nouns in B.**

A		B	
1	stormy	a	smile
2	heated	b	manner
3	icy	c	discussion
4	sunny	d	relationship
5	breezy	e	stare

b **Can you guess what the phrases mean? Use a dictionary to help you.**

5 **What kind of weather do you think would be most appropriate for:**
1 a romantic encounter?
2 a quarrel with your best friend?
3 a long car journey?
4 a holiday in the mountains?
5 a trip in a sailing boat?

MODULE 4
Challenges

Overview

- **Reading:** multiple choice (Paper 1 Part 1)
- **Language development 1:** narrative tenses; time conjunctions
- **Writing:** story (Paper 2 Part 2)
- **Speaking:** collaborative task (Paper 5 Part 3)
- **Listening:** multiple matching (Paper 4 Part 3)
- **Language development 2:** quantity; determiners
- **Use of English 1:** key word transformations (Paper 3 Part 4)
- **Use of English 2:** multiple-choice cloze (Paper 3 Part 1)
- **Language development 3:** adjectives often confused; phrasal verbs with *take*

Lead-in

- The photos show people in challenging situations. Which situations would, for you, be the hardest/easiest? the most satisfying? the most interesting?
- What's the most challenging situation you've faced in your school, college or working life?

51

Personal challenges

Reading (Paper 1 Part 1)

Before you read

1 Look at the photo opposite. Where do you think the man is? What's he doing?

Skimming

▶ Reading strategy Module 2A, page 24

2 Look at the title of the article and the introduction. Then write down at least three questions you would like to find the answer to in the text. **EXAMPLE:** *How does he prepare for this?*

Multiple choice

▶ page 178

3 Skim the text to find the answers to your questions.

4 a For questions 1–7 below choose the option A, B, C or D which you think fits best. Follow the task strategy. Question 1 has been done for you. The highlighted words show how the answer was found.

Task strategy

- Read the questions and mark key words. Don't look at the options yet.
- Find and mark the parts of the text that contain the information you need.
- Read the options. The correct option will match the meaning of the text but use different words.

b Compare and justify your answers.
  1 Which part of the text helped you to answer each question?
  2 Which parallel words or phrases helped you identify the correct answer A, B, C or D?

5 a What do the underlined phrasal verbs in the text mean?

b Discuss these questions.
  1 What have <u>you</u> taken to like a duck to water?
  2 Have you ever put yourself through something really difficult? Are you glad you did?

Vocabulary and discussion

---

1 **As a child, Pugh's ambition was to be**
   A a sailor   B a lawyer   C a swimmer   D an explorer

2 **Why did Pugh make travel a priority?**
   A to improve his knowledge of the seas
   B to achieve something never done before
   C to find out how far it was possible for him to swim
   D to swim amongst the world's most dangerous animals

3 **What was so extraordinary about Pugh's achievement in 2005?**
   A He broke the record for the fastest cold water swim.
   B He swam in absolutely dreadful weather conditions.
   C He was the first person to swim so near both the North and South Poles
   D He is the only human ever to dare to swim near polar bears in the Arctic.

4 **What is so unusual about Pugh?**
   A He is able to make himself warm when he needs to.
   B He is able to put on weight before an important swim.
   C He has the kind of skin which can tolerate extreme cold.
   D He has trained his body not to be affected by freezing water.

5 **What motivates Pugh to do what he does?**
   A his determination not to be beaten
   B his love of competitive swimming
   C his obsession with any form of sport
   D his fascination with the Polar regions

6 **What do we learn about Pugh from the last paragraph?**
   A He no longer feels the need to beat world records.
   B He is putting all his energy into saving the environment.
   C He feels he has achieved all he wants to as a swimmer.
   D He is not prepared to say what he might be doing next.

7 **What does Pugh believe that everyone should do?**
   A learn to overcome any personal fears
   B prevent global warming by any means possible
   C do dangerous things in order to feel more alive
   D continue to do things that people have never done before

In at the deep end

British explorer Lewis Pugh wants to conquer some of the most inhospitable, dangerous places in the world in his own unique way – by swimming through them.

Brought up on a diet of stories about Ernest Shackleton, Captain Cook and Sir Edmund Hillary, Lewis Pugh's childhood dreams were filled with his heroes' ground-breaking expeditions to the Poles, Australia and Mount
5 Everest . The son of a Royal Navy officer, Pugh was 17 before he learned to swim but he took to it, literally, like a duck to water and from then on the British lawyer decided he would combine his passion for adventure with his other love: swimming. Just one month after his first
10 lesson, Pugh decided to do something normally reserved for experienced athletes: the five mile crossing from Robben Island (the island where Nelson Mandela was a prisoner) to Cape Town in water of 16 degrees centigrade. Five years later Lewis swam across the English
15 Channel, the biggest challenge for most extreme swimmers.

Twenty years ago a large chunk of the world's waters had still not been swum so Pugh decided that, while getting on with his studies in maritime law, he'd spend as
20 much time as he could going around the world to collect 'firsts'. Some of these achievements are impressive because of their distance, like the longest cold water swim (204 kilometres down Norway's longest fjord). Others would make even the greatest animal lover tremble with
25 fear: crossing African lakes filled with hippopotamuses and crocodiles or swimming round the southernmost tip of Africa in shark-infested waters. But for Pugh, each challenge has to be greater than the last.

This attitude ended up taking him to the most
30 inhospitable regions in the world; in August 2005 Pugh made world-wide headlines when, ignoring the threat of polar bears, he broke the world record for the most northern swim, as he plunged into the near frozen waters of the Arctic near the North Pole and swam for a
35 kilometre. Four months later he went on to do the same for the most southern part of the Antarctic. This time there were icebergs around, the water was at freezing point and it was snowing, yet despite these more extreme conditions he did the same distance in even less time. His
40 incredible achievement was broadcast by more than 500 TV channels around the world.

'The first dive in Antarctica was an unforgettable experience. You get a terrible headache and your breathing speeds up until you can't control it. Then the
45 skin gets terribly burned. After five or ten minutes you start losing the feeling in your fingers and toes,' says Pugh, known as 'The Polar Bear' because of his ability to swim in temperatures which, physiologically, should be impossible. Like the seals and polar bears that live in these freezing
50 conditions, Pugh has to insulate his body by putting on 15 kilos before a swim in order to up his fat levels. However, it is his unique ability to raise his core body temperature by as much as two degrees in anticipation of the water by the power of his mind that has made him a medical
55 phenomenon.

It is incredible enough that anyone would choose to put themselves through the experiences he does, especially as, to raise the game, he wears only swimming trunks, a cap and goggles. So what drives him? 'Sometimes
60 we set boundaries for ourselves in life, or even worse, we allow others to do so. In many cases these boundaries are just in our mind and need to be pushed away. If you worry about sharks and things like that, the fear will paralyse you. You have to do maths problems or think about
65 something else, otherwise you will fail.' He insists that everyone – however ordinary – is capable of extraordinary things if you can do this.

By swimming more than 1 km in all five oceans of the world Pugh has fulfilled every swimmer's dream. So his
70 latest adventure – swimming down the Thames in London – might seem a little tame, until you realise that this was the full length of the river – 325 km in 21 days – in a heat-wave. As well as collecting another 'first', he used this as a publicity opportunity for a concern very close to his
75 heart; during his swim members of his team put on polar bear costumes and gave out leaflets to educate passers-by about ways of preventing global warming. Although he is currently planning his next round of adventures, he remains tight-lipped about them. 'It may be that I'll quit
80 the aquatic world for a change,' he told us. 'But trust me: no matter what I do, it'll be something that no one has ever seen before.'

Language development 1

Narrative tenses

1 a Read the first sentence of this student's story. How do you think it continues?

> I was unlocking my front door when I heard a noise inside the house.

b Read the next part of the story and compare. Does it continue the way you thought it would?

> I closed the door again quickly and ran out into the street. Then I tried to call the police but my mobile phone wasn't working, because I'd been talking to people all day and the battery had run down.

c Mark the different past verb forms in the story so far.

d Match the meanings in the list a–d to the sentences in the story. Then complete the table below.
   a an activity in progress at a point in the past
   b a single action which happened before a point in the past
   c an action or event at a point in the past
   d an activity which happened before a point in the past

2 Now complete the rest of the story with the correct forms of the verbs in brackets. Sometimes there may be more than one possible answer.

I **(1)**..................... (*run*) down the street to a payphone, but someone **(2)**......................... (*talk*) on the phone. I think she **(3)**........................... (*argue*). After I **(4)**........................... (*wait*) for about ten minutes, she **(5)**........................... (*come*) out. I could see from her eyes that she **(6)**........................... (*cry*).

I **(7)**........................... (*tell*) the police officer what **(8)**........................... (*happen*). But then, while I **(9)**........................... (*talk*) to him, a friend of mine **(10)**........................... (*come*) out of my house. He **(11)**........................... (*carry*) balloons. Then I realised what **(12)**........................... (*go*) on. Of course! It **(13)**........................... (*be*) my birthday, and my friends **(14)**........................... (*wait*) in the house to give me a surprise birthday party!

I **(15)**........................... (*explain*) everything to the officer. When I **(16)**........................... (*go*) into the house, everyone **(17)**........................... (*laugh*), and they **(18)**........................... (*start*) to sing Happy Birthday. I **(19)**........................... (*feel*) very stupid about the way I **(20)**........................... (*react*) ...

Form	Meaning	Example
A Past simple	....	....
B Past continuous *was/were* + *-ing*	....	....
C Past perfect simple *had* + past participle	....	....
D Past perfect continuous *had been* + *-ing*	....	....

▶ Grammar reference pages 188–189

| The battery had run down (3) | | I tried to call the police (1) | | now |

(4)
ᴧᴧᴧᴧᴧᴧᴧᴧᴧ
I'd been talking to people all day

(2)
ᴧᴧᴧᴧᴧᴧ
My mobile phone wasn't working

Time conjunctions

A *As, while, when*
- A longer activity happening 'around' a short event:
  ***As/While/When** I was watching a horror movie, I heard a noise outside.*
- Two longer activities happening at the same time:
  ***As/While/When** I was working, my brother was sitting on the beach.*

B *When*
- A short event in the middle of a longer activity:
  *I was watching a horror movie **when** I heard a noise outside.*
- A short event immediately before another short event:
  ***When** he crossed the finish line, everybody cheered.*

C *Before, after*
- *Before* always goes with the **second** action in the sequence:
  ***Before** we left, I filled up/had filled up with petrol.*
  (= first: I filled up, second: we left)
  *I filled up/had filled up with petrol **before** we left.*
- *After* always goes with the **first** action in the sequence:
  ***After** I filled up/had filled up with petrol, we left.*
  (= first: I filled up, second: we left)
  *We left **after** I filled up/had filled up with petrol.*

D *As soon as*
- *(= immediately after)*
  ***As soon as** he went/had gone outside, it started raining.*
  *It started raining **as soon as** he went/had gone outside.*

E *By the time*
- *(= before)*
  ***By the time** the police arrived, the robbers had run away.*
  *The robbers had run away **by the time** the police arrived.*

3 Read the information about time conjunctions in the box and decide which answer A, B, C or D best fits each space.

1 .... Joe arrived at the cinema, the film had finished.
   A While   B As soon as   C By the time   D As
2 .... we were sitting in a traffic jam, our plane was taking off.
   A As soon as   B While   C After   D By the time
3 .... I phoned Sara, she said she had been ill.
   A While   B Before   C When   D By the time
4 She fell asleep .... she was reading her book.
   A as soon as   B before   C by the time   D while
5 .... I turned on the TV, the programme ended.
   A While   B As soon as   C By the time   D Before
6 Mechanics had checked the cars .... the race started.
   A before   B while   C as   D after
7 The police searched us .... we arrived.
   A when   B by the time   C while   D before
8 I felt so relieved .... I found my missing purse.
   A while   B before   C by the time   D after

4 a Complete these sentences about yourself. Use the past simple, past continuous or past perfect.
   1 When I left school, I … .
   2 I was … when I saw … .
   3 I had been … when I … .
   4 I had … but I … .
   5 When I heard the news about …, I … .

b Compare your sentences with other students.

5 Join the sentence pairs. Use the time conjunctions in brackets and make any other changes necessary. You may need to change the order of the sentences.
   1 I heard the news. Then I phoned my sister. (*as soon as*)
   2 I went to see a friend. Then I went home. (*after*)
   3 I waited for around an hour. Then he eventually arrived. (*by the time*)
   4 The boss resigned. Then the business collapsed. (*when*)
   5 I was gardening for hours. Then she phoned me. (*when*)
   6 His owner was talking. At the same time, the dog ran into the road. (*while*)
   7 The plane left. Then we got to the airport. (*by the time*)
   8 I never ate caviar. Then I went to Russia. (*before*)

6 Think of a different ending for the story in Exercise 1. Continue your story from the opening sentence.

Writing Story (Paper 2 Part 2)

Lead-in 1 a **What kind of stories do you like?**

> love stories ☐   ghost stories ☐   adventure stories ☐
> crime stories ☐   science fiction ☐

b **What makes a good story for you?** EXAMPLE:*Interesting characters …*

2 **Read the task below and answer the questions.**

Understand the task

1 What KIND OF STORY from Exercise 1a above will your readers expect?
2 What will make it a GOOD story? A strong storyline? Interesting characters? Vivid language?
3 What EFFECT do you want to have on the readers? To make them laugh, move them emotionally or frighten them?

> You have been asked to write a **story** for a student magazine. Your story must begin with the words:
>
> That day, my life changed forever.
>
> Write your **story** in **120–180** words.

Plan your story 3 a **Brainstorm ideas for a story. Use these pictures to help you.**

DONATE FUNDS NOW OR OUR HOSPITAL WILL CLOSE!

To raise funds, why not take part in our 6-day 90km sponsored walk of the Great wall of China

b **Now make notes under these headings.**

Paragraph 1:	Set the scene (people and place)
	Who? What? When? Where?
	(What sort of people? How old?)
Paragraphs 2–4:	Say what happened (action)
	What? When? Where? Why? How?
	(How did it happen? How long did it last? How did they feel?)
Paragraph 5:	Bring it to a conclusion
	What? How? Why?

Language and content

4 a Which of these opening paragraphs would have most impact on the readers? Why?

> A That day my life changed forever. Our local children's hospital needed to raise money or it would close, so I decided to take part in a six-day sponsored walk along 90 km of the Great Wall of China. At the time I didn't realise what an incredible personal challenge it would be.

> B That day my life changed forever. Our local children's hospital wanted money to stay open. I decided to do a sponsored walk in China.

b Which of these closing paragraphs would have most impact on the readers? Why?

> A I was OK in the end. I enjoyed the walk. I got the money I wanted and next year I'll probably do something similar.

> B I learned so much from that wonderful experience that every year now I challenge myself to do something different. Next year I'm planning to cycle across Cuba!

c Look at the phrases in the table for sequencing events. How would you continue at least <u>one</u> of the phrases from each section for your story?

Beginning	At the beginning … (I had been …).	That was when … (I realised …)
	At the time … (I didn't realise …)	Then one day … (I decided I would …)
	Before I went … (I'd thought …)	
Middle	Right from the start …	To my amazement … Luckily … (I managed to …)
	Before long I'd … Eventually …	Naturally … (I was very pleased …)
	At the end of the first day …	
End	After it was all over … . In the end … (when I got back …).	Of course … (I was … but …).

d Underline the correct adverb.
1 I was *absolutely/fairly* horrified when I realised it might close.
2 *Precisely/Unfortunately*, it had too little money to stay open.
3 I decided to take two weeks off work *at once/absolutely*.
4 I don't remember *closely/exactly* how many steps there were in each section.
5 *Luckily/Extraordinarily*, I started to enjoy the walk on the third day.
6 I had *positively/definitely* had one of the most amazing experiences ever.

Write your story

5 Now write your story, using some of the language and ideas above. Write your answer in 120–180 words.

Check and improve your story

6 Edit your story using this list. Check your:
- plan (Is the story clear and interesting?)
- use of narrative tenses and linking expressions
- range of adjectives, adverbs and verbs (Is the story vivid?)
- number of words.

▶ Writing reference page 201

LANGUAGE SPOT: making a story vivid

Complete these extracts from a story with more vivid equivalents of the words in brackets.

1 Yesterday it was a .... (*nice*) sunny morning.
2 There had been a .... (*large*) snowfall the night before.
3 Zoe left her friends and .... (*went*) off on her own.
4 When she got to the top, she was .... (*very tired*).
5 People .... (*not often*) go to that part of the mountain.
6 .... (*finally*) she came to the frozen lake.

Speaking (Paper 5 Part 3)

Vocabulary: sports

1 Look at the photos.

a Name each of the sports in the photos.

b Describe what each person is doing. Which person is using a racket? Which person is playing on a court?

c For each photo complete this chart.

SPORT	PLACE	EQUIPMENT

2 Which sports do you do? Do you train seriously or do you do them for fun?

3 a Match the expressions in A with the sports in B.

A	B
do the backstroke	tennis
win by two laps	golf
serve an ace	boxing
win with a knock-out	rugby
take three putts	swimming
make a tackle	athletics

b Choose the correct alternative.

Have you seen last night's football (**1**) *results/grades* in the paper this morning? There were a lot of important international (**2**) *plays/matches*. Brazil (**3**) *won/beat* France one-nil, Spain (**4**) *drew/lost* against England two–all and Russia (**5**) *hit/scored* four goals against Switzerland and (**6**) *won/beat* four–one. I saw some of the Northern Ireland–Spain (**7**) *game/competition* but I thought Spain were the better (**8**) *group/team*. They were one up at (**9**) *the first half/half-time* but in the second half the (**10**) *referee/umpire* sent one of their players off and gave Northern Ireland a (**11**) *penalty/shot*. Healy hit a brilliant (**12**) *shot/drive* in the corner of the net and later he headed in a second goal!

4 You are thinking about taking up a sport. Look at the different sports in the photos. Think of one advantage and one disadvantage of each one, in your situation.

EXAMPLE: *Tennis is good for meeting people, but it's very expensive in my town.*

Sample answer

5 a 🎧 Listen to the examiner's instructions. What <u>two</u> things do the students have to do?

EXAMINER: *First* .... *Then* ....

b 🎧 Now listen to the two students doing the task. Which sport do they choose, and why?

c 🎧 Listen again and tick (✓) the expressions in the table that the students use.

Starting a discussion	*Why don't we start by …?* *Shall we … first?* *Let's begin with … .* *We could start by talking about … .*
Interrupting/Showing you want a turn	*Can I just say…?* *Sorry to interrupt, but … .* *Yes, and as well as that, … .*
Involving the other person	*What do **you** think (about) …?* *Do you agree with that?* *What would you say?*
Bringing the discussion to an end	*So let's decide which … .* *Shall we make a decision?* *Anyway, we have to decide … .*

▶ Functions reference page 215

Collaborative task

▶ page 181

Task strategy

- Listen carefully to the examiner's instructions.
- Talk to your partner, not the examiner.
- Take an active part in the discussion, but involve your partner too.
- Talk about more than one option before making a decision, or you will finish too quickly.

6 Work in groups of three.

STUDENT 1: You are the examiner. Give the instructions (look at page 209) and stop the discussion after three minutes.

STUDENTS 2 AND 3: You are Candidates A and B. Follow the examiner's instructions. Read the task strategy before you start.

7 Discuss the task you have done.

EXAMINER: Did Candidates A and B listen and respond to each other? Did they both put forward ideas?

CANDIDATES: Did you come to a conclusion? Did you run out of time or have too much time?

Listening (Paper 4 Part 3)

Before you listen

1 a Do you think some sports are more risky than others? Why do you think people want to do them? Write down as many 'extreme sports' as you can.

b Look at the reasons for taking up a sport in 2a. Which sports do you think they are going to mention?

c Read the task in Exercise 2a.
1 How many speakers will you hear? What will they talk about?
2 Compare **your** reasons for taking up a sport with those in **A–F**. Which are the same?

Multiple matching

▶ page 191

Task strategy

- Read the task and mark key words in each option A–F.
- The first time you listen, focus on each speaker's main point.
- Match the main points with the closest options and note down your answers.
- During the second listening, check that the statement matches exactly what the speakers say.

2 a 🎧 You will hear five different people giving their reasons for taking up a sport. For questions 1–5 choose from the list A–F what each speaker says. Use the letters only once. There is one extra letter which you do not need to use. Listen to the recording twice. Follow the task strategy.

A I was persuaded by other people.

Speaker 1 [1]

B I was advised to take more exercise.

Speaker 2 [2]

C I did it to raise money for charity.

Speaker 3 [3]

D I wanted to give my family a surprise.

Speaker 4 [4]

E I needed to find a way to relax.

Speaker 5 [5]

F I wanted to prove to someone that I could do it.

b Compare and justify your answers. Listen to the recording again if necessary.
1 How was the main point in each extract expressed?
EXAMPLE: 1C – *get people to give donations to a medical research organisation*
2 Did you need to change any answers the second time you listened?

Vocabulary: idiomatic expressions

3 In the sentences, replace the words in italics with an expression from the following list. (All the expressions were on the recording.) Make any other changes necessary.

fancy (something)   sign up (for something)   from the word go
give (something) a go   (be) into (something)

1 I really enjoyed playing tennis *from the moment I took it up.*
2 My cousin has always been *keen on* snooker.
3 Shall we *enrol* for the judo course on Fridays?
4 Do you *like the idea of* joining the netball team?
5 She has never tried diving but she is happy to *try it.*

Discussion

4 Discuss these questions.
1 *Do you fancy* going scuba diving or doing parachute jumping? Why/Why not?
2 What sports have you always *been into from the word go?*
3 Which sports would you like to *give a go?* Have you ever tried skiing or horse-riding?
4 Have you ever *signed up* for something and then given it up? Why?

Language development 2
Quantity

> A Countable nouns have singular and plural forms:
> *Tiger Woods is a great **golfer**.*
> *He is one of the greatest **golfers** of all time.*
>
> B Uncountable nouns only have one form:
> *He has a lot of **confidence**.*
>
> C Some nouns can be countable or uncountable, depending on the meaning:
> *Golf has become a **sport** for everyone.* (countable – a particular sport)
> ***Sport** is big business these days.* (uncountable – sport in general)
>
> ▶ Grammar reference page 183

1 a **Decide whether each of these nouns is countable, uncountable or both. Use a dictionary if necessary. Which noun in each group is different from the other two? Why?**

1	spectator	fan	excitement
2	advice	fact	information
3	skiing	athletics	football
4	money	salary	coin
5	racket	equipment	glove
6	temperature	weather	sunshine
7	exercise	tracksuit	trainer

2 Correct the mistakes in these sentences.
1 Our trainer gives us good advices.
2 I've heard the results. The news are very bad.
3 People likes Tiger Woods.
4 Some footballers have long hairs.
5 It was a terrible weather so the match was cancelled.
6 Beckham has very expensive furnitures in his house.
7 My shorts was very dirty after the match.
8 I had to do some hard works to beat the champion.
9 The national team stayed in a luxury accommodation.
10 I need informations about tickets.

Determiners

> A Plural countables
> • *(a) few/fewer*
> • *many; a great many; very many; not many*
> *There were **a few** people at the match but **not many**.*
> • *Several*
> ***Several** players were injured.*
> • *small/a good/a large/a great number of*
> *A **large number** of fans watch matches on Saturdays, but only **a small number** go on Wednesday evenings.*
>
> B Uncountables
> • *(very) little/not much*
> *There was**n't much** interest in the village cricket match.*
> • *a good/a great deal of; a small/a large amount of*
> *The club spent **a great deal of** money on their star player, so they only had **a small amount** left to improve facilities for spectators.*
>
> C Uncountables and plural countables
> • *a lot of/lots of/plenty of*
> *There's been **a lot of** improvement in her tennis.* (uncountable)
> *She's got **a lot of** fans.* (countable)
> • *no … at all; none*
> *He takes **no** pride **at all** in his appearance.*
> • *a lack of*
> *There's **a lack of** honesty in sport these days.*

3 Read the information about determiners in the box and mark the correct word(s) in each pair in the text.

> **(1)** *Many / Much* famous sportspeople get injured for unexpected reasons. For example, the English footballer Rio Ferdinand managed to injure himself by watching TV for **(2)** *a number of / a great deal of* hours with his leg on a coffee table. And after the cricketer Chris Lewis shaved his head he spent too **(3)** *many / much* time in the sun and got sunstroke.
>
> But the worst accident occurred in 1913 when the racing driver Camille Jenatzy took **(4)** *several / a small amount of* friends hunting for boars. They didn't see **(5)** *no / any* boars, so the group went back to the house and had **(6)** *lots / too many* to eat and drink. Jenatzy was convinced they would soon have **(7)** *many / much* better luck and offered **(8)** *much / a lot of* money as a bet that they would be shooting in the next **(9)** *little / few* hours. After everyone had gone to bed, he crept outside, walked **(10)** *few / a few* metres away from the house and made **(11)** *a few / a little* sounds like a wild boar to wake up his friends. Unfortunately, his friends opened the window and shot him by mistake.

Use of English 1 (Paper 3 Part 4)

Lead-in

1 **Look at three completed transformations. What area of grammar is tested in each one?**
   a time conjunctions
   b determiners
   c present perfect + *since/for*

   1 Not many staff attended the meeting.
   number
   Only … *a small number of* …. staff attended the meeting.

   2 He wasted no time looking for a new car.
   soon
   He looked for a new car … *as soon as he* … possibly could.

   3 Sally moved here ten years ago.
   living
   Sally … *has been living here* … for ten years.

Key word transformations

▶ Task strategy Module 1B page 20

HELP

➤ **Question 1**
You need four words. (Remember that contractions = two words.) Will you need an adjective or a noun?

➤ **Question 2**
You will need an indefinite article.

➤ **Question 6**
Is the verb singular or plural?

2 **Now do the task below. Follow the task strategy and use the Help clues if necessary.**
Complete the second sentence so that it has a similar meaning to the first sentence, using the word given. **Do not change the word given.** You must use between two and five words, including the word given. Write only the missing words.

   1 The children were not very interested in what the guide said.
   much
   There ……………… among the children in what the guide said.

   2 I think he's rather nice.
   quite
   I think he's ……………… person.

   3 When I was younger I would play football with my father.
   used
   When I was younger my father and I ……………… football together.

   4 There weren't any volunteers to do the job.
   lack
   There ……………… volunteers to do the job.

   5 She's worked very hard in the garden.
   deal
   She's done a ……………… in the garden.

   6 I don't know why golf is so popular.
   people
   I don't know why ……………… golf so much.

   7 'This car's not mine,' said the old man.
   belong
   'This car ……………… ,' said the old man.

   8 There don't seem to be as many tourists around this year.
   fewer
   There seem ……………… tourists around this year.

3 **Answer the questions about the task.**
Which questions test:
   • quantity expressions? • determiners? • verb forms? • adverbs of degree?

Use of English 2   (Paper 3 Part 1)

Lead-in

1 **Discuss these questions.**
 1 In which sports is it very easy to hurt yourself? Why do people take part?
 2 Do you know any new sports that people have started playing?

Multiple-choice cloze

▶ page 179

▶ Task strategy Module 1B page 21

2 **a Read the title and text quickly and answer the questions. (Ignore the spaces at this stage.)**
 1 What is Parkour?   2 What recent changes have there been?

 b Do the exam task. Follow the task strategy and use the Help clues if necessary.

 Read the text below and decide which answer **A**, **B**, **C** or **D** best fits the space. There is an example at the beginning (0).

PARKOUR

Parkour (from the French 'parcours', meaning 'course') is a new activity which (0) ...C..... in towns. The aim is to get over, under or through (1) .... obstacles like hedges, or man-made objects like buildings, in the fastest, most direct manner possible. The sport demands great agility and (2) .... athletics, dance and acrobatics. Participants in the sport are (3) .... 'traceurs' and are (4) .... to improvise their movements rather than rehearse them. However, in order not to cause themselves (5) .... injury as they run up walls or jump from rooftop to rooftop, they have to learn good jumping and landing techniques.

In the UK the sport really (6) .... after it was featured on television but it actually (7) .... in the suburbs of Paris in 1988. In its (8) .... days there were no tricks for their own sake but (9) ...., after the sport became really popular, some participants started doing interesting things for show like mid-air flips. However, many 'traceurs' (10) .... that unnecessary moves are not part of real parkour.

Of course, anyone interested in (11) .... the sport has to be young and athletic but (12) .... all they need is a good pair of shoes!

HELP

➤ **Question 5**
 Only one of these adjectives goes with *injury* in context.

➤ **Question 8**
 An adjective that can mean *near the beginning of a period* and combines with days.

➤ **Question 11**
 A phrasal verb that means *start to do something for pleasure*

	0	**A** goes off	**B** gets up	**C** takes place	**D** comes about
	1	**A** native	**B** natural	**C** usual	**D** accustomed
	2	**A** jumbles	**B** ties	**C** combines	**D** fixes
	3	**A** proposed	**B** marked	**C** signed	**D** called
	4	**A** hoped	**B** demanded	**C** needed	**D** expected
	5	**A** grim	**B** strict	**C** serious	**D** cruel
	6	**A** got out	**B** took off	**C** turned on	**D** came out
	7	**A** originated	**B** made	**C** derived	**D** resulted
	8	**A** beforehand	**B** previous	**C** early	**D** preceding
	9	**A** following	**B** later	**C** next	**D** presently
	10	**A** claim	**B** request	**C** confess	**D** show
	11	**A** bringing on	**B** setting up	**C** taking up	**D** putting on
	12	**A** alternatively	**B** instead	**C** however	**D** otherwise

 c Make a note of the verbs, phrasal verbs and adjective + noun combinations you want to remember in your vocabulary book.

Language development 3
Adjectives often confused

---

1 The **actual** origins of Parkour were in the suburbs of Paris. ✓ (= real)
   The ~~current~~ origins of Parkour were in the suburbs of Paris. ✗ (= present)

2 The sport demands **great** agility. ✓ (= large amount of)
   The sport demands ~~big~~ agility. ✗ (= large in size)

3 In **ancient** times some sports were far more dangerous. (= many centuries ago)
   In ~~old~~ times some sports were far more dangerous. ✗ (= not young or new)

---

1 **Match the words to the definitions. They are in pairs.**

1	pleasant	a	understanding other people's problems
2	sympathetic	b	friendly, easy to talk to
3	sensitive	c	understanding other people's feelings
4	sensible	d	practical and able to judge things well
5	nervous	e	happy because something good is happening
6	excited	f	worried about something that is happening
7	usual	g	having the normal features of a group
8	typical	h	the same as what happens most of the time

2 **Answer these questions about yourself.**
   1 Are you sensitive or sensible? Or both?
   2 When do you get nervous? Or excited?
   3 Who's the most sympathetic person you know?

3 **What is the difference between *-ing* and *-ed* adjectives? Look at the examples from the Use of English text on page 63.**
   1 *Some participants started doing **interesting** things for show.*
   2 *Of course, anyone **interested** in taking up sport.*

   ▶ Grammar reference page 183

4 a **Complete the sentences with an adjective formed from the words in brackets.**
   1 Golf is so .... (*bore*)!
   2 The team felt .... (*disappoint*) not to win the final.
   3 Professional football looks glamorous, but it's .... (*tire*).
   4 The crowd got .... (*annoy*) because the game was so bad.
   5 I've never tried skiing. It looks .... (*terrify*) to me.
   6 The team captain is .... (*depress*) about his injuries.
   7 I'm not at all .... (*interest*) in sport.
   8 It was very .... (*amuse*) when a dog ran onto the field!

b **Answer these questions about yourself.**
   1 What do you find interesting/amusing?
   2 When was the last time you felt annoyed/disappointed?
   3 What's the most boring/terrifying thing you've ever done?

Phrasal verbs with *take*

5 **Find an example of a phrasal verb with *take* in the Use of English text on page 63.**

6 **Phrasal verbs sometimes have more than one meaning. Rewrite the phrases in italics in these sentences using *take* and the particles in the list.**
   after   to   up   over   off
   1 The darts player Bobby George *started a new career in* acting after he was discovered by a film producer during the World Darts Championship.
   2 Andy Murray's tennis career *began to be successful* after he played at Wimbledon.
   3 The England soccer team improved enormously after a foreign manager *became responsible*.
   4 Damon Hill *did the same thing as* his father, Graham Hill, and became a racing driver.
   5 Although Sonny Liston was a great boxer, the general public never really *felt a liking for* him as they did Mohammed Ali.

7 **For you, which is the best way to keep a record of phrasal verbs – by topic, verb or particle? How do you record a phrasal verb with more than one meaning?**

MODULE 5
Discovery

Overview

- **Reading:** multiple matching: (Paper 1 Part 3)
- **Language development 1:** future forms
- **Writing:** email (Paper 2 Part 1)
- **Speaking:** collaborative task and discussion (Paper 5 Parts 3 and 4)
- **Listening:** sentence completion (Paper 4 Part 2)
- **Use of English 1:** key word transformations (Paper 3 Part 4)
- **Language development 2:** reflexives; structures with question words
- **Use of English 2:** word formation (Paper 3 Part 3)
- **Language development 3:** forming nouns; phrasal verbs with *come*

Lead-in

- Look at the photos. What benefits have these inventions and discoveries brought?
- How would our lives be different without them?
- When is 'progress' not necessarily a good thing?

Reading   (Paper 1 Part 3)

Before you read

1 a Match the fields of science in the list below to the definitions 1–6.

psychology   genetics   astronomy
forensic science   linguistics   archaeology

1 the study of the stars and planets
2 the study of ancient societies by examining what remains of their buildings, graves, etc.
3 the study of how the mind works
4 the study of language
5 the study of the characteristics that living things pass on from one generation to the next
6 methods used for finding out who is guilty of a crime (study of blood, hair, fingerprints, etc.)

b Look at the title of the article opposite and the subheadings A–D. What are you going to read? What field of science do you think each book is about?

Skimming

2 Skim each text and check your answers to Exercise 1b.

Multiple matching:

▶ page 178

3 a For Questions 1–12 choose from the book titles (A–D). There is an example at the beginning (0). Follow the task strategy. For the first four questions, the key words in the questions and text have been highlighted for you.

Which review states that the book:

Task strategy

- Read the lead-in line very carefully. (**Which review states** ...)
- Read the questions and mark the key words.
- Predict which sections of the text contain the answers.
- Scan the relevant section, looking for parallel phrases and parts of sentences.
- Read that part carefully to check it answers the question.
- If you can't find the answer, leave it for the moment and go on to the next question.

- follows on from the author's earlier book ?	0 C
- includes a number of funny stories ?	1
- is not difficult for the non-scientist to read?	2
- would make a good gift for someone?	3
- contains a wide range of examples?	4
- talks about a theory that has been disproved?	5
- puts forward the author's own ideas about the subject?	6
- mentions a part of the body that improves as you get older?	7
- discusses research carried out on young babies?	8
- reflects the writer's wider educational aims?	9
- covers important topical issues?	10
- is intended to go with a filmed documentary?	11
- has very effective illustrations?	12

b Compare and justify your answers.

1 Why is **A not** the answer to example question **0** although it refers to *earlier books*?
2 Which key words did you mark in the questions?
3 What related phrases or parts of sentences did you find in the text?

Four Popular Science Books

Oliver Mansell reviews four books, all of which tell us more about ourselves.

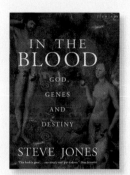

A In the Blood *by Steve Jones*

This is the book for anyone who wants to keep up-to-date with the latest influential theories. Did you know, for example, that whoever our parents may be, we are all united by DNA, 'the basic stuff of life', which contains our genes? And did you know that most of the
5 population of the world may have descended from fewer than 100 people?

New and surprising discoveries like this are being made almost every week, which is why genetics is now at the forefront of twenty-first-century science. Before they'd heard of genes, people believed that family traits were carried in the blood. Today we know that they were wrong. Issues like these are among those discussed in this thrilling new book by
10 Professor Jones. As with his earlier books on other subjects, you will find it hard to put down, even if you don't have a scientific background.

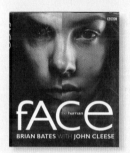

B The Human Face *by Brian Bates with John Cleese*

This fascinating book collects together the findings of various scientific studies, old and new, concerning the human face. One of these has shown that 30 minutes after birth, when
15 our eyes can hardly focus, we gaze at faces rather than anything else. And it seems that we continue to be fascinated with them all through life. There have been a number of psychological tests designed to investigate beauty, but their conclusions only prove what the Ancient Greeks always knew – a beautiful face is one with regular features.

So, maybe this is not the book to buy if you want to be surprised with new facts, but it
20 does provide some fascinating insights into how faces have developed over the years, and whether one can judge a person by their appearance alone. Although rather serious in places, the book is packed with eye-catching photos, making it an ideal birthday present even for the most reluctant student of science.

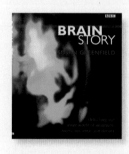

C Brain Story *by Susan Greenfield*

25 As Director of the Royal Institution of Science, Susan Greenfield's main objective is to encourage the greater public understanding of scientific ideas. In this book, she introduces us to the inside of our heads and shows the kind of enthusiasm about the brain that other writers reserve for fine art or football. The idea of 'intelligence' worries her, however, because this suggests that a person's 'brain power' is pre-determined. She agrees with those
30 who insist that the brain, which is capable of amazing things, is constantly developing, and gets better and better with age, providing you look after it. Although this book develops the ideas introduced in her previous one, *The Private Life of the Brain*, it clearly has television audiences in mind (a tie-in series has just begun on BBC1) and as a consequence it is rather shorter on detail, focusing instead on one or two interesting examples.

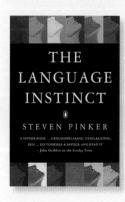

35 **D The Language Instinct** *by Steven Pinker*

Where does our feeling for language come from? How do we learn to speak it so effortlessly? Why is it so hard for adults to learn a foreign language? Cleverly structured, with many amusing anecdotes, linguist Steven Pinker's book examines why we use language and where this ability comes from. His personal belief is that language is as
40 instinctive to us as flying is to geese, and that we use it to great effect in order to communicate. He illustrates his theory with examples of language taken from various sources, including children's conversations, pop culture and politicians' speeches. A clever user of language himself, Pinker has packed his book full of original thoughts. Because of this, it does not make for light reading, but it will nonetheless appeal both to specialists and
45 anyone who is interested in language and human beings in the widest sense.

Discussion

4 **Discuss these questions.**

1 Based on the reviews, which of these books would you most and least like to read? Why? What else would you like to know about the subject?

2 Do you ever read popular science books or watch science programmes on TV? Why/Why not?

Language development 1

Future forms

1 a Read the extracts. Guess who is talking to who, and what the situation is.

EXAMPLE: 1 A child talking to a parent, in a car. The child is feeling travel-sick.

1
> I don't feel well. I think I'm going to be sick.

4
> I know what she's like. If you tell her, she'll tell everyone.

2
> I can't, I'm afraid! I'm taking my driving test tomorrow.

5
> Hurry up! It starts at eight.

3
> Did I tell you it doesn't work? I'm going to take it back to the shop.

6
> That bag looks heavy. I'll carry it for you.

b Mark the verb forms in Exercise 1a that express the future.

c Match the meanings in the list a–f to each extract above. Then complete the table below.

a planned, decided earlier (intention)
b unplanned, decided now (e.g. an offer, a promise)
c planned, a definite arrangement (e.g. in a diary)
d prediction: we notice something in the present that will make something happen
e planned, fixed event (e.g. a public timetable)
f prediction: we expect something to happen (it is our opinion or we have experience of it)

Time Clauses

Use the present simple in time clauses with a future meaning.
Which example below is **not** correct?

1 *I'll give her the message **as soon as** she **arrives**.*
2 ***When** everyone **is** on the coach, it will leave.*
3 *Are you going to have a drink **before** the show **will start**?*
4 ***After** we **move** offices, we'll start on the new project.*

2 Mark the most likely verb form in each pair.

1 He adapts quickly; I'm sure he *will be / is going to be* fine in his new job.
2 Sorry, I can't. I *'ll go and visit / 'm going to visit* Tom in hospital tonight.
3 We'll call you as soon as we *'ll get / get* there.
4 It says here that the play *starts / is going to start* at seven.
5 You look tired. You rest, and I *'ll cook / 'm going to cook* dinner tonight.
6 I'd love to come tomorrow but I *have lunch / 'm having lunch* with my brother.
7 Have you heard the news? Tara *'ll have / 's going to have* a baby.
8 Just before you *go / will go*, can you check this for me?

3 a Read the quotation below and mark examples of the future continuous and the future perfect.

> 'I am confident that in 50 years' time we will have established a permanent base on Mars and that later this century people will be having holidays in space.'
> *Martin Rees, astronomer.*

	Form	Meaning	Example
A	Present continuous	....	....
B	Present simple	....	....
C	*Going to* + infinitive (two meanings)	....	1 .... 2 ....
D	*Will/Shall* + infinitive (two meanings)	....	1 .... 2 ....

▶ Grammar reference pages 189–190

b   Which verb form in the box below refers to an action:
   • which will be complete by a point in the future?
   • which will still be in progress at a point in the future?

A   Future continuous: *will/won't be + -ing*
     People **will be having** holidays in space.
B   Future perfect: *will/won't have + past participle*
     We **will have established** a permanent base …

---

4   Complete these predictions for the year 2100. Put the verbs in brackets in the future continuous or the future perfect.

1   We .... (*find*) life on other planets before then.

2   We .... (*travel*) around in aerial vehicles, like flying saucers.

3   Long before then, scientists .... (*discover*) how to make fresh food last for years.

4   Many people .... (*live*) in space, which will help with the overpopulation problem.

5   The Internet .... (*take over*) most teachers' jobs and .... (*provide*) most of our entertainment.

6   Scientists and engineers .... (*make*) parts of the body routinely. When we're sick, we .... (*go*) to mechanics, not doctors!

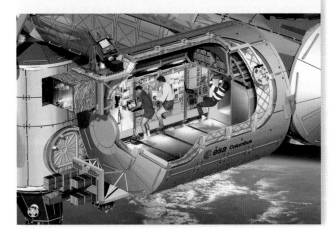

5   a   Read the statements and decide which are:
   • very certain
   • fairly certain
   • not very certain at all
   1   *I am confident that* in fifty years' time we will have established a permanent base on Mars.
   2   *We may have* found life on other planets, *but I doubt it.*
   3   *I think it's quite likely that* scientists will be making blood.
   4   *There could be* holidays in space.
   5   *We should be* travelling in aerial vehicles.

b   Use the expressions to comment on the predictions in Exercise 4.

c   What other things do you think will be possible in a hundred years' time? Think about these questions.
   1   What will we be eating?
   2   What progress will have been made in medicine and technology?
   3   What changes will have taken place in education and entertainment?

6   a   Complete these sentences with information about yourself. Think about your arrangements, plans, hopes and dreams.
   1   At the weekend … .
   2   In the next few days … .
   3   For my next holiday … .
   4   On my birthday … .
   5   In the future I hope … .
   6   By this time next year … .
   7   Within the next ten years … .

b   Discuss your arrangements, plans, hopes and dreams from Exercise 6a with other students.

7   Correct the mistakes in this piece of student's writing.

After I will finish the last year of university, I am definitely going to have a long holiday. I expect I am going with my friend, Luis, to a place where we will be doing lots of sport and relaxing in the sun to recover from all our hard work.

But before that there is a lot of work. My exams will start on the 15 June and they are lasting two weeks. The results will not have been here before the end of August, so I am having a long time to wait. For the next month I will study for two hours every evening and I am not going out during the week.

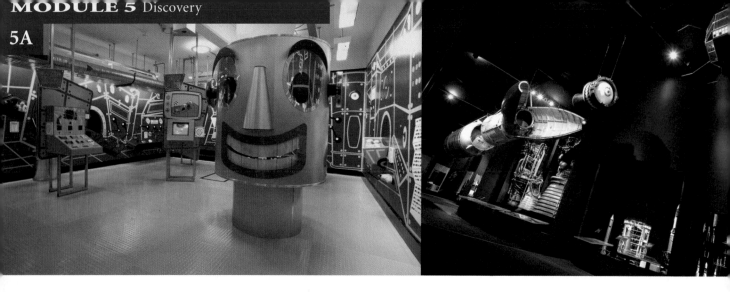

Writing

Email (Paper 2 Part 1)

Lead-in

1 Discuss these questions.

1 What would you expect to find in a museum? What's the best museum you've ever been to?

2 If you had to organise a visit by your college to a local museum, what things would you have to consider?

Understand the task

2 Read the task below and answer the questions.

1 WHO are you writing to?

2 WHY are you writing?

3 WHAT information will you include?

4 HOW will you write? In what style? (Remember who you are writing to.)

You are the secretary of your college Science Club. You have seen this advertisement FOR YOUR LOCAL MUSEUM and are interested in organising a group visit. You have written some questions to ask the museum. Read the advertisement and the questions carefully. Then write an email to the groups' organiser of the museum explaining what you would like to do and asking for the information you need.

COME TO YOUR LOCAL MUSEUM
AND FIND OUT ABOUT YOUR FUTURE.

•••••••

Over 300 exhibits showing recent exciting discoveries that will affect the way we live.

Refreshments – snack bar or picnic space available?

Booking – necessary for groups? How far in advance?

•••••••

The exhibition is open daily. 10 a.m. – 6 p.m. (including weekends) Special discounts for educational groups.

•••••••

Number of people in the group – any maximum?

Write an **email** of between **120–150** words. You must use grammatically correct sentences with accurate spelling and punctuation in a style appropriate for the situation.

Plan your email   3   a   Number these key points in a logical order for the email.
- asking about eating
- asking about booking
- conclusion
- saying why you're writing
- introducing myself
- asking about numbers

b   Write the key points from the list above in this paragraph plan.
Paragraph 1: ...introducing myself...   Paragraph 3: ....

....

Paragraph 2: ....   Paragraph 4: ....

....

Language and content   4   a   Complete the expressions in the table for the email.

Requesting	*I would be grateful …*
Asking for information/ permission	*Could you …?* *Would it be possible … ?* *I would also like … .*
Introducing a request	*We will (probably) be arriving … so … .* *Since we will (probably) be coming for the whole day … .* *When we arrive, can we …/will we be able to …?* *Our group is quite large so … .*

b   Complete these opening and closing sentences.
Opening: *I am the … . I saw your … and I was wondering if I could ask … .*
Closing: *I look forward to … .*

c   **Which word or phrase from the list below will you use to close the email?**
Goodbye   Yours faithfully   Cheers!   All the best

Write your email   5   Now write the email, using the ideas and some of the language above. Avoid copying whole phrases from the question. Do not write any postal addresses. Write your answer in 120–150 words.

Check and improve your email   6   When you edit your email, what things will you check? Refer to the checklist in the Writing reference.

▶ Writing reference page 197–198/200

LANGUAGE SPOT: polite questions

Look at the examples of polite questions.

Where's the café? ➔	Do you think I wonder if I would be very grateful if	you could tell me	where the café is(?)
Is the café open? ➔	Could you (please)	tell me let me know	whether the café is open?

Make each question more polite using a phrase above, including the word in brackets.

1   Where can we leave our bags? (*think*)
2   Is there a toilet on this floor? (*could*)
3   How much will we have to pay? (*grateful*)
4   When does the museum close? (*wonder*)
5   Where's the cloakroom? (*tell*)
6   What time does the museum close? (*grateful*)
7   Can we pay by credit card in the shop? (*tell*)
8   Who's the person in charge? (*wonder*)

5B | Technology

(Paper 5 Parts 3 and 4)

Vocabulary: technology

1 a Look at the pictures opposite and name the inventions. Which could you describe as
   - *a common household appliance*
   - *a useful gadget*
   - *a ground-breaking invention*
   - *a labour-saving device*
   - *an important recent development*
   - *an unnecessary luxury*

b Which syllable is stressed? Put each word in italics into the correct column. (Compound words count as one word. Don't worry about the syllables after the stressed syllable.)

● .   . ●

HOUSEhold   *aPPLIance*

Which word is most stressed in each phrase?

c Where is the stress in these words and phrases? Say each in a sentence (e.g. *I've just bought a…/I've got a…*) to check.

> a laptop   a microwave oven   a food blender
> an electric toothbrush   a hairdryer   a washing machine
> a mobile   a dishwasher

d Answer these questions.
   - Which of the above items have you got? Do they have any disadvantages?
   - Which do you think is the least useful?

2 a Which of the items in Exercise 1c do you associate with these words or phrases?

> keyboard and mouse   long-distance call   e-commerce
> blogging   virtual reality   headphones   get cut off
> social networking   get the wrong number   re-charge

b The words in Column A are all actions you might do on a computer. Match the verbs in A with the definitions in B.

A		B	
1	download (music/videos)	a	make a copy of your files
2	log on	b	produce a written document
3	click on (an icon)	c	work from home and communicate online
4	cut and paste (a document)	d	copy from the Internet
5	telework	e	start using an operating system
6	back up (data)	f	move to a different place
7	wordprocess	g	perform an action by clicking the mouse

3 a What things are best done by computer? What things are not done well by computers at the present time?

b What do you use a computer for?

4 Look again at the pictures. Which piece of technology do you think is the most important?

Sample answer (Part 3)

5 a 🎧 Listen to the examiner's instructions and the candidate's response.

   1 Complete the examiner's instructions.

   EXAMINER: First .... Then ....

   2 What does Igor say to check he has understood?

   ....

▶ Functions reference page 215

  b 🎧 Listen to the candidates doing the task and number the photos above in the order in which they are mentioned. Did both candidates participate equally in the task?

  c 🎧 Listen to the end of the discussion again, and answer the questions.

   1 What language do the candidates use to report their decision?

   2 Does it matter that the candidates don't completely agree?

   3 What does the examiner say to end this part of the test?

Sample answer (Part 4)

6 a Look at the questions the examiner might ask about modern technology in this Part 4. Which ones do you think you would find easy or difficult to answer?

   1 Can you imagine a world without mobile phones?

   2 How has technology changed our lives?

   3 Which household appliances get used most in your house?

   4 Are some appliances and gadgets an unnecessary luxury?

   5 What are the advantages and disadvantages of technology for our health?

   6 What item of technology would you like someone to invent?

  b 🎧 Listen to the Part 4 discussion and tick (✓) the questions the examiner asks. Did both candidates participate equally in the discussion?

Three-way discussion

▶ page 181

7 a Work in groups of three.

   STUDENT 1: You are the examiner. Ask each candidate one question.

   STUDENTS 2 AND 3: You are Candidates A and B. Answer the examiner's questions and develop your ideas. Read the task strategy before you start.

  b Change roles and repeat the task in Exercise 7a.

Task strategy

• Listen carefully to the questions.

• Don't just answer questions with *yes* or *no*. Give your opinions, justify them and develop your ideas.

8 Did you follow the advice given in the task strategy?

Listening (Paper 4 Part 2)

Before you listen

1 Do you think this is a typical modern family? Which of the items in the picture are important to you and your family? What are they used for?

Sentence completion

2 a 🎧 You will hear a radio interview with Nina Cooke about modern technology and her family. For questions 1–10, complete the sentences. Follow the task strategy.

The domestic chore Nina dislikes most is _____(1).

Nina doesn't like buying her own _____ (2) on-line.

Nina still buys a newspaper because of the _____ (3).

Lizzie communicates with her friends by sending _____ (4).

Tom is very keen on _____ (5).

Tom goes on _____ (6) to stay in touch with his cousin.

Nina mentions the _____ (7) facility, which is helpful for checking homework.

Nina is concerned about the effect Lizzie's _____ (8) may have on her hearing.

Dan really appreciates the _____ (9) which came with his new car.

Nina points out that you can now pay bills or _____ (10) at any time of the day and night.

b Compare and discuss your answers.

Task strategy

- Read the sentences and decide what kind of information is missing.
- Listen and complete the sentences with a word, number or short phrase from the recording. Write no more than three words. Only use words from the recording.
- Check your answers during the second listening. Don't leave any blanks.
- Check your spelling and grammar.

Vocabulary: collocations

3 Complete the gaps with these verbs from the listening text in the correct form.

try   pay   do   take   book   save

With more and more people now (1) _____ the computer for granted, it is possible to avoid shopping as people do everything online, from (2) _____ bills to (3) _____ holidays. It can (4) _____ a lot of time if you are busy, and a lot of money, too. Going to the library may also become a thing of the past, too, as young people usually (5) _____ research for their studies on the web. However, many people still prefer to go shopping for their own clothes as they prefer to (6) _____ them on and see what they look like before they buy.

Discussion

4 Discuss these questions

1 What modern technology do you take for granted and would find it hard to live without?

2 Do you prefer to do most of your shopping and business on-line? Why/Why not?

3 What are the advantages and disadvantages of texting and chatrooms for young people?

4 Do you think that modern technology will mean that more and more people will work from home?

Use of English 1   (Paper 3 Part 4)

Lead-in

1 **Correct the errors in these completed answers and say what areas of language are tested in each one.**

1 I can't speak Mandarin Chinese.
   how
   I don't know ......*how speak*...... Mandarin Chinese.

2 Nobody helped her clean the house last week.
   herself
   She ...*by herself cleaned the house*...... last week.

3 Jane decided to wait and only hand in her work at the last minute.
   put
   Jane decided to ...*put up handing*...... in her work until the last minute.

Key word transformations

▶ Task strategy Module 1B page 20

2 **Now do the task below. Follow the task strategy if necessary.**
Complete the second sentence so that it has a similar meaning to the first sentence, using the word given. **Do not change the word given**. You must use between **two** and **five** words, including the word given. Write only the missing words.

1 I don't live with anyone else in this house.
   own
   I live .... in this house.

2 It won't help if Tania goes to see the manager.
   point
   There's .... to see the manager.

3 He loves her and she loves him very much.
   each
   They .... very much.

4 It was only after she left that I realised that she was famous.
   wasn't
   It .... that I realised that she was famous.

5 Unfortunately, nobody painted this room for me.
   myself
   I .... , unfortunately.

6 I don't know which person to talk to in the bank.
   who
   I ....talk to in the bank.

7 The holiday I enjoyed the most was the one we had in Greece.
   pleasure
   The holiday which .... was the one we had in Greece.

8 Caroline was too tired to work any more so she stopped.
   carry
   Caroline .... any more because she was too tired.

3 **Answer the questions about the task.**
Which questions test
   • phrasal verbs?
   • reflexives?
   • structures with question words?
   • time clauses?
   • noun phrases?

MODULE 5 Discovery

5B

Language development 2
Reflexives

A Reflexive pronouns
- when the subject and object of a transitive verb are the same:
  *He **hurt himself** when he fell off the chair.*
  (Compare: *He hurt his sister when he bumped into her.*)
- = without the help of others:
  *I repaired the television **myself**.*
- with *enjoy* when there is no direct object:
  *They **enjoyed themselves** at the party.*
- with *by* to mean alone.
  *She went to the cinema **by herself**.*

B *Own*
- = without the help of others:
  *I repaired the television **on my own**.*
- = *alone:*
  *She went to the cinema **on her own**.*
- = belonging to no other person:
  *My (very) **own** room.*
  *I saw it with **my own** eyes.*

C *Each other/One another*
- = each of two or more does something to the other:
  *They talked to **each other/one another**. They talked to ~~themselves~~.*

LOOK Find correct examples of this language in the Use of English text on page 75.

1 a Tick (✓) the correct sentences. Correct the incorrect ones.
   1 I used to work myself abroad.
   2 My printer turns itself off.
   3 Can you help myself?
   4 Robots can't talk to each one another.
   5 This was her very own invention.
   6 Have you enjoyed you?
   7 He found himself in trouble.
   8 Relax yourself!
   9 I built the model my own.
   10 Clare and Rob met themselves last year.

b Complete the text opposite with reflexives where possible (see the box above), and pronouns (e.g. *me, them*).

2 Discuss these questions.
   1 What things do you prefer to do yourself?
   2 Do you like being on your own?
   3 Do you and your best friend ever argue with each other?

ROBOTS

Robots are not new. As long ago as 400 BC, the philosopher and mathematician Archytus built a wooden bird that could fly on (1)............... And in the seventeenth century, Johann Muller created both an iron fly and an artificial eagle that could take to the air by (2)............... These days of course robots are everywhere, but I sometimes ask (3)............ whether they are a good thing. There are even robot dogs that we can have as pets, but I can't imagine buying one (4).............. For a start, I can't believe we'd ever manage to communicate with (5).............., unlike real animals. I suppose there is some point in having a robot helping (6)............. in our daily lives – like doing the household chores that some people can't do (7)............., or doing a mechanical job in a factory – but I wouldn't want a robot carrying out a delicate operation on (8)............. in hospital, would you? I'd rather the surgeons did it (9)...............!

Structures with question words

A Question word + *to*-infinitive: *He didn't know **what to do**.*
B Question word + clause:
  *They never found out **why it had happened**.*
  *Do you know **how to programme** the video?*

3 a Complete the second sentence so that it has a similar meaning to the first sentence, using the word given.
   1 Mike can't use a camcorder. **how**
     Mike doesn't .... camcorder.
   2 When you've done the things I want you to do, you can go out. **what**
     You can go out when .... want you to do.
   3 We don't know the right places to find the information. **where**
     We aren't sure .... information.
   4 I'm not sure which person I should believe. **who**
     I don't .... believe.

b Complete these sentences about yourself.
   1 Next year I have no idea what … .
   2 I can't explain why … .
   3 I wish I could decide where … .
   4 It would be useful if I knew how to … .

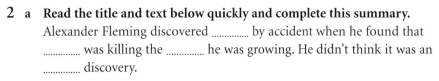

Use of English 2 (Paper 3 Part 3)

Lead-in

1 Do you know who discovered a) penicillin; b) the water displacement principle; c) gravity?

Word formation (A)

▶ page 179

▶ Task strategy Module 2B page 35

2 a Read the title and text below quickly and complete this summary.
Alexander Fleming discovered .... by accident when he found that .... was killing the .... he was growing. He didn't think it was an .... discovery.

b Read the text below. Use the word given in capitals at the end of some of the lines to form a word that fits in the space in the same line. There is an example at the beginning (0).

The Discovery of Penicillin (1928)

One of the most **(0)** .amazing. advances ever made in medicine   AMAZE
began with an **(1)** .... event. Sir Alexander Fleming had   EXPECT
been looking into the **(2)** .... of finding a better way of   POSSIBLE
killing germs when he came upon something **(3)** .... in his   PUZZLE
laboratory. Some mould that had **(4)** .... landed on one of   ACCIDENT
the dishes appeared to be killing the bacteria he was growing.

   At first he was **(5)** .... about his   EXCITE
(6) .... and grew more of the mould, giving it the name of   DISCOVER
penicillin. However, in his view it was only really **(7)** .... as   EFFECT
an antiseptic against skin **(8)** .... and soon lost interest. It   INFECT
wasn't until ten years later that two other **(9)** .... managed   SCIENCE
to isolate the substance that killed the bacteria, and
(10) .... began to save people's lives with it.   SUCCESS

c How many nouns and adverbs did you have to make? Which words required a prefix?

HELP

➤ Question 1
Did he expect it or not?

➤ Question 2
Is the suffix *-ness* or *-ity*?

➤ Question 4
Is this an adjective or adverb?

Word formation (B)

3 Read the title and the text quickly and find out why 'Lucy's Baby' is important to many scientists. Then do the task.

'Lucy' (1974) and 'Lucy's baby' (2006)

The 3.3-million-year-old remains of a human-like child were
(0) ...originally.... found in a block of sandstone in 2000 but it   ORIGIN
took over five years of **(1)** .... work to free the bones   CARE
without doing any damage. Judging from the **(2)** .... of her   LONG
teeth the infant was probably about three years old when she
died. According to **(3)** ....working in this area, these   RESEARCH
remains are **(4)** .... because of their completeness and   USUAL
this will give us a great opportunity to study the **(5)** .... of   DEVELOP
one of our distant ancestors. Earlier **(6)** ...., such as the   DISCOVER
3.2 million-year-old fossil of an adult female known as 'Lucy',
are still regarded as **(7)** .... significant but their remains   HIGH
are less well-preserved. Since the species has a **(8)** .... of   MIX
ape-like and human-like qualities, scientists say that these
findings are telling us a lot about our early ancestors.
However, their conclusions have come in for **(9)** .... from   CRITICISE
some people. They say there is **(10)** .... evidence to regard   SUFFICIENT
the remains as the missing link between apes and humans.

HELP

➤ Question 3
Singular or plural?

➤ Question 5
Is the suffix *-ment* or *-ance*?

➤ Question 10
Positive or negative?

Language development 3
Forming nouns

1 a Look at the examples in the table of nouns formed from verbs.

-ment	-ure	-ance	-ence
achievement	failure	assistance	presence
equipment	departure	appearance	existence
amusement	pleasure	performance	correspondence

(t/s)ion	-y	-er	-or
decision	delivery	explorer	sailor
organisation	recovery	employer	supervisor

b Add nouns from the Use of English texts on page 77.

2 a Do the quiz below. Guess the answers if you don't know.

EXPLORERS' QUIZ

1 Who reached the South Pole first?
a) Captain Robert Scott ☐
b) Roald Amundsen ☐

2 Who discovered Hawaii?
a) the Polynesians ☐
b) Captain Cook ☐

3 Who sailed round Africa first?
a) Magellan ☐
b) Vasco da Gama ☐
c) the Phoenicians ☐

4 Who crossed the Gibson Desert in Western Australia in 1873?
a) Alfred Gibson ☐
b) Dr Livingstone ☐

b Read the information below and check your answers. Complete the sentences with nouns formed from the verbs in brackets.

1 Norwegian Roald Amundsen reached the South Pole in 1911, with the .... (*assist*) of a determined team and through brilliant .... (*organise*).
2 The Polynesians discovered Hawaii In 400 AD, nine hundred years before the Europeans knew of its .... (*exist*). Making such a journey by canoe was a remarkable .... (*achieve*).
3 The Phoenicians were the first .... (*sail*) to travel round Africa. They completed their journey in the seventh century BC, without the technical .... (*equip*) which is available today.
4 The Gibson Desert is named after the .... (*explore*) Alfred Gibson, who died after his .... (*fail*) to reach a camp in search of help.

3 a Copy and complete the table below with nouns formed from the adjectives in the list.

able   long   kind   generous   dark   strong
sad   equal   ill   real   popular

-ness	-th	-ity
loneliness	truth	activity

b Add one noun from the Use of English texts on page 77.

4 Complete the sentences with nouns formed from the words in brackets.

1 The .... (*popular*) of travelogues has increased recently.
2 The best travelogues have always been .... (*describe*) of cultures which are new to the writer.
3 The *Hai-Lu*, a Chinese traveller's account of the west, was written in the eighteenth century by the writer Hsieh Ch'ing Kao, who had the .... (*able*) to write vividly about Europe from a Chinese point of view. Its .... (*important*) has recently been recognised.
4 In the fourteenth century, Moroccan writer Ibn Buttuta spent 29 years travelling and making .... (*observe*) about Africa, Asia and Europe. We can only imagine the .... (*lonely*) he must have felt at times.

Phrasal verbs with *come*

5 a Match this phrasal verb from the Use of English text to the correct definition:
They have come in for criticism ... .
a given   b asked for   c received

b Match the phrasal verbs to the definitions.

1	come across	a	visit (somebody) at home
2	come off	b	find by chance
3	come up	c	happen
4	come round	d	succeed
5	come up with	e	get uncovered
6	come out	f	get mentioned
7	come about	g	suggest

6 Complete the sentences with phrasal verbs from Exercise 5b in the correct form. Use each verb once only.

1 Did anything important .... at the meeting?
2 Tania .... last night but you weren't in.
3 I'm sure the truth will .... one day.
4 We .... some old school photos the other day.
5 How did the accident ....?
6 Jackson's attempt to break the record didn't ....
7 Has anybody .... any new ideas?

MODULE 6
Enjoying yourself

Overview

- **Reading:** multiple matching (Paper 1 Part 3)
- **Language development 1:** relative clauses; reduced relative clauses
- **Writing:** review (Paper 2 Part 2)
- **Speaking:** individual long turn (Paper 5 Part 2)
- **Listening:** extracts (multiple choice) (Paper 4 Part 1)
- **Use of English 1:** open cloze (Paper 3 Part 2)
- **Language development 2:** adjectives and nouns + preposition; *be used to/get used to + -ing*
- **Use of English 2:** word formation (Paper 3 Part 3)
- **Language development 3:** word formation: entertainment; word formation: prefixes; verbs and nouns

Lead-in

- Which of the following are especially important to you and why?
  music   books   cinema   dancing   theatre
- Do governments have a responsibility to support and develop the arts, or should this be left to private enterprise?

6A Music

Reading (Paper 1 Part 3)

Before you read

1 **Look at the title and introduction of the text opposite.**

   a **Which of the following kinds of music do you associate with a) 'easy listening' and b) 'youthful rebellion'? Add any other types you can think of.**

   > reggae   rock   hip hop   country and western   rap   folk   blues
   > jazz   R&B   salsa   swing   disco   heavy metal

   b **What types of music do you associate with these instruments? (E.g. the trumpet and saxophone are played in jazz bands.) Add more examples of instruments.**

   > acoustic guitar   flute   trumpet   piano   xylophone   electric guitar
   > tabla   drums   violin   sitar   saxophone   keyboard   clarinet   harp
   > accordion   harmonica   banjo

Skimming

2 **Skim the text to find out what kind of music genre each person is known for.**

Multiple matching

▶ Task strategy Module 5A page 66

HELP

➤ Question 1
Global is the same as *worldwide*

➤ Question 2
Celebrities might include *famous actors* and *models*

➤ Question 3
Doing a gig is idiomatic for *performing live*

➤ Question 4
If you *dress up*, you wear special clothes

➤ Question 6
A different *genre* could be *rock* or *pop*

3 a **You are going to read a magazine article about four young musicians who are well known for the type of music which was very popular in their parents' or grandparents' day. For questions 1–15 choose from the people (A–D). The people may be chosen more than once. Use the Help clues if necessary.**

   b **Compare and give reasons for your answers.**

   Which musician

is globally very successful?	1
has a celebrity following?	2
has had a wide and varied experience of performing live?	3
likes to dress up when doing a show?	4
admits their music is not fashionable with younger fans?	5
plays music which is a mixture of different genres?	6
was trained as a classical musician?	7
feels they only perform the kind of music they love?	8 9
sings songs with other people?	10
wants to use their music as a political message?	11
wants to appeal to a wider audience?	12
receives a mixed reaction to their music?	13
wanted to offer an alternative to the usual music on offer?	14 15

FEELS NOTHING LIKE
TEEN SPIRIT

The albums chart is filled with some of the least offensive music ever made and rock critics are wondering whatever happened to youthful rebellion, as embodied by punk rock and grunge. The stars of easy listening see things differently.

A When 26-year-old **Jamie Cullum** was a teenager, music was his hobby and he worked his way through college doing every kind of gig possible – weddings, cruise liners, parties – and playing in every band going, from heavy metal to freestyle hip hop. Backed by experienced professionals on double bass and drums, the charismatic vocalist and pianist brings a contemporary broad approach to jazz. 'What I'm doing isn't pure jazz. Pop, rock, dance, hip hop – everything gets thrown together.' He covers heroes of his own generation like Coldplay and Radiohead as well as those of the past by doing jazzy new interpretations of their songs but also writes songs of his own with modern themes in old styles. A gifted but self-taught performer, Cullum, who can't read music and plays by ear, provokes extremes of love and loathing amongst record buyers and jazz purists but says, 'What I do is totally true to me. I put my heart and soul into it.'

B **Michael Bublé**, at 27, has achieved over a million worldwide sales for his album of old dance band favourites from the 1930s and 40s. He discovered swing through his Italian grandfather. 'While I was growing up,

40 this music would be everywhere. Of course, I heard modern stuff too, but there wasn't enough melody for me. Swing is all about rhythm. When I was growing up, kids weren't given any
45 choice so this was my rebellion. I like rap, pop and R&B but for too long there's only been room for that and nothing else.' So does this on-stage 'smooth' behaviour come naturally to
50 him? 'I wasn't born in the 30s and I don't smoke cigars in real life. I don't want to be a copycat – I'm not really Frank Sinatra. It's just part of the performance in the same way that an
55 actor doesn't have to take drugs in order to play a junkie.'

C In 2004, **Katie Melua**, then 19, spent most of the year as number one in the album charts. Her music is not
60 easily categorised but she laughs at the idea that she is conservative. 'If everyone else was doing jazz, blues and folk in the charts then you could accuse me of this. But everyone's
65 doing R&B and hip hop, and I feel there should be another option.' Haven't some of her contemporaries accused her of being a little unexciting? 'All I can say is that my
70 music is completely from my heart and it's what feels right. OK, it happens not to be hip and cool, but I'm not suddenly going to get an electric guitar out just to attract the kids.
75 Perhaps my music appeals to an older

generation because I myself listen to artists such as Ella Fitzgerald, Bob Dylan and Eva Cassidy. When I heard Cassidy's 'Over the Rainbow' it
80 opened my eyes, because it sounded old-fashioned but also fresh and new.' So would she ever consider using her fame to write a song about the wrongs of the world, as Dylan
85 did? 'I already have. This kind of protest can be a powerful tool with young people and it's been neglected in the current popular charts.'

D Being in a band which does
90 cover versions of old songs is rarely cool or glamorous, but **Marcella Puppini**, as one third of one of the most interesting vocal acts around, includes supermodel Kate Moss
95 amongst her famous fans. Marcella met the other two 'Puppini Sisters' at the Royal College of Music, where they studied singing and various instruments including the
100 piano, saxophone, violin, harp and accordion. All accomplished musicians, they decided to turn the clock back 60 years to form a three-part harmony group. As well
105 as creating up-to-date interpretations of favourites from the 1940s, they also translate 'modern' songs and reinterpret them in the 1940s style. Helped by
110 the present vogue for all things retro they have achieved a cult following in the coolest, trendiest clubs and festivals in the UK, wearing clothes and make-up in
115 keeping with the songs they sing. 'I would now like the band to cross over to the 'pop' charts. I think they may be ready for something
120 different,' says Marcella.

Discussion

4 **Discuss these questions.**

1 Do you agree that contemporary music is not 'rebellious'? What kind of music do people of your age buy?

2 Do you like singers to write their own songs or do you prefer them to do 'covers'?

3 Do you like any 'retro' music?

The Rolling Stones

Abba

The Sex Pistols

Gladys Knight and the Pips

Bob Marley

The Black-eyed Peas

Language development 1

Relative clauses

1 a These bands belong to different genres in the history of popular music. Match the pictures with the music genres.

1	rock	4	reggae
2	disco	5	soul
3	punk	6	hip hop

b Discuss these questions.
1 Can you think of
   - any other artists for each genre?   • any other genres?
2 Have you heard the people in the pictures?

2 a Read about the history of popular music over the last 50 years. Answer these questions.
1 When were these genres popular: reggae, punk, hip hop?
2 Where did hip hop develop?

b Complete the information in the box with examples from the text.

> *The bands which dominated Western popular music* in the 1960s were the Beatles and the Rolling Stones, although *the one singer who had the most influence* was probably the 'protest' singer Bob Dylan. In the 1970s and 80s popular music moved in different directions. There were singers like *Elton John, whose piano-based pop songs were hugely popular*, the reggae artist, *Bob Marley, who had a huge hit with 'No woman, No Cry'*, and there was highly-polished disco music. In reaction, punk bands, and *the records they made*, were crude and aggressively anti-establishment. In the 1990s and the 2000s, *decades in which 'boy bands' and 'girl bands' became popular*, music fashion was heavily influenced by *hip hop, which was an Afro-American musical movement* from New York *that first emerged in the 1970s*.

Relative clauses

A   Defining relative clauses add essential information.
   Examples:
   1 ....
   2 ....
   3 ....
   Use *who* for people, and *which* or *that* for objects.

B   The relative pronoun can be omitted when the clause defines the object of the clause.
   EXAMPLE: C Non-defining relative clauses add extra, non-essential information and separated by commas.

   Examples:
   1 ....
   2 ....
   3 ....
   Use *who* for people, and *which* for objects.
   Whose is the possessive relative pronoun.

▶ Grammar reference page 186

3 Complete the sentences with a pronoun from the list below and add commas if necessary. Show where two different pronouns could be used, and where the pronoun could be omitted.

that   who   whose   where   which

1 The singer Nelly Furtado .... parents emigrated to Canada from the Azores in the 1970s grew up in the quiet town of Victoria in British Columbia. Furtado .... can speak English, Spanish, Portuguese and Hindi incorporates cross-cultural sounds into her music.

2 The British girl band Girls Aloud were discovered on *Popstars* .... was an international reality television programme in .... boy bands and girl bands were created on TV.

3 The rock band Snow Patrol was formed in 1994 in Scotland .... two of its original members were studying at the time. Both of them were born in Ireland so it's not surprising that the band .... they admire most is the Irish rock band U2.

4 Shakira .... means 'grateful' in Arabic was born in Columbia .... she grew up among the Lebanese and Italian communities. Her song 'Hips Don't Lie' reached No 1 in almost every country in .... it was sold.

5 Justin Timberlake was one of several singers .... were first discovered on the popular TV show *The Mickey Mouse Club* .... first began in the 1950s. Other Club singers .... went on to become famous were Britney Spears and Christina Aguilera.

6 Oasis .... major musical influence was the Beatles was one of several bands in the 1990s to .... the media gave the label *Britpop*. Their current drummer is Zak Starkey .... father, Ringo Starr, was drummer for the Beatles.

4 Join these pairs of sentences with relative clauses. Add commas to the non-defining relative clauses.

1 I saw a poster. It was advertising a gig for a new rock band.
2 I phoned the box office. It was in London.
3 There was an answering machine. It was telling me to call another number.
4 I spoke to a man on the other number. He told me there were only expensive seats left.
5 I booked two tickets. They cost 90 Euros each.
6 I paid by credit card. This is a very convenient way to pay.
7 On the day, we went to the theatre. It overlooks the River Thames in London.
8 We couldn't get into the theatre. It had been closed because of technical problems.
9 I went home with my friend. She was very disappointed.
10 Next day I phoned the theatre. They were very helpful and offered replacement tickets.

5 Expand the sentences about the Latin American dance music salsa by adding the extra information in brackets.

1 Salsa is a mixture of Spanish Caribbean rhythms and styles. (*'salsa' means sauce in Spanish*)
2 The salsa band Sonora Carrusales was formed in Colombia in 1995. (*their songs are played in salsa dance clubs everywhere*)
3 The singer Gloria Estefan uses salsa rhythms in many of her songs. (*she was born in Cuba but now lives in the USA*)
4 The Puerto Rican American Victor Manuelle is often thought of as a romantic salsa singer. (*his career began when he was discovered by salsa superstar Gilberto Santa*)
5 The album *Travesia* was a huge success with Manuelle's fans. (*on it he improvises vocals and lyrics within a salsa tune*)

Reduced relative clauses

Some relative clauses can be 'reduced' to participle clauses.

A A present participle clause (*-ing*) can replace:
• a relative clause in the present or past continuous.
The woman **singing** that song is a famous actress.
(The woman **who is singing** …)
The car **going** round the corner was the new BMW.
(The car **that was going** …)
• a relative clause describing a permanent state.
The people **living** in that house work in the theatre.
(The people **who live** …)
The flat **belonging** to my brother was the nicest.
(The flat **which belonged** …)

B A past participle clause can replace a passive relative clause.
• All TVs **sold** in this shop have a one-year guarantee.
(All TVs **which are sold** …)
The video **released** last week has sold a million.
(The video **which was released** …)

6 Look at the information in the box above. Join the pairs of sentences 1, 3, 5 and 7 in Exercise 4. This time use reduced relative clauses.

7 Look at Exercise 4 again. Make notes about a time when <u>you</u> went to see a musical event. Write pairs of sentences. Then talk about it, using relative clauses and reduced relatives to link your sentences.

Writing a review
Review (Paper 2 Part 2)

Lead-in

1 Discuss these questions.

1 How do you decide which singers and bands to see?
2 Do you read reviews of live performances? Do you follow their advice?

Understand the task

2 Read the task below and answer the questions.

1 What is the PURPOSE of the review? (e.g. to inform, persuade, to entertain, to teach)
2 How many PARTS are there to the question?
3 Which of these are you being asked for in each part:
   • an opinion   • an anecdote   • facts   • to describe the situation?
4 What STYLE will you use? Neutral, formal, informal?

> You have just seen this advertisement:
>
> ### INTERNATIONAL MUSIC MAGAZINE
>
> **Have you been to a music concert recently? If so, could you write us a review of the concert you went to?**
>
> Include information on the band or singer, the music, and say whether you would recommend the concert to other people. We will publish some of the best reviews next month.
>
> Write your **review** for the International Music Magazine in **120–180** words in an appropriate style.

Plan your review

3 Complete the paragraph plan below with the topics below.

   • brief description of the person/band   • what you don't like
   • conclusion • attention-grabbing introduction   • what you like
   • recommendation

Paragraph 1: ....
Paragraph 2: ....
Paragraph 3: ....
Paragraph 4: ....
Paragraph 5: ....

Language and content

4 a Choose the best opening paragraph.

> A My favourite singer is Beyoncé. She's very good.

> B What a performer! Beyoncé's spectacular concert will get you on your feet dancing.

b Choose the best closing paragraph.

> A Throughout the concert Beyoncé showed why she is the new princess of pop. Get tickets if you can.

> B I think you will like the concert. I did.

c   Complete some of the sentences in the table for your favourite singer, musician or band.

Catching the reader's attention (para. 1)	*Have you seen/heard … ?* *I have to tell you about my favourite singer/musician/band … .* *They give/They've made one of the best … .*
Describing the performers (para. 2)	*He/She is … They are … who/whose … .* *On stage/On disc … .*
Saying what you like (para. 3)	*What an incredible … .* *Both … and … .* *As the show started …/The first track on the disc … .* *… are/were amazing.*
Saying what you don't like (para. 4)	*The only thing I'm not/wasn't really happy about was … .* *It's/was … .* *I must admit that … .*
Conclusion/ Recommendation (para. 5)	*Judging from this (CD/show), (he/she/they)'ll be (one of) the best … .* *If you like (disco music of the 1980s) you'll love … .* *Although some of … (it's/they're/he's/she's) still a great … .* *You really must/should (buy it/try and catch one of their shows).*

Write your review

5   Now write your own review, using the ideas and some of the language above. Write your answer in 120–180 words.

Check and improve your review

6   Edit your review using this list. Check your:
- plan (Have you covered everything?)
- style (Is it lively and interesting?)
- language (Is it varied and interesting?)
- use of relative clauses.

▶ Writing reference page 205

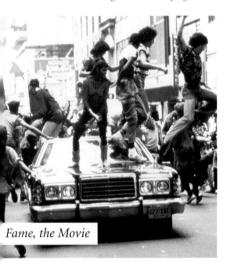
Fame, the Movie

LANGUAGE SPOT: avoiding repetition

a   **What do the words in italics refer to?**
   Fame – the musical
   Good musicals make sure *their* audience feel good when *they* leave the theatre. In *this* musical the acting and singing are wonderful. The actors hit *their* notes with gusto and give *the show* all *they*'ve got. The youngest *ones* are the best. *You* won't know *their* names but *they*'re as good as any professional. However, *these* are the plus points. The plot is less than satisfactory. *It*'s very thin and *this* is the reason *we* don't really care about the characters or what happens to *them*.

b   **Change the words in brackets to avoid repetition.**
   1   I like *Phantom of the Opera* and *Les Miserables*. (*Phantom of the Opera* and *Les Miserables*) are both musicals.
   2   *Phantom of the Opera* is on at the Adelphi. (The Adelphi) is a lovely theatre. We've been (to the Adelphi).
   3   I'd love to see *Grease* but I can't afford (to see *Grease*).
   4   Can you get me tickets for Friday? I've got a day off (on Friday).
   5   These seats are quite near the stage, but the (seats) over there are nearer.

Art and entertainment

Speaking (Paper 5 Part 2)

Vocabulary: art and entertainment

1 a **Look at the photos which show two kinds of art and answer the questions.**
   - Which one is *modern* and which one is *classical*?
   - Are the paintings *oil paintings* or *watercolours*?
   - Do you go to *art galleries* and *art exhibitions*?

b **Choose the correct word in these sentences.**
   1 I'm very *interested/keen* on landscape painting.
   2 I *can't see the point/couldn't care less* of abstract painting.
   3 I thought his portraits were *fascinating/fascinated*.
   4 Those sketches really *appeal/interest* to me.
   5 This watercolour is nothing *special/wonderful*.
   6 I *absolutely/completely* adore her drawings.
   7 She's really *into/onto* sculpture in a big way.

c **Divide these words into those with the stress on the first syllable and those with the stress on the second syllable. Then use the words to talk about a work of art you know.**

   > enjoyable   boring   amusing   shocking   depressing   moving
   > powerful   awful   brilliant   exciting   dreadful

2 a **What do we call someone who:**
   1 paints?   2 makes sculptures?   3 dances?
   4 produces a TV programme?   5 writes a review?

b **What do these people do: *a choreographer, a comedian*?**

3 **Match these kinds of TV programmes with the extracts from a TV listings below.**

   > soap opera   reality TV   quiz show   documentary   chat show
   > sitcom   current affairs

1	10.35	**Jonathan Ross** talks to Julio Iglesias and Ben Affleck.
2	7.00	**EastEnders** Andy tries to destroy Kat and Alfie's marriage.
3	10.00	**Question Time** Four public figures answer your questions on political subjects.
3	8.00	**The Royle Family** Another hilarious episode in the life of the Royles.
4	9.00	**Celebrity Big Brother** Which celebrity will you vote out of the house tonight?
5	6.30	**The Weakest Link** Nine new contestants. Anne Robinson asks the questions.
6	11.00	**Panorama** A new investigation into teenage crime.

4 **Which is the odd one out?**
   1 audience, front row, interval, viewers, stage
   2 adverts, switch on, channel, final act
   3 rehearsals, cartoon, performance, clap/boo, reviews
   4 turn off, box office, screen, remote control, live programme
   5 horror, thriller, trailer, comedy, sci-fi

5 Look at the two photos, which show two different kinds of art. Which do you prefer?

Sample answer

6 **a** 🎧 Listen to the examiner and complete the instructions.

EXAMINER: *I'd like you to compare and contrast these photographs, and say which* ....

b 🎧 Listen to Alice doing the task and answer the questions.

1 Does she give enough time to both parts of the task?
2 Does she make full use of the minute?

c 🎧 Listen to the first part again, and tick (✓) the expressions she uses to speculate about the photos.

> *The statue could be/might be … . It can't be … .*
> *It must have/must have had … . I get the impression that … .*

▶ Functions reference page 224

d 🎧 Listen to the second part and complete her personal opinions.

ALICE: *Well, I like .... but if ...., I think I .... because ....*

Short response

7 🎧 Listen and complete the examiner's question and Robert's answer.

EXAMINER: *Robert, are you ....?*

ROBERT: *I'm .... art. I prefer ....*

Individual long turn

▶ Task strategy Module 3B page 45

Task strategy

Student B, remember: Just give a brief response to the question, maximum 20 seconds.

8 **a** Work in pairs. Do Task 1 (on this page). Then turn to page 210 and follow the instructions for Task 2.

Task 1

Look at the photographs above.

STUDENT A: Compare and contrast the photographs, and say which type of art you think is more interesting.

STUDENT B: Listen to Student A without interrupting. Stop him/her after one minute, and say briefly whether you are interested in art.

b Did you follow the strategy on page 45?

c What language did you use to compare and contrast, speculate and give personal opinions?

Listening (Paper 4 Part 1)

Before you listen

Extracts (multiple choice)

▶ page 180

Task strategy

- Focus on the speaker's main idea – you don't need to understand every word.
- Choose one of the options after listening the first time.
- Check your answer during the second listening. Make sure the other options are wrong.
- Guess the answer if necessary.

1 Look at the listening task in Exercise 2. The extracts are not related. What kind of information does each question 1–6 ask for? Mark key words.

2 a 🎧 **You will hear people talking in six different situations. For questions 1–6, choose the best answer A, B or C.**

1 You overhear a woman talking on her mobile phone. What is she doing when she speaks?
  A thanking a friend who's done something for her
  B asking a friend for information about an event
  C inviting a friend to an event she's organising

2 You hear part of an arts programme on the radio. What is the speaker talking about?
  A a film
  B a stage play
  C a novel

3 You hear an extract from a radio play. Where is this scene taking place?
  A in a restaurant
  B in a hotel reception
  C in a motorway café

4 You overhear two teenagers discussing a film they have just seen. How does the boy feel about it?
  A uninterested in the storyline
  B disappointed by the acting
  C unimpressed by the photography

5 You overhear two people talking. Who are they talking about?
  A a close friend
  B a colleague
  C a relation

6 You overhear a man talking about an art exhibition. What does he criticise?
  A the way it is laid out
  B the information available to visitors
  C the quality of the works of art on show

b **Compare and discuss your answers. Listen to the recording again if necessary. What words and phrases give the answer?**
  EXAMPLE: 1B – *So do they give the exact dates?*

Use of English 1 (Paper 3 Part 2)

Lead-in

1 Discuss these questions.

1 Both of these pictures are from the Edinburgh Festival in Scotland. Which kinds of events do you prefer and why?

2 Do you like going to cultural events?

Open cloze

▶ Task strategy Module 2B page 33

2 a Read the title and text quickly. Are these statements *True* or *False*?

1 The 'Fringe' is separate from the main International Festival.

2 Performances are carefully selected for the Fringe.

3 Comedy is becoming more popular.

b Do the task. Follow the task strategy and use the Help clues if necessary.

Read the text below and think of a word which best fits each gap. Use only one word in each gap. There is an example at the beginning (**0**).

THE
EDINBURGH FESTIVAL

If you are at all interested (**0**) ...*in*.... the arts, Edinburgh in August is the place to be. Apart from the main International Festival (**1**) .... is what is called the Fringe, which offers 1,800 different shows in over 260 venues throughout the city, many of (**2**) .... are free. Visitors are often surprised (**3**) .... the range of shows on offer, including comedy, classical as well as cutting edge theatre, dance, children's shows and music – in fact plenty (**4**) .... everyone! As there is no selection committee, (**5**) .... kind of event is possible and the quality varies. While many high-profile performers take part, the vast majority (**6**) .... a mixture of unknown professionals, actors and students, (**7**) .... use the festival as a way of bringing their talents (**8**) .... an audience for the first time. Indeed many members (**9**) .... the Monty Python team and Rowan Atkinson first appeared there (**10**) .... student productions. In recent years a large proportion of new audiences are drawn almost exclusively to stand-up comics and some regular visitors are disappointed (**11**) .... this trend, but since comedy is very much in fashion at the moment, others recognise that they will simply have to get used (**12**) .... it.

HELP

➤ **Question 2**
This is a relative clause.

➤ **Question 3**
Which prepositions collocates with *surprised*?

➤ **Question 6**
Singular or plural?

c Which questions test:

• adjectives + prepositions? • verbs + prepositions? • verb forms?

d Which did you find the most difficult, and why?

3 Make a note of the word + preposition combinations you want to remember. You can record them by main word (A), by preposition (B), or by example sentence (C):

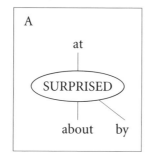

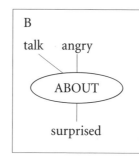

A
at
SURPRISED
about by

B
talk angry
ABOUT
surprised

C
He's angry about the result.
Everyone's talking about it. I'm surprised about that.

Language development 2
Adjectives and nouns + preposition

> A Adjective + preposition
> *I'm **tired of** walking around this exhibition.*
> *It's **unusual for** him to be late.*
>
> **LOOK** at the Use of English text on page 89 and find examples of adjectives with a preposition.
>
> B Noun + preposition
> ***Congratulations on** an excellent performance!*
> *I have no **doubt about** the artist's talents.*
>
> C Some adjectives and nouns go with different prepositions.
> *He's **good at** acting. (= he is skilful)*
> *Relaxation is **good for** you. (= it benefits you)*
> *That's very **good of** you. (= you are kind and thoughtful)*
> *My sister's **good with** children. (= she deals with them well)*

1 a Mark the correct preposition in each sentence.

1 What was the result *for/on/of* the competition?
2 Audiences often feel sorry *for/by/with* the good guy!
3 I have a lot of respect *of/in/for* the artist's talents.
4 There's no comparison *of/with/between* those two comedians.
5 I'm puzzled *by/with/in* what the play meant.
6 Moira always gets involved *on/in/of* discussions about art.
7 I have difficulty *for/in/by* understanding modern dance.
8 Your ideas are quite similar *in/of/to* mine.
9 Ellie was annoyed *with/on/in* her husband for forgetting the tickets.
10 That comedian's got no hope *from/to/of* getting an award.

b Complete the article with the correct prepositions. There may be more than one possibility.

Carlos Acosta

Anyone interested (1) .... ballet will be excited (2) .... the news that the great ballet star, Carlos Acosta, will be back in his native Cuba for this year's Havana Ballet Festival. Acosta's background was unusual (3) .... a ballet dancer. As a boy from a very poor family he mixed with some rough kids and had a huge natural talent (4) .... street dancing. It was only after strong encouragement (5) .... his father that he enrolled in ballet school.

As a dancer, Acosta is famous (6) .... his perfect control, and he is capable (7) .... jumping high and long in the air. Acosta has shown that he's also good (8) .... choreography and recently was responsible (9) .... the dance drama *Tocaroro*, which combined classical discipline with lively Cuban music. Acosta has had great success (10) .... his career and if the critics are right (11) .... how he has improved since establishing a permanent relationship (12) .... the Royal Ballet in London, we are in for a treat!

2 Answer these questions about yourself.

1 What are you shocked by/keen on/bad at?
2 Who are you impressed by/scared of/worried about?
3 What are you puzzled by/excited by/tired of?
4 Who are you sorry for/annoyed with/similar to?

be used to/get used to + -ing

> **LOOK** at this example from the Use of English text:
>
> *... others recognise that they will simply have to **get used to** it.*
> *I'm **used to eating** spicy food. (= accustomed to it)*
> *I'm **not used to eating** spicy food. (= it's new and strange for me)*
> *I can't/couldn't **get used to driving** on the left. (= become accustomed to, it was difficult)*
> *I left home last year. I had to **get used to living** alone.*
> Compare: *I **used to watch** TV a lot when I was younger but I don't now.*

3 Complete the sentences. Mark the correct form of *used* and use the correct form of the verb in brackets.

1 He *used / is used / get used* to (*live*) .... in Hollywood but he moved to Cannes in July.
2 It took him a long time to *used / be used / get used* to (*live*) .... in France.
3 Katie got tired quickly. She *didn't used / wasn't used / didn't get used* to (*film*) .... so early.
4 If you want to be an actor, you'll have to *used / be used / get used* to (*hear*) .... criticism of your work.
5 Newspapers *weren't used / didn't use / couldn't get used* to (*print*) .... such awful stories.
6 These days we *aren't used / don't used / can't get used* to (*watch*) .... films in black and white.
7 When he became famous, he had to *be used / get used / used* to people (*stare*) .... at him in the street.
8 I'm exhausted. I *don't used / didn't use / 'm not used* to (*go*) .... round art galleries.

4 What things do you have to *get used to* when you:

- get married?
- start work?
- go on a diet?
- go travelling?
- change college?

Use of English 2 (Paper 3 Part 3)

Lead-in

1 Who is your favourite comedian? Who did you used to like?

Word formation (A)

▶ Task strategy Module 2B page 35

2 a What advice would you give someone doing the word formation task below? Check your answer with the task strategy on page XX.

b Do the task. Follow the task strategy and use the Help clues if necessary.
Read the text below. Use the word given in capitals at the end of some of the lines to form a word that fits in the space in the same line. There is an example at the beginning (0).

HELP
➤ Question 2
What suffix do you need?
➤ Question 5
Do you need a prefix, a suffix or both?
➤ Question 7
Is it a suffix or a prefix you need?

The perfect comedy face

Ricky Gervais is a highly **(0)** ..inventive.. British comedian, who	INVENT
wrote and acted in an **(1)** .... funny TV mock-documentary	EXTREME
series called The Office. In it, Gervais plays the highly **(2)**	EMBARRASS
boss of a paper supply company, whose **(3)** .... high opinion	FANTASY
of his managerial skills and his sense of humour is not shared	
by his group of **(4)** .... Now, having analysed the facial	EMPLOY
characteristics of 20 top comedians, scientists have come to	
the **(5)** .... conclusion that the perfect comedy face must be	EXPECT
(6) .... soft and feminine, with a small forehead, wide nose,	PARTICULAR
large lips and high cheekbones. They say we should not **(7)**	ESTIMATE
the **(8)** .... of how comedians come across when we first see	IMPORTANT
them. Their **(9)** .... to appear agreeable and obliging puts us	ABLE
at our ease and encourages us to relax – in fact, the ideal image	
has an incredible **(10)** .... to Ricky Gervais!	SIMILAR

c Which were the hardest answers, and why?

Word formation (B)

3 Do the task below.

A serious actress

Penelope Cruz's career in movies has been **(0)** extraordinarily..	EXTRAORDINARY
successful, although she feels she has always had to struggle for	
(1) .... as a serious actress because of her looks. As she says,	RECOGNISE
'No one will take you **(2)** .... once you are known as	SERIOUS
the 'pretty woman'.' Nevertheless, in her best films, which she	
has made in her native Spain, she has managed to play some	
well-rounded, **(3)** .... characters. In 2000, Cruz was	BELIEVE
(4) .... to resist the call of Hollywood and early on appeared	ABLE
in one or two **(5)** .... films such as All the Pretty Horses.	DISAPPOINT
Now she is an **(6)** .... international performer who appears	IMPRESS
in both Spanish and English language films and many regard her	
recent **(7)** .... in Almodovar's film Volver as one of her best	PERFORM
films. In it she plays a woman who not only has **(8)** .... looks	CREDIBLE
but also great **(9)** .... of character. Not just a talented	STRONG
actress, Cruz gives generously to charitable	
(10) .... , such as Mother Teresa's Missionaries of Charity,	ORGANISE
and has spent months as a volunteer in Uganda.	

HELP
Two of the words require a prefix. You have to make **four** nouns.

Discussion

4 Discuss these questions.
1 Have you ever acted on the stage? What part did you play?
2 Which male or female actor do you most admire?

91

Language development 3
Word formation

1 a Discuss these questions.
1 What are events like this called?
2 What is their purpose?

b Complete this article with the correct form of the nouns in brackets.

I think awards ceremonies make good television
(1) .... (*entertainer*). Every year MTV gives awards
to talented (2) .... (*music*) and (3) ....
(*song*) and the fans get the chance to see some of their
heroes perform. In Hollywood, the Academy Awards
gives over twenty Oscars, including one to the best film
(4) .... (*direction*) and the best film (5) ....
(*acting*) and the show is watched by millions around the
world. I also enjoy theatre and television awards, where
they give an award to the person they consider the best
(6) .... (*drama*) and even one to the person who
the public votes as best television news (7) ....
(*presentation*). However, the ceremonies I like most are
when gifted (8) .... (*comedy*) get awards, which is
not (9) .... (*surprise*) really as most of them are
good live (10) .... (*performance*) and some of
their speeches can be very funny.

2 a Find three adjectives with negative prefixes in the Use of English texts on page 89 and write them in the correct place in the table.

un-	in-	dis-
unpleasant	inconvenient	dissatisfied
im-	**il-**	
impossible	illegal	

b Choose the correct negative prefix for each of the adjectives in the box. Copy and complete the table.

> polite   loyal   experienced   tidy
> patient   honest   fair   literate   practical
> fit   secure   satisfactory   logical

3 a Choose an adjective from Exercise 2 to describe:
1 a child who never puts his things away.
2 a man who can't cook or change a tyre on a car.
3 a good student who feels her homework is not good enough.
4 homework which is not good enough.
5 someone who can't read or write.
6 a graduate who has just started in her first job.
7 a man who is exhausted after running for a bus.

b Answer these questions.
1 Are you ever impatient, impolite or unfair?
2 What's the most illogical or impractical thing you've done?
3 Is your room untidy?

Verbs and nouns

> Look at these verb + noun combinations with *say, tell, speak* and *talk.*
>
> - *say*
>   anything/something
>   (to someone)
>   a few words
>   yes/no
>   a prayer
>   hello
>   your name
> - *speak*
>   a language
>   your mind
> - *tell*
>   someone
>   the time
>   the truth/a lie
>   a joke/a story/a secret
>   someone's fortune
> - *talk*
>   sense/nonsense/rubbish
>   business/sport/politics

4 a Read the information in the box above and correct the mistakes in these sentences.
1 The teacher spoke us a horror story.
2 I can't stand it when artists say politics.
3 We all talked a prayer together.
4 Excuse me, could you say me the time?
5 My brother talks three languages.
6 Tell hello to Rosie for me.
7 Mike said the police what he had seen.
8 Don't trust him. He's always speaking lies.

b Now complete this email with the correct form of *say, tell, speak* or *talk.*

> ● ● ●   New Message
>
> Why don't we go to Spain together – for a holiday
> perhaps – I (1)............... a little Spanish and it would
> be fun. Please (2)............... yes, but don't (3)............
> anything to Jason – he'll be very jealous. I like Jason
> but sometimes he (4)............... a lot of rubbish. Last
> week he (5)............... me that he had seen the music
> *Le Cirque d'Hiver Bouglione* in Paris but I knew he w
> (6)............... a lie – he's never been to France. I didn
> (7)............... anything to him at the time because I wa
> in a hurry but when I get the chance I'll (8)...............
> my mind and (9)............... him exactly what I think
> about him and his lies.
> OK, I've got to go now. Hope you can come!

5 Make sentences about yourself, using the prompts and *say, tell, speak* or *talk.*
1 I/languages   3 I/politics   5 I/no
2 I/lies   4 I/jokes

MODULE 7
Keeping up with the fashion

Overview

- **Reading:** multiple choice (Paper 1 Part 1)
- **Language development 1:** permission and necessity: present and past; advice and recommendation
- **Writing:** email (Paper 2 Part 1)
- **Speaking:** collaborative task, discussion (Paper 5 Parts 3 and 4)
- **Listening:** multiple matching (Paper 4 Part 3)
- **Language development 2:** speculation and deduction
- **Use of English 1:** key word transformations (Paper 3 Part 4)
- **Use of English 2:** multiple-choice cloze (Paper 3 Part 1)
- **Language development 3:** prepositional phrases; verbs with similar meanings

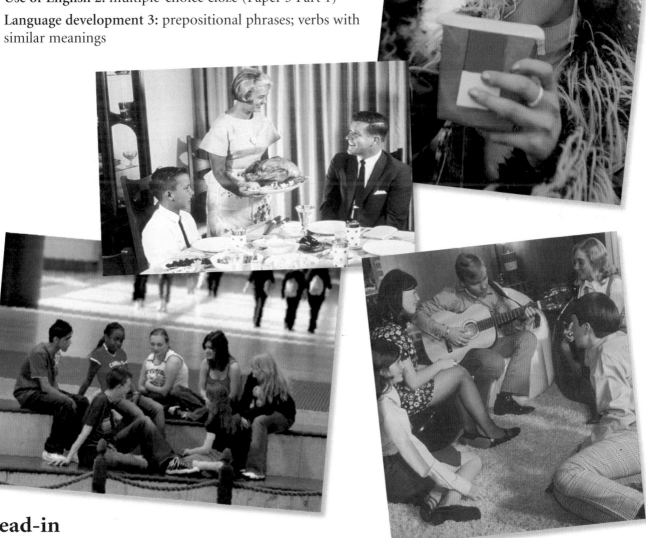

Lead-in

- Look at the photos. How have fashions changed over the last 25 years in your country in these areas?

  a) food and how we eat it   b) clothes and dress codes

- 'There's never a new fashion but it's old.' (Geoffrey Chaucer 1342–1400)
  What does this quotation mean? Do you agree with it?

Reading (Paper 1 Part 1)

Before you read 1 Look at the title and subtitle of the article and think of three things you would like to know about the current fashion for competitive eating.

Skimming 2 Skim the text to find the answers to your questions.

Multiple choice 3 For questions 1–8 choose the answer A, B, C or D which you think is best according to the text. Follow the task strategy and use the Help clues.

▶ Task strategy Module 4A page 52

HELP

➤ Question 1:
Unlikely is a similar word to surprising. What does the writer find unlikely?

➤ Question 2:
Where did Sonya first hear about the competition? What was her reason for entering it?

➤ Question 3:
Find another word for *enlarge*.

1 What does the writer find surprising about Sonya?
  A her nickname   C her determination
  B her appearance   D her attitude to men

2 Why did Sonya first get involved in competitive eating contests?
  A She was keen to take up a challenge.
  B She wanted to find a way of leaving her job.
  C She heard about it through her work at a fast food restaurant.
  D She needed to earn some money to finance her eating habits.

3 What makes a successful competitive eater?
  A being used to eating lots of meals
  B having a roll of fat around the middle
  C knowing how to enlarge the stomach
  D having the ability to drink a lot of liquid

4 *that many* in line 32 refers to
  A calories   C crab cakes
  B minutes   D competitions

5 Taking part in eating competitions
  A has been proven to be harmful for your general health.
  B can be dangerous if the food is swallowed too quickly.
  C means that there is no point in taking any kind of exercise.
  D does not appear to have affected the weight of most competitors.

6 What does the writer say about the fashion for competitive eating?
  A It has always been very popular in the US.
  B It is widely accepted as a sport these days.
  C It does not have a following in other countries.
  D There are uncomfortable moral issues involved.

7 Sonya's main goal for the future is to
  A own her very own restaurant.
  B earn vast amounts of money.
  C try to become world famous at a sport.
  D become the Number 1 eater in the world.

8 The choice of the word 'straightfaced' in the context emphasises that
  A Sonya is convinced that eating is a sport.
  B Sonya is trying very hard not to laugh out loud.
  C the writer thinks that Sonya is not telling him the truth.
  D the writer thinks it is ridiculous to take eating so seriously.

The craze for competitive eating

Crab cakes, hot dogs and chicken wings. We meet Sonya Thomas – the woman who has taken the male world of competitive eating by storm – and watch her in action.

When you first see Sonya Thomas you wonder whether she might be blown away by the breeze. Yet she is a tough nut. Unlikely as it may seem, this tiny woman, who weighs no more than 46 kilos, ranks second in the world for competitive eating. Indeed, she is America's number one who currently holds over 26 eating records, including 162 chicken wings in 12 minutes and 52 eggs in five minutes. Known as 'the Black Widow', (after the female spider which destroys the males of the species) she routinely humiliates hulking men three times her size as she wolfs down her food, leaving them watching her in bewilderment, unable to keep up.

There's something about being paid to eat large quantities of (usually fast) food in a short time period that speaks volumes about consumerist values in 21st century Western society. And yet Sonya was born and raised in South Korea, to a poor family who struggled to afford to satisfy their daughter's appetite. After emigrating to the US, she took a job at Burger King but it wasn't until she saw the World Hot Dog Eating championship on television that she finally found a channel for the competitiveness that had always been part of her nature. Curious to see how she would do, Sonya signed up for the competition straightaway, and ended up breaking the record for the fastest eating female.

In today's competition she is trying to break her own record for eating 40 highly calorific crab cakes in 12 minutes and I wonder how anyone, let alone a slightly built woman, can put away that many in one sitting. Many people subscribe to the 'belt of fat' theory which suggests that abdominal fat prevents stomach expansion so that the skinny eaters have the advantage. For pre-event training the Japanese world champion Kobayashi, also very thin, supposedly trains by expanding his stomach with cabbage and water. In Sonya's case, she finds drinking huge amounts of cola tends to have the same effect.

The competition is, without question, the most disgusting thing I have ever seen and I hear someone in the crowd mutter, 'What the hell are these people doing to themselves?' It's a good question. At today's competition, Sonia will consume around 11,000 calories in her quest for the $1,500 first prize, and put on around four and a half kilos in the process. But despite this, her policy of undereating – only one (huge Burger King!) meal every day – and regular running or walking enables her to keep very slim. The same cannot be said for the majority of contestants, who tend to be absolutely huge! And while it is true that there has been no conclusive evidence that competitive eating causes health problems, there have been instances in Japan of people choking while speed eating and ending up in intensive care, which is why paramedics are always on hand during competitions and why competitive eating is no longer shown on television in that country.

Watching the competition, you don't have to be unduly sensitive to find yourself thinking that the amount of food consumed here would represent the difference between life and death for a substantial number of people in the world's poorest countries. I discovered that this so-called sport dates back decades to events held at country fairs, where the idea was simply to dispose of left-over food. However, unlike Japan, which has been a stronghold of the competition since the 1990s, it has only taken off in a big way in the US fairly recently. The US now holds around 150 eating events a year and there are those who are convinced that it will get bigger, even becoming part of the Olympics. The majority of people that I spoke to, though, regarded it as a sign of the decay of society and an example of stupidity rather than sport.

Despite that, Sonya still hopes that one day in the future she will be thought of in the same way as an international sports star like Tiger Woods. She also tells me – completely straightfaced – that she studies video footage of her rivals' performances for clues to improve her technique and claims that even if there were no money involved she would still compete, both for the sheer joy of winning, and the opportunity to become a celebrity. However, although money may not be central to her life, it will come in useful if she is going to fulfil her dream of buying a franchise for her very own fast food outlet. In the meantime she still works full-time at Burger King, as efficient and energetic as ever, despite her new-found fame.

Discussion

4 Discuss these questions.

1 How much effect do you think what you eat has on your health?

2 In what ways can people become celebrities in your country?

3 Do you like fast food, or are you more interested in the 'slow food' movement, which encourages fresh ingredients, and a leisurely approach to eating meals?

Language development 1

Permission and necessity: present

1 a Look at these comments made in a restaurant. Which ones are more likely to be made by a waiter, and which ones by a customer?

1 We're not allowed to smoke, are we?

2 You don't have to give them a tip.

3 I'm afraid you can't s there – it's reserved

4 You're allowed to smoke in this area.

5 Excuse me, sir, children over 12 mustn't use the play area.

6 Steve, you're not supposed to use your mobile phone here. Turn it off.

7 I'm sorry, but you have to wear a tie to eat here.

8 I must try one of the desserts – they look delicious.

9 You can choose any table on this side, madam.

10 I think we are supposed to leave a tip.

b Write the words and phrases in italics 1–10 in the correct place in the table below.

Function	Example
A Giving permission	1 ....
	2 ....
B Prohibiting	1 ....
	2 ....
	3 ....
	4 ....
C Expressing obligation	
• the speaker feels it's necessary	1 ....
• the rules or situation make it necessary	2 ....
	3 ....
D Expressing lack of necessity	....

▶ Grammar reference pages 200–201

2 a Complete the sentences with the correct form of the words in brackets. You may need to make the verb negative.

1 They're very busy at the weekend, so we (*must/book*) .... a table.

2 It's a formal dinner. You .... (*can/wear*) jeans.

3 Lorna's a club member. Of course she (*allow/come*) .... in!

4 I think we (*suppose/wait*) .... for a waiter to show us to our table.

5 You (*have to/have*) .... a starter if you don't want one.

6 You (*must/bring*) .... your own food or drink to this restaurant!

7 Children under 16 (*allow/drink*) .... alcohol; they're too young.

8 You (*can/pay*) .... by cash, cheque or credit card.

b What rules are there in a café or restaurant that you know?

Permission and necessity: past

3 a Read the extract from a letter about a new restaurant and answer the questions.
1 Was it necessary to wear a suit?
2 What was the worst thing about the restaurant?

> We went to that new restaurant yesterday. It's very big, so we didn't have to book a table. John wore a suit because he thought it would be very formal, but in fact it wasn't, so he needn't have dressed so smartly. Of course, the children couldn't play in the restaurant but they were allowed to use the play area outside. The meal was very expensive though – we had to pay by credit card because we didn't have enough money with us. And worst of all, I wasn't allowed to smoke!

b Complete the table with examples from the letter.

Meaning	Example
It was permitted.	....
It was prohibited.	1 .... 2 ....
It was necessary.	....
It wasn't necessary.	....
It was done but it wasn't necessary.	....

▶ Grammar reference pages 190–191

4 a Mark the correct forms in each pair.

> When I was a student I worked as a waiter during the holidays. The best thing was that I **(1)** *needn't have paid / didn't have to pay* for my meals, as they were all free. We **(2)** *were allowed to / had to* eat as much as we wanted during breaks, but the work was tiring because we **(3)** *could / had to* work long hours. And although customers **(4)** *had to / could* give us tips, we **(5)** *couldn't have kept / couldn't keep* the money – we **(6)** *had to / were allowed to* share it with the other staff. I was nervous when I started because they said that sometimes I would **(7)** *need to have cooked / have to cook* the food, but I **(8)** *couldn't worry / needn't have worried* because I **(9)** *was allowed to / didn't have to* cook at all while I worked there.

b What rules about food and eating did your family have when you were a child?

Advice and recommendation

5 Find and correct the mistakes in these sentences.

> 1 You ought complain about that soup – it's cold.
> 2 You shouldn't having a dessert if you're full up.
> 3 If you don't like pasta, you'd better to have a pizza.
> 4 You must have try that new restaurant in Castle Street.

▶ Grammar reference page 191

6 Replace the words in italics in the letter below with words from the list in the correct form.

> can   must   have to   had better

Dear Melanie,

Thanks for agreeing to look after our house while we're away. Just a few things to remember:
    Be careful with the front door lock. *It's necessary to* (1).............................. pull it up before turning it. But *it's very important not to* (2).............................. force the key or it'll break!
    Please feed the cat twice a day. You *are allowed to* (3).............................. give him anything from the bottom shelf.
    It's not necessary for you to (4).............................. pay us to use the phone, and the kids *are permitted to* (5).............................. use the PlayStation. *We strongly recommend you* (6).............................. try the local restaurant. *It's a good idea to* (7).............................. book though.

Have fun,
Louise

7 Complete these sentences about yourself.
1 This year I really must … but I mustn't … .
2 At college / work we have to … but we don't have to … .
3 When I was younger I could … but I wasn't allowed to … . I had to … but I didn't have to … .

Writing   Email (Paper 2 Part 1)

Lead-in   **1   Discuss these questions.**
1 Have you been to a meal or a party on a river-cruise boat?
2 Would you like to? Why/Why not?

Understand the task   **2   Read the task below. What four things must you decide before you start writing? Look back at Module 3A, page 42, Exercise 2, if you need help.**

You work for a language school in the UK. A group of students is coming next month and you have organised a lunch cruise for them on a river near the school. You have sent the programme to their group leader, who has written back to you with some questions. Read the questions and the notes you have made. Then write an email to her, giving all the necessary information.

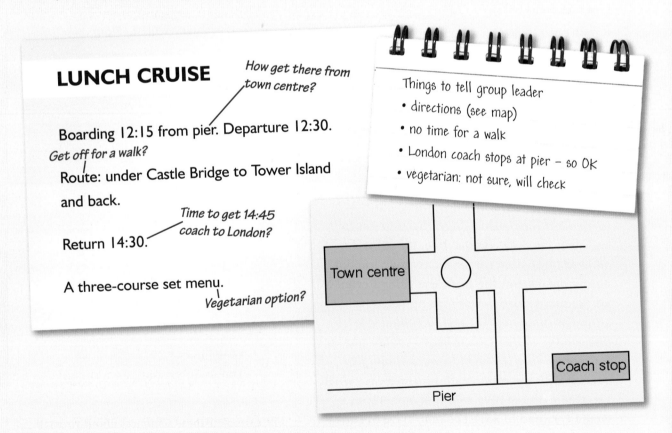

LUNCH CRUISE   *How get there from town centre?*

Boarding 12:15 from pier. Departure 12:30.
Get off for a walk?
Route: under Castle Bridge to Tower Island and back.
Time to get 14:45 coach to London?
Return 14:30.

A three-course set menu.
Vegetarian option?

Things to tell group leader
• directions (see map)
• no time for a walk
• London coach stops at pier – so OK
• vegetarian: not sure, will check

Town centre   Coach stop   Pier

Write an **email** of between **120–150** words. You must use grammatically correct sentences with accurate spelling and punctuation in a style appropriate for the situation.

Plan your email   **3   a   Make a list of key points to include in the email.**

            b   How many paragraphs will you have? What will you include in

Language and content

4 a How could you continue these sentences for the opening paragraph?

Thank you very much for … . Here are the … .

b Which of these expressions for giving directions would be appropriate in this email?

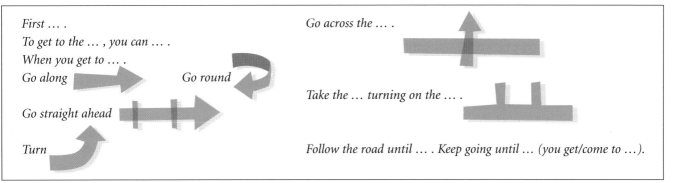

First … .
To get to the … , you can … .
When you get to … .
Go along   *Go round*

Go straight ahead

Turn

Go across the … .

Take the … turning on the … .

Follow the road until … . Keep going until … (you get/come to …).

c Match the expressions in this list to the correct functions below.

- *We should manage to … .*
- *You asked about … .*
- *We might be able to … .*
- *I'm afraid there won't be … .*
- *You wanted to know whether … .*
- *Unfortunately, I don't think … .*

Referring to questions	*As for (X) itself … .*
Talking about possibilities	*You'll be able to … .*
Apologising	*I'm very sorry but … .*

d Complete some of the expressions in the table to use in your email.

e How will you close the email?

Write your email

5 Now write your email, using the ideas and some of the language above. Avoid copying whole phrases from the question.

Check and improve your email

6 Edit your work.

▶ Writing reference pages 197–198

LANGUAGE SPOT: giving directions

a Mark the correct preposition in each sentence.

1 There's a bus *in / on / over* the corner.
2 Get off *on / between / at* the cinema. I'll be waiting for you outside.
3 The car park is right next *to / at / by* my house.
4 Go *past / on / at* the supermarket.
5 You'll see the café *at / on / in* the right at the end of the road.
6 Drive *on / across / at* the bridge.
7 Turn sharp right *in / on / at* the crossroads.
8 Follow the road *across / past / over* the police station at the bottom of the hill.

b Mark the more informal alternative in each pair.

1 I've never *visited / been to* your house before. Could you *give me directions / tell me the way*?
2 *Where do we go / Which direction do we take* once we get to the top of the hill?
3 *You should / I think you ought to* be able to *find the route without any difficulty / find the way OK*.
4 *There's no need / It isn't necessary* to get a taxi but *it is possible that you will / you might* have to wait *a short time / a bit* for a bus.
5 When you *get there / arrive at your destination* you *will notice / 'll see* my house on the other side of the road.

How do I look?

Speaking (Paper 4 Part 3 and Part 4)

Vocabulary: clothes

1 a Look at the pictures on the opposite page. In which picture can you see the following …?

> a stripy jumper   baggy trousers   high heels   a white silk blouse
> ankle boots   a plain leather belt   trainers and tracksuit   wedges
> a grey pleated skirt   a strappy dress   flat pumps   green cords

b In your opinion, which person is …?

- smart • casual • well-dressed • fashionable • scruffy

2 a When do people wear these?

> a bow tie   flip-flops   a parka   shorts   a fur coat   slippers
> sandals   a suit   pyjamas   a vest top

b In which situations would you …?

> • dress down • dress up • get changed • try on something
> • tuck something in • hang up something • get a bigger size
> • get something taken in

3 a Which clothes do you associate with these styles and fabrics?

> roll-neck   denim   suede   bootleg   cashmere   cotton
> moleskin   chunky   three-quarter length

b Practise saying the style/fabric + clothes combinations in 3a. Which is the syllable with the most stress?

4 a The table shows the usual order of adjectives describing clothes. Complete the table with the words in the box and any other words from Exercises 1–3.

> linen   fitted   patterned   old-fashioned   navy   viscose   Italian
> short-sleeved   tight   woollen   checked

opinion	size/shape	colour	pattern	origin	material
elegant	straight	khaki	striped	French	silk

b Use some of the words to help you describe what the people in the photos are wearing. Add your own words to the table.

c Look around your classroom. What styles and colours seem to be most popular in your group?

1 2 3 4 5 6

Collaborative task

▶ Task strategy Module 4B page 59

5 a **Work in groups of three.**
STUDENT 1: You are the examiner. Turn to page 210 and read the instructions.
STUDENTS 2 AND 3: You are Candidates A and B. Look at the photos on this page. Follow the examiner's instructions.

b **Look at the task strategy on page 59. Did you follow each piece of advice?**

Discussion

6 Look at the six Part 4 questions below. Which questions ask you to:
a give an opinion?   d make a comparison?
b give personal information?   e describe an experience?
c make a prediction?   f talk about likes or dislikes?

1 Do you enjoy shopping for clothes?
2 Have you ever bought clothes which you didn't like later, or never wore?
3 How much do you spend every month on clothes?
4 How much do you think the media decides what clothes we buy?
5 Do you notice a big difference in the way different generations dress?
6 Do you think clothes will generally be more or less casual in ten years' time?

Sample answer (Part 4)

7 a 🎧 **Listen to Julia and Paul answering Exercise 5 above. Do you agree with what they said?**

b **Who gave a better answer? In what way was it better?**

c **Which of these expressions did Paul use to begin his answer? Why did he use it? What is wrong with the other two expressions?**
1 *I really haven't a clue. Can I have a different question?*
2 *To be honest, I haven't thought much about it but … .*
3 *I don't know.*

d **Julia added her opinion to what Paul said. Was she agreeing or disagreeing? Which of these expressions did she use? Tick (✓) them. Which of the others could she use?**

> *Apart from that … .*   *Not only that … .*
> *And there's another thing … .*   *Actually … .*

Three-way discussion

▶ Task strategy Module 5B page 73

8 a **Work in groups of three. Take turns to be the examiner and ask two questions each from Exercise 6.**

b **When you have finished, discuss these questions.**
1 Did you give your partner an opportunity to respond to what you said?
2 Did you develop all your answers fully?

Listening   (Paper 4 Part 3)

Before you listen

1   How important are clothes to you? Read the task in Exercise 2a. Discuss each statement A–F and decide how true it is for you.

EXAMPLE: *I sometimes dress to look smart. It depends what I'm doing. For instance, I have to look reasonably well turned-out at work.*

Multiple matching

▶ Refer to task strategy Module 4B
page 60

2   a   🎧 You will hear five people talking about the clothes they like to wear. For questions 1–5, choose from the list A–F what each speaker says. Use the letters only once. There is an extra letter which you do not need to use.

A   I dress to look smart

B   I buy good quality clothes

C   I don't care what I wear

D   I choose clothes that are easy to look after

E   I wear fashionable clothes

F   My priority is to be comfortable

Speaker 1

Speaker 2

Speaker 3

Speaker 4

Speaker 5

b   🎧 Compare and give reasons for your answers. Listen to the recordings again to check.

1   What phrases helped you choose your answers?

EXAMPLE: *1A fairly stylish clothes … businesslike … . I don't feel right in casual clothes.*

2   Did you need to change any answers the second time you listened?

Discussion

3   Discuss these questions.

1   What kind of clothes are best to buy as an investment?

2   Speaker 5 says that she isn't a fashion victim. What does she mean? Why do you think people become fashion victims?

3   Do you ever buy clothes in sales or charity shops? What is the best bargain you have had?

4   What is it 'cool' to wear these days in your country if you are a young person?

Language development 2
Speculation and deduction

Use	Present: modal + verb	Past: modal + *have* + past participle
A *must* Certainty (we are sure it's true)	*The light's on. Ken* **must be** *at home.*	*Helen's late. She* **must have missed** *the train. He* **must have been going** *to work. That's why he was in a hurry.*
B *can't/couldn't* Certainty (we are sure it's **not** true)	*Jamie* **can't/couldn't be** *in the library. It's closed.*	*It* **can't/couldn't have rained/been raining***. The roads are dry.*
C *may/might/could* Possibility (we are less sure)	*Sally* **may/might/could be** *at home. I don't know.* *They* **may/might/could be watching** *us.*	*She* **may/might/could have left** *already. I'll check.* *The train may have been delayed. Who knows?*

Present speculation and deduction

1 **a** **Look at the first two columns (Use and Present) in the table above and correct the mistakes in the sentences below.**
   1 Marlie's in her pyjamas. She can be going to bed.
   2 It mustn't be his jacket – it's too small.
   3 That might be Kate. I recognise that voice.
   4 I think that's John's case, so he couldn't be here.
   5 She's decided not to buy those shoes. She could have enough money.
   6 Mike must work in a clothes shop – he knows nothing about fashion!

b **Look at these bags and make guesses about each owner.**
   1 *It … a woman. She … rich because … . She … because … .*
   2 *It … someone on holiday or … because … .*
   3 *It … either a man or a woman … . I think they … because … .*

Speculation/deduction in the past

2 **Look at the third column (Past) in the table. Complete the conversations with modals of deduction in the past and the verbs in the list in the correct form.**

steal   be   have   go   leave   cost   buy

   1 A Have you seen my make-up box in the bedroom?
     B No, you .... it there. I've just tidied up and I didn't see it.
   2 A What happened to Sarah's necklace?
     B Nobody knows, but it ....
   3 A Those shoes are so elegant! They .... you a lot of money.
     B Not really – I got them in a sale.
   4 A Why is Mark looking so suntanned?
     B He .... to the beach yesterday or else he .... a sunlamp!
   5 A I saw Frank at the gym this morning.
     B Oh. So his illness .... very serious!
   6 A Jane's nose looks completely different.
     B She .... plastic surgery!

3 **Complete these sentences about yourself and the class, and speculate using modals.**
   EXAMPLE: *The road outside sounds noisy. There must be a lot of people going home from work.*
   1 The teacher looks … . He/She … .
   2 The classroom feels … . It … .
   3 The student next to me seems … . He/She … .

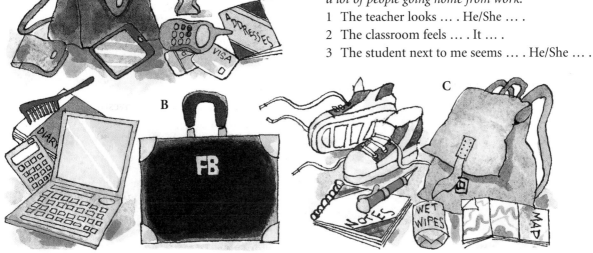

Use of English 1   (Paper 3 Part 4)

Lead-in   1 a **Look at the three completed transformations below. In what way has the candidate not followed good exam strategy in each one?**

> 1 I'm sure Sue was pleased when she saw the coat you bought her.
>   **been**
>   Sue ...~~must be pleased~~... when she saw the coat you bought her.
> 2 I'd love to go to the cinema tonight, but I've got to do the ironing.
>   **wish**
>   I ...~~wish I could go with you to~~... the cinema tonight, but I've got to do the ironing.

b **Check your answers by looking back at the task strategy on page 20.**

Key word transformations
▶ Task strategy Module 1B page 20

2 a **Now do the task below. Follow the task strategy and use the Help clues.**

Complete the second sentence so that it has a similar meaning to the first sentence, using the word given. Do not change the word given. You must use between two and five words, including the word given. Write only the missing words.

1 There's someone at the door, but it's too early for Kate.
   be
   There's someone at the door, but .... because it's too early.

2 I'm sure Tom's tired because he's yawning a lot.
   must
   Tom .... because he's yawning a lot.

3 I'm hungry because the last time I ate was five hours ago.
   not
   I'm hungry because I .... five hours.

4 He's so relaxed, I'm sure he's just got back from holiday.
   been
   He's so relaxed, he .... holiday.

5 I'm not fit enough to go in for a marathon.
   too
   I'm .... go in for a marathon.

6 It was possible that he was having a shower, so he couldn't hear the bell.
   may
   He .... shower, so he couldn't hear the bell.

7 You can borrow my computer, but you must look after it.
   as
   You can borrow my computer .... look after it.

8 I'm sure she hasn't left because her coat's still here.
   have
   She .... because her coat's still here.

HELP
➤ **Question 1:**
  You need to use a modal.
➤ **Question 3:**
  Be careful. You need to change the tense.
➤ **Question 6:**
  You need to add a preposition.
➤ **Question 7:**
  An expression which means *provided that.*

b **Answer the questions about the task.**
   1 Which questions test modals of speculation and deduction?
   2 Which modals are in the present and which are in the past?
   3 What do the other questions test?

Use of English 2 (Paper 3 Part 1)

Lead-in

1 Discuss these questions.
  1 Which of these hairstyles do you like best?
  2 What kind of hairstyles do you think look best on men? And on women?

Multiple-choice cloze

▶ Task strategy Module 1B page 21

2 a Read the title and text quickly and answer the questions. (Ignore the spaces.)
  1 Why do people change their hairstyles?
  2 How have hairstyles in the UK changed since the 1960s?

  b Do the task. Follow the task strategy and use the Help clues if necessary.
   Read the text below and decide which answer A, B, C or D best fits each space. There is an example at the beginning (0).

   0 A seeing   B watching   C looking   D showing

HAIRSTYLES

Hairstyles are not just about (0) ....*C*...... smart – we also use them to (1) .... statements about ourselves. We can (2) .... our hair longer or shorter than other people to give the (3) .... that we are different or we can style our hair in imitation of a pop celebrity and (4) .... that people will think we are fashionable.

In the UK in the early 1960s, the Beatles' 'mop-hair' style was copied by boys who, on the whole, wanted and (5) .... to shock their parents. Later, middle-class 'hippies' let their hair grow long to (6) .... their commitment to an alternative lifestyle. In the 1970s, 'skinheads' shaved their heads and (7) .... to represent the working class; and for those who felt themselves part of a multi-cultural society dreadlocks were (8) .... fashion.

In (9) .... years, though, men's hairstyles have been more dictated by fashion icons like the footballer David Beckham, who changes his look every few months, (10) .... from styles anywhere in the world.

In fact, one consequence of the Beckham phenomenon is that boys spend as much time and money (11) .... their appearance as girls and it's not (12) .... for boys to cover their hair in so much gel that it's rock solid!

HELP
➤ **Question 4**
All of these verbs can combine with *that* but only one makes sense in context.
➤ **Question 5**
In this context the verb means *believe that it is likely*.
➤ **Question 11**
Which preposition comes after *spend*?

	A	B	C	D
1	do	cause	make	give
2	wear	support	hold	carry
3	thought	meaning	design	impression
4	propose	hope	wish	suggest
5	required	expected	supposed	assumed
6	explain	create	perform	show
7	allowed	admitted	claimed	said
8	in	with	at	by
9	present	recent	current	latest
10	borrowing	using	lending	operating
11	for	about	on	of
12	occasional	few	insufficient	uncommon

  c Which questions test preposition + noun combinations?

Discussion

3 Discuss these questions.
  1 When you buy something new to wear, do you care what other people think?
  2 Would you consider completely changing your image (e.g. through a new hairstyle, different clothes, tattoos or body-piercing)?
  3 What do you think of people who are always changing their image?

Language development 3
Prepositional phrases

 LOOK at these examples of prepositional phrases from the Use of English text on page 105.

*The style was copied by boys, who, **on the whole**, wanted to shock their parents.*
*Dreadlocks were **in fashion**.*

1 a Mark the correct phrase in each pair.

Before I was sent to Milan to write an article for *Fashion Week*, I hadn't realised that it was one place where you are expected to look good **(1)** *at all times/at the moment*. So, when I arrived in scruffy jeans and with my hair all over the place, people stared at me as if they were **(2)** *in danger of/in favour* of contracting some dreadful disease. Things went **(3)** *from time to time/from bad to worse*. When I got to my hotel, **(4)** *at least/at first* the receptionist assumed I had walked in **(5)** *by mistake/ by the way* and **(6)** *to my surprise/to my advantage* asked the porter to give me directions. When she realised I was a guest she apologised but **(7)** *by that time/by heart* I was **(8)** *in a very loud voice/in an extremely bad mood*.

However, I had learnt my lesson. **(9)** *From time to time/From then on* every morning **(10)** *without fail/without notice* I would spend hours in front of the mirror making sure I looked good before I went out.

b Which noun in each group does <u>not</u> combine with the preposition? Cross it out.
1 **on:** sight   purpose   the beginning
2 **for:** fun   conclusion   a change   nothing
3 **in:** uniform   the end   luck   time to time
   conclusion   fashion
4 **out of:** date   fashion   sight   purpose   breath

c Replace the words in italics with a phrase from Exercise 1b.
1 Ellen didn't turn up, so *finally* I decided to go in by myself.
2 My clothes were no longer *a popular style*.
3 The doorman said my pass was *no longer valid*.
4 I'm sorry, I didn't do it *deliberately*.
5 Please be honest with me *in contrast with your usual behaviour*.
6 You're *fortunate* today – I've found your wallet.

Verbs with similar meanings

2 Look at these examples from the Use of English text on page 105 and mark the correct verb in each pair.

1 … we also use them to **make / do** statements about themselves.
2 … we can style our hair in imitation of a pop celebrity and **expect / hope** that people will think we are fashionable.
3 … boys **buy/spend** as much money on their appearance as girls.

3 a Complete the phrases with *make* or *do*.
1 your hair   7 a difference
2 friends   8 a job
3 a suggestion   9 an excuse
4 a course   10 something for a living
5 the washing-up   11 a profit
6 a phone call   12 a good impression

b Complete the text below with these phrases.
it would be comfortable   feel so good
a lot of money on it   to show my friends
in cash   trying it on   an Armani suit

I've just bought **(1)**............... . I spent **(2)**............... , and paid **(3)**............... not by credit card. I was looking forward to **(4)**............... in the shop and I hoped **(5)**............... , but I wasn't expecting it to **(6)**............... . And of course it looks great – I can't wait **(7)**............... !

4 Mark the correct word in each pair.
1 That fashion company's profits didn't *raise / rise* at all last year.
2 It all started when Johnson *became / grew* the Director.
3 It soon emerged that he *earned / won* $20 million a year.
4 Their reputation was badly *damaged / injured* by the scandal.
5 He was forced to *retire / resign* and look for another post.
6 But the company's wounds have still not *cured / healed*.

5 Complete the text with an appropriate verb in the correct form.

After I **(1)**............... from work at 60, I decided to **(2)**............... some money on a day at Royal Ascot, the most popular horse race meeting in the UK. I didn't **(3)**............... to get a ticket for the Royal Enclosure, but I **(4)**............... the decision that I would **(5)**............... my best to look good. So I **(6)**............... a dress from a London store and paid a designer to **(7)**............... me a hat. On the day, my hat **(8)**............... such a great impression that I was invited to the Royal Enclosure and met the Queen!

MODULE 8
The important things in life

Overview

- **Reading:** gapped text: (Paper 1 Part 2)
- **Language development 1:** reported speech and verbs
- **Writing:** essay (Paper 2 Part 2)
- **Speaking:** interview (Paper 5 Part 1)
- **Listening:** multiple choice (Paper 4 Part 4)
- **Use of English 1:** open cloze (Paper 3 Part 2)
- **Language development 2:** ways of expressing ability
- **Language development 3:** phrasal verbs with *get*
- **Use of English 2:** key word transformations (Paper 3 Part 4)

Lead-in

- Look at the photos. Which important things in life do they illustrate? Which are the most important for you? Do you think you devote the right amount of time to each?
- 'The man who goes alone can start today; but he who travels with another must wait until that other is ready.' (Henry David Thoreau 1817–1862) What do you think the quotation means? Which is better: to go alone or to wait for the other?

Relationships

Reading (Paper 1 Part 2)

Before you read

1 a Where or how do people usually make new friends in your country? For example:
- in a bar/nightclub
- at work
- through a dating agency
- on public transport
- through friends
- through their family.

Skimming

b Read the title and introduction to the article opposite.
1 Where did this couple first meet? How do you think it happened?
2 What does the title mean?

Gapped text

▶ page 178

2 Skim the text to see if your answers to the questions in 1b were right. (Ignore the gaps at this stage).

3 a Seven sentences have been removed from the article. Choose from the sentences A–H the ones which fit each gap (1–7). There is one extra sentence which you do not need to use. Do the task. Follow the task strategy and use the Help clues if necessary.

b Compare and give reasons for your answers.

Discussion

4 Discuss these questions.
1 What is your reaction to the way Wendy and Dennis met? Do you think this is a true story?
2 Do you believe that everyone has one 'soul mate' who is just right for them?
3 Which of these things do you think is most important in a successful relationship?

appearance   shared interests   age   education   sense of humour

Vocabulary

5 a What preposition is used with these verbs? How do they translate into your language?
- go out .... someone
- get on .... someone
- fall in love .... someone

b The text contains a lot of vivid words and phrases. Find the ones that mean:
1 extremely full (para. 2)
2 fell asleep (para. 2)
3 stood up (para. 4)
4 wrote in a hurry (para. 6)
5 confused and nervous (para. 6)
6 go somewhere very quickly (para. 7)

HELP

➤ Gap 2
Which sentence in the box explains who *the man sitting opposite* was?

➤ Gap 3
Which paragraph in the box mentions the sleeping businessman?

➤ Gap 4
Which sentence in the box explains where Wendy was at the time?

➤ Gap 5
Read the sentence after the gap. What does this tell you about Wendy's reaction?

MEANT TO BE

Five minutes later, and Wendy would never have met Dennis on the tube. Wendy Hatton, 39, and her husband Dennis, 32, live in London. She works in publishing and he is a scientist.

I On 18 October, Dennis and Wendy celebrated their second wedding anniversary – three years to the day after they first met on a crowded underground train in London. However, it was only a chance in a million that they got to know each other at all. Wendy had intended to get a taxi home that night. [1 _____] It was a decision that was to change her life.

2 She remembers: 'The train was packed. There was only one seat free – next to a businessman in a smart suit who had dropped off to sleep. As I pulled out my book, I caught the eye of the man sitting opposite, who gave me a little nod. [2 _____] 'Late night trains are horrible enough without strange men staring at you,' he says. Wendy smiled briefly and got on with her reading, but she could feel herself blushing.

3 Meanwhile, the businessman's head was slowly moving towards Wendy's shoulder as he fell into a deeper sleep. Suddenly, to her horror, it was resting on her arm. Wendy was very embarrassed, but didn't know what to do. [3 _____] It woke him up, and Wendy smiled her appreciation.

4 As Wendy reached her stop and got to her feet, Dennis pushed a note into her hand with his phone number on it. To this day, he doesn't know what made him do something so totally out of character, but he felt he couldn't just let her disappear into the night. [4 _____] She hadn't gone far before she felt a tap on her shoulder.

5 'I'm sorry,' said Dennis, who had run after her. 'I honestly don't make a habit of chatting up women on trains but would you come for a coffee with me? [5 _____] There was, however, nowhere open at that time of night, so they ended up going back to Wendy's flat for a drink. As she recalls: 'He was so non-threatening that I felt instantly comfortable with him.' They sat and talked for hours, both realising they had met someone special. When Dennis left, he asked Wendy to phone him.

6 Five minutes later, on his way home in a taxi, he rang her. 'I was worried that I might never see you again,' he said, and started to explain. When he'd scribbled down his mobile number on that scrap of paper in the train, he'd been feeling very flustered. Suddenly the horrible truth had just hit him. He hadn't given her the right number! He could never remember his own number, and without thinking he'd written down the number of his ex-girlfriend! [6 _____] They got on so well that two weeks later, realising they were made for each other, Dennis proposed.

7 'To me, it seemed too soon to be thinking of anything like that,' said Wendy. 'But later that night Dennis had a bad fall – he slipped on some wet stairs at home and knocked himself out. At the hospital they found my number on a slip of paper in his wallet, and called me. I dashed straight round. It was when I saw him lying there on that hospital trolley that it really hit me – I had fallen in love with him. [7 _____] Fate must have been on my side when I decided against getting that taxi, because there's no way we'd have met at any other time.'

They got married the following year. Wendy is still stunned by her good fortune.

A So I really had met my Mr Right on an underground train.

B Wendy's heart was pounding as she stepped onto the platform, clutching the scrap of paper.

C Seeing this, Dennis suddenly felt irritated and gave the man's briefcase a kick.

D As Wendy explains: 'I know it seems ridiculous, but it never occurred to me to refuse.'

E Fortunately, Wendy saw the funny side of it and they started going out together.

F This came as a shock to Wendy, who told him it was out of the question.

G It was Dennis, who had noticed Wendy as soon as she got on, but was trying not to make it too obvious that he found her attractive.

H Seeing the long queue, though, she changed her mind and got the tube instead.

Language development 1

Reporting exact words

1 a Read the following and discuss the questions below.

Irene, who is British, first met her Romanian husband, Ilie, while she was on holiday in Bucharest. They now live in Bucharest.

*   Do you think it's a good idea to marry someone from a different country? Would you do it? Do you know anyone who has?
*   Would you be happy to live in his/her country?

b Read what Irene says and answer the questions.

1   How did she meet her husband?
2   Is she happy?

I was staring at a painting in the National Art museum when this amazingly attractive man came up and asked me if I liked the painting. I replied that I'd seen it before in a book I have at home. He then said he'd been looking at me for the last few minutes and that he found me very attractive. I was embarrassed and told him to leave me alone. I said I didn't talk to strange men in art galleries. He asked me what the matter was and explained that he was just trying to be friendly. Then he smiled and asked me to join him for a coffee. I don't know why but I said I would, and that was the beginning of our romance. Somebody asked me last week if I regret marrying a foreigner and living abroad and I replied, 'Certainly not' and that I'm the happiest I've ever been in my life.

c Complete the table with the exact words each person used.

Present simple	Past simple
1 'I .... ?'	She said she didn't talk to strange men.
Present continuous	**Past continuous**
2 'I .... friendly.'	He said he was just trying to be friendly.
Present perfect (continuous)	**Past perfect (continuous)**
3 'He .... the painting before .'	She replied that she'd seen the painting before.
4 'He .... at me.'	He said he'd been looking at you.
Imperative	***tell* + object + *to* + infinitive**
5 '.................................... alone.'	I told him to leave me alone.
Request	***ask* + object + *to* + infinitive**
6 '...................... join him?'	He asked me if I would join him.
Yes/No **question**	
7 '...................... painting?'	He asked me if I liked the painting.
Wh-**question**	
8 'What .... the matter?'	He asked me what the matter was.
No tense change	
9 '........... marrying a foreigner?'	They asked me if I regret marrying a foreigner.
10 'I .... happiest I've ever been.'	I replied that I'm the happiest I've ever been.

d Why is there no tense change in examples 9 and 10?

e What does the past simple usually change to in reported speech?

f What do these words and expressions usually change to?

> today   tomorrow   yesterday   last week
> next month   this   here   come   bring

2 Read the conversation, then complete the text below.

TIM: Hi Sarah, it's Tim. What are you doing tonight?

SARAH: You're nosy! Anyway, I'm studying.

TIM: That's boring – come out for a meal instead.

SARAH: Well, I've nearly finished, I suppose. Which restaurant do you have in mind?

TIM: That new Indian one. I went there last week – it's great.

SARAH: OK, then. Can you pick me up?

TIM: Sure. I'll be there at seven.

SARAH: Great. I must be back early though.

> Tim took me out last night – he called and asked me **(1)**............................. doing, so I said that **(2)**............................. studying. He said **(3)**............................. boring, and asked me **(4)**............................. for a meal instead. I replied that **(5)**............................. finished and asked him which restaurant he **(6)**............................. in mind. He told me that he **(7)**............................. the new Indian restaurant the previous week, and that **(8)**............................. great. I asked him **(9)**............................. up, and he said he **(10)**............................. there at seven. I said I **(11)**............................. back early.

3 a Tell each other about a person, place or pet that is important to you. As you listen, ask each other questions and make notes.

b Report your conversations to the rest of the group.

Reporting verbs

4 a Complete the 'report' of Sarah and Tim's conversation with these verbs.

accused   agreed   explained   persuaded   suggested

1 Sarah .... Tim of being nosy.
2 Tim .... Sarah to go out for a meal.
3 She .... to go out for a meal.
4 Tim .... going to the new Indian restaurant.
5 He .... that he'd been there before.

b Write the verbs in Exercise 4a in the correct place in the table.

verb + *to*	
verb + object + *to*	
verb + *-ing*	
verb (+ object) + prep + *-ing*	
verb (+ object) + *that* + clause	

c Now write these verbs in the correct place in the table.

admit   advise   apologise   decide   deny   insist   offer   refuse   remind   recommend   warn

d Which verbs in Exercises 4b and c could go into more than one place in the table?

▶ Grammar reference page 197

5 Report what the people say, using a reporting verb from Exercise 4.

1 'You shouldn't get married yet,' Jane's father told her.
Jane's father ....

2 'I started the argument,' Nadia said.
Nadia ....

3 'I don't care what you say, I'm cooking dinner tonight,' Paul said.
Paul ....

4 'Don't go out with Mike, he's not nice,' Adela told her sister.
Adela ....

5 'I'm sorry if I hurt your feelings,' Nick told his girlfriend.
Nick ....

6 'Why don't we stay in this weekend?' Mark said.
Mark ....

7 'I'll carry that bag for you,' Marta said to her mother.
Marta ....

8 'I'm not listening!' Carol said.
Carol ....

6 Complete these sentences about yourself.

1 Once I had to apologise … .
2 … asked me if … .
3 … persuaded me … .
4 I've decided … .

7 Make sentences from these words.

1 Sometimes people / suggest / marriage / old-fashioned idea.
2 Parents often / persuade / children / get married.
3 Some people / insist / get married / while / still teenagers.
4 One couple / admit / get married / for financial reasons.
5 Some couples / refuse / have / religious wedding.
6 A few women / decide / not / change their surname.

Writing   Essay (Paper 2 Part 2)

Lead-in   **1 Discuss these questions.**

1 Would you prefer to live alone or with someone else? Why?
2 What are the advantages and disadvantages of each? Make notes.

Understand the task   **2 Read the task below and answer the questions.**

1 WHO is going to read the essay and what is its PURPOSE?
2 Will you just give your OPINION, or will you give both sides of the argument (FOR and AGAINST)?
3 What STYLE will you use?
4 What do you think makes a GOOD essay?

> After a class discussion on different kinds of relationships, your teacher has asked you to write an essay, giving your opinions on the following statement.
>
> Living alone is more enjoyable than living with someone else.
>
> Write your **essay** in **120–180** words in an appropriate style.

Plan your essay   **3 a Look at your notes from Exercise 1 and decide on the two most important advantages and disadvantages.**

b This is a possible paragraph plan for the essay. Which of your points would you include in each paragraph?

Paragraph 1:   **Introduction**
A general statement/rhetorical question
Qualifying the argument

Paragraph 2:   **Advantages**
Introduction
Advantage 1   →   Reason   →   Specific example
Advantage 2   →   Reason   →   Specific example

Paragraph 3:   **Disadvantages**
Introduction
Disadvantage 1   →   Reason   →   Specific example
Disadvantage 2   →   Reason   →   Specific example

Paragraph 4:   **Conclusion**
Summing up/Balancing the argument
Your overall point of view

Language and content   **4 a Choose the best statement for the essay from each pair below.**

A 1 On balance, despite the various advantages, it would be difficult to live alone.
   2 Fine, yes there are good things about it, but overall, no, not really.

C 1 I like being with my mates, don't you?
   2 Most people would find it lonely and miss the friendship.

B 1 I agree with this statement.
   2 Nowadays more people are deciding to live by themselves.

D 1 There is nobody to tell us what to do.
   2 We make the decisions – no one else.

b Match the statements (A–D) to the paragraphs in Exercise 3.

c   Complete some of the expressions below with your own ideas for the essay.

Introducing the topic	First of all I'd like to say that … . The first point I'd like to make is … . I'd like to begin by … . Many people think that … . Some people say/claim … . Why do some people believe … ? However, if that is the case, then why … ?
Advantages	In the first place … . The main advantage is that you are free to … . There is no one else to … . Then there is … . What's more … . Another advantage is that … .
Disadvantages	On the other hand … . Secondly, … . Another disadvantage is … . Last but not least, … .
Summarising	In conclusion (I believe that) … . To sum up, there are arguments … . However, in my view … .

Write your essay   5   Now write your essay, using the ideas and some of the language above. Write your answer in 120–180 words.

Check and improve your essay   6   Which of the statements are true about your essay?

- I have answered the question.
- The sentences and organisation are clear and logical.
- Arguments are followed by reasons and examples.
- Both sides of the argument are given equal treatment.
- It is clear what I think by the end.
- The style is consistent and neutral.
- I have checked: length, grammar, spelling, punctuation and linking expressions.

▶ Writing reference page 203

LANGUAGE SPOT: linking expressions

Mark the correct phrase in each pair.

1   Flatmates often don't get on very well at first. *In addition / In fact*, they can have a lot of arguments.

2   Flats in my city are very expensive for one person. *In addition / In other words*, I like sharing.

3   Most people share household tasks. *For instance / That is to say*, they take it in turns to wash up.

4   I haven't got room for a flatmate. *Moreover / For example*, I like living on my own.

5   I think that house would be too expensive. *Similarly / Besides*, it's a long way from the centre.

6   He's a nice guy to live with. *Nevertheless / What's more*, he needs to help out more.

7   The flat's on the fifth floor, and there's no lift. *Because of this / Even so*, we decided to rent it.

8   It's not very big. *Even so / On the other hand*, it's right in the centre.

8B Hobbies

Speaking (Paper 5 Part 1)

Vocabulary: Spare-time activities

1 Look at the photos on the opposite page. Which person do you think does the following?
- plays Scrabble
- knits
- goes car-racing
- plays jazz piano
- keeps pigeons
- does archery

Check page 210. Are you surprised? Why do you think they have these hobbies?

2 a Match a verb from box A with a leisure activity from box B. Then match with the pictures.

A

| play   collect   learn   go   do   make |

B

| models   how to draw   amateur dramatics   Monopoly |
| waterskiing   rare coins |

b Which is the odd one out?
1 do (a bit of/some) *gardening, darts, yoga, drawing*
2 collect *autographs, old sport cars, pool, stamps*

c What other free-time activities go with the verbs in Box A?

3 a One of these words/phrases is stressed on a different syllable from the others. Which is it?

backgammon   paragliding   folk dancing   bird watching
wind-surfing   scuba diving   photography   dominoes
rock-climbing   train spotting

b Which of the activities in Exercise 1 and 2a is the most …?
- relaxing
- exciting
- time-consuming
- expensive
- unusual
- dangerous
- energetic
- rewarding
- popular in your country

4 Discuss these questions.
1 Which free-time activity are you most *keen on*?
2 Is there any free-time activity which
- helps you *unwind*?
- you *dabble in*?
- you are *obsessed with*?
- you would like to *take up*?

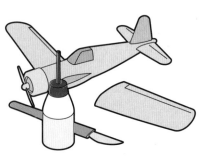

5 What is your favourite board game?

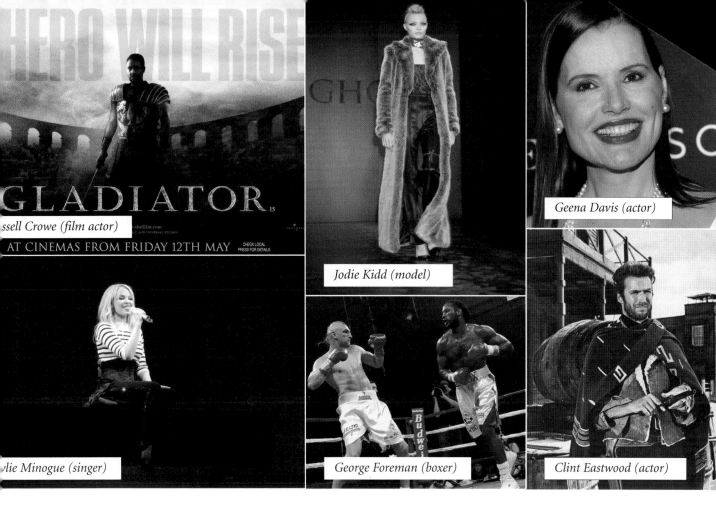

HERO WILL RISE

GLADIATOR

ssell Crowe (film actor)

AT CINEMAS FROM FRIDAY 12TH MAY
CHECK LOCAL PRESS FOR DETAILS

Jodie Kidd (model)

Geena Davis (actor)

lie Minogue (singer)

George Foreman (boxer)

Clint Eastwood (actor)

6 In Part 1 of the exam you may be asked questions about:

- your home town
- your family
- your job or your studies
- your spare-time activities
- your future plans.

a Write two possible questions for each topic above. Make notes about your answers to the questions.
EXAMPLE: Home town: Do you live in ....? Yes – here all life.

b Practise asking each other the questions.

Sample answer **7 a** 🎧 Listen to Anna and Giorgio's Part 1 Interview and answer the questions.

1 What topics did they each talk about?
2 Do you think they made a good first impression?

b 🎧 Listen again. Which two words didn't they know? How did they explain them?

Interview ▶ page 181

Task strategy

- Try to be calm and make a good first impression.
- Give full answers, but don't speak for too long.
- If you don't know a word, express it in a different way.
- Listen when your partner speaks.

8 a Work in groups of three. Take turns to be the examiner (asking the questions), the assessor (listening to and assessing the candidate) and the candidate.
EXAMINER: Ask some of your questions from Exercise 6a. Don't repeat questions already asked.
ASSESSOR: Make notes on the candidate's performance.
CANDIDATE: Answer the questions. Try to follow the task strategy.

b Discuss the task.

1 How well did you each do?
2 Did you give full answers?
3 Were any answers too short or too long?
4 Did you have to think of different ways of saying things?
5 What would you do differently next time?

Listening (Paper 4 Part 4)

Multiple choice

1 a 🎧 You will hear part of a radio programme with a journalist who is talking about the psychology of hobbies. For questions 1–7, choose the best answer A, B or C. Follow the task strategy.

1 According to Simon, what can you learn by knowing about people's hobbies?
   A what kind of job they have
   B what kind of person they are
   C what kind of skills they have

2 What do celebrities' hobbies often have in common?
   A They take place outdoors.
   B They are connected to music.
   C They involve being part of a group.

3 On film sets, the most popular way for actors to spend their time is
   A playing competitive board games.
   B helping each other with crosswords.
   C doing creative activities by themselves.

4 What is unusual about the Dalai Lama?
   A He loves old movies.
   B He collects vintage cars.
   C He is always mending things.

5 What does Bill Wyman get most pleasure from?
   A collecting antique jewellery
   B writing archaeological books
   C looking for items of historic interest

6 Simon says that the hobbies of world leaders are often
   A dangerous.
   B obsessive.
   C embarrassing.

7 What does Simon say about ordinary people who are fanatical about their hobbies?
   A They are usually a little strange.
   B Luckily, they are the exception.
   C It can be hard for others to put up with them.

b 🎧 Compare and give reasons for your answers. Listen to the recording again and check.

Discussion

2 Discuss these questions.
   1 Tell each other about your free-time activities. What interesting experiences have you had?
   2 What do your own hobbies tell people about your personality?

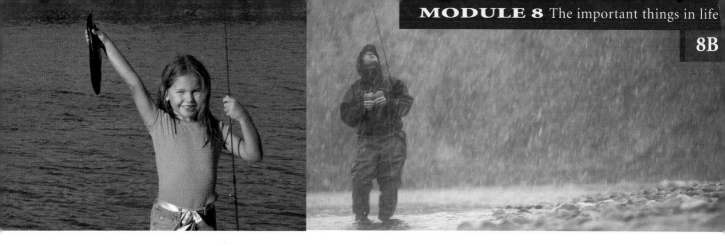

Use of English 1 (Paper 3 Part 2)

Open cloze

▶ Task strategy Module 3B page 47

Discussion

HELP

➤ **Question 2**
Which auxiliary is needed here?
What form is it in?

➤ **Question 4**
A 'dummy' auxiliary is needed here, which refers back to *catch*.

➤ **Question 10**
Which preposition combines with *succeed*?

1 Discuss these questions.

1 Why do people go fishing as a hobby?
2 Have you been fishing? What do you/don't you like about it?
3 Is fishing popular in your country?

2 a Read the title and text quickly. Answer these questions.

1 What type of fishing is 'angling'?
2 How many types of angling are there?
3 How is angling changing in the UK?

b Do the task. Follow the task strategy and use the Help clues if necessary.
Read the text below and think of a word which best fits each gap. Use only **one** word in each gap. There is an example at the beginning (**0**).

Angling

It is difficult to know why angling (fishing with a rod, line and hook) is (**0**) ..**one**.. of the most popular outdoor pursuits in the UK, with anywhere between two and four million taking part on (**1**) .... regular basis. For a father, (**2**) .... able to spend some 'quality' time with his son must be a big attraction, but why should grown adults, on (**3**) .... own, spend hours in the wind and rain, looking at the water, or standing waist-high in waterproof boots in the hope they catch a fish? When they (**4**) ...., they will probably throw it back anyway!

For the benefit of beginners, (**5**) .... are two types of angling: coarse fishing, where you dangle a worm in the water and hope that you manage (**6**) .... attract a passing fish, or fly-fishing, where you drag colourful, artificial flies across or just below the surface of the water to lure the fish.

Even though a woman holds the record (**7**) .... the biggest salmon (**8**) .... caught, until recently 98% of all anglers (**9**) .... male. However, the Environment Agency has lately succeeded (**10**) .... getting far more women to take (**11**) .... angling and a number of female celebrities, including Madonna, (**12**) .... learning how to fish.

c Which questions test
• verb forms? • verbs + prepositions?

1 Some people say fishing for fun is cruel. Do you agree?
2 Why don't more women go fishing?

Language development 2

Ways of expressing ability

A   Present: *can*
   Can is more common than *be able to* in the present:
   Can you play tennis? No, I can't.

Note: *can* also expresses future ability, if we are deciding now about the future:
I can play tennis tomorrow if you want.

B   Past: *could/was able to*
   - Use *could* for general past ability:
     Could you play chess when you were a child?
   - Use *was able to*, not *could*, for ability in a specific situation:
     I was finally able to finish my model plane last weekend.
   - Use *wasn't able to* or *couldn't* for both general and specific ability:
     I couldn't/wasn't able to beat Tom at squash yesterday.

C   Future/Perfect tenses/Infinitive form: *be able to*
   Can has no infinitive or past participle, so we use *be able to:*
   I will be able to play more tennis in the summer.
   Has he ever been able to finish a marathon?
   I might be able to go hiking next weekend.

D   Other ways of expressing ability
   *I **know how to** play chess.* (I have learned the skill)
   *I **succeeded in** beating my sister last week.* (suggests some difficulty)
   *I **managed to** beat my brother as well.* (suggests a lot of difficulty)

 LOOK   at the Use of English text on page 117 and find examples of two of the above.

1 a   Mark the correct form in each pair. Sometimes both options may be correct.

1   I *can / manage to* play the piano quite well.
2   Last week I *was able to / could* get away for a few days.
3   I *could / have been able to* ride a bike from a very early age.
4   When I was at school, I *couldn't / wasn't able to* draw very well.
5   In the last month I *have managed to / knew how to* get some outdoor exercise every weekend.
6   Once the exams are over, I *will be able to / can* spend more time on my favourite hobby.
7   I *could / managed to* beat my father at chess eventually, but it wasn't easy.
8   I was very pleased when I finally *managed to find / succeeded in finding* a salsa class.

b   Which of the sentences in Exercise 1a are true for you and your partner?

2   Complete the sentences with the correct forms of the words in brackets.

1   If Paul doesn't get some help, he .... that model. (*able/finish*)
2   How do you .... so slim? (*manage/stay*)
3   After five years Nico has .... his driving test. (*succeed/pass*)
4   I'm afraid I .... to the party on Saturday night. (*can/come*)
5   After making three big mistakes, Tara realised she .... the match. (*could/win*)
6   We .... (*know/play*) chess. Can you teach us?
7   Sergio .... (*able/stay*) ahead at the end, so he lost the race.
8   I .... (*could/swim*) until I was twelve, but then I learned very quickly.

3   Complete the sentences with the verbs in brackets and *can, could, be able to, succeed* or *manage* in the correct form. There may be more than one possibility.

I've been making models all my life. When I was nine I had my first Lego set – you know, those plastic pieces which you **(1)**........................... (use) to make machines – and everyone was amazed that I **(2)**...........................(put together) cars that moved.
   Later I **(3)**........................... (build) a larger car which **(4)**........................... (reach) quite high speeds. I also built a radio-controlled machine that looked like a plane, but unfortunately it **(5)**........................... (not/fly). Now I make radio-controlled robot machines that battle with other machines. Last year I **(6)**........................... (get) 'Victor', my warrior robot, onto the TV programme Robot Wars and we actually **(7)**........................... (win) every battle. I hope I **(8)**........................... (carry on) making machines for many years to come.

anguage development 3

hrasal verbs with *get*

a Read these weblogs and match them to the pictures.

nily

...idn't **get off to** a very good start with the ...dy Combat classes because my shoes were ...o heavy and not very comfortable. Also I ...d to miss a couple of sessions and found it ...fficult to **get back** into the routine. But ...erything's fine now and the trainer says I'm ...tting on really well.

eira

..., guys! I just have to tell you what I've been ...tting up to since I last made an entry on this ...g. Remember last time I was **getting over** ...e death of my pet rat and my dad wouldn't ...me have another pet? Well, I managed to ...t round him in the end – it took me two ...eeks and I had to promise to do better at ...hool – and he's bought me a bearded dragon ...look after!!!! How cool is that!!!

ck

...ove singing in the choir. We **get together** ...rly Friday evening, which means I have to ...t off work a couple of hours early. When I ...t there, we usually chat for a bit before we ...t down to serious rehearsals. I know I'm not ...ery good singer but I **get by**.

b Look at the verbs and expressions with *get* in bold and decide if these statements are *True* or *False*, according to the texts. The first one has been done for you.

1 Emily's Body Combat classes began badly. *True*
2 It was hard to start doing the Body Combat classes again.
3 Emily is making good progress in her classes.
4 Keira is saying what she's been doing recently.
5 She forgot to mention the death of her pet.
6 She eventually persuaded her father to buy her a new pet.
7 Jack's choir meets on a Friday evening.
8 Unfortunately, he can't leave work early.
9 They only rehearse seriously after a chat.
10 He doesn't really sing well enough to be in the choir.

c What do you think of how the people spend their free time?

2 Choose the correct paraphrase A or B for each sentence below.

1 It takes ages to get through to the complaints department.
   A Contacting the complaints department takes a long time.
   B Travelling to the complaints department takes a long time.
2 This weather is beginning to get me down.
   A The weather's making me happy.
   B The weather's making me unhappy.
3 To his surprise, he got away with a fine.
   A He thought his punishment would be less.
   B He thought his punishment would be more.
4 He always manages to get his ideas across.
   A He is a good communicator.
   B He gets his ideas mixed up.
5 I get along very well with my sister.
   A My sister and I have a good relationship.
   B My sister and I often go out together.
6 They got behind with their work.
   A They lost their work.
   B They didn't do as much work as they should have done.

3 a Complete the questions with a phrasal verb from Exercises 1 and 2.

1 How often do you .... with friends from your previous school/job?
2 What kind of things .... you .... ? What do you do to cheer yourself up again?
3 Have you ever done anything wrong and .... it?
4 How well do you .... with your parents?
5 How much money do you need to .... ?
6 What will you be .... this weekend?
7 What time do you .... lessons today?

b Ask a partner the questions.

Use of English 2 (Paper 3 Part 4)

Lead-in **1** **Look at the three completed transformations below. What vocabulary is tested in each one?**
  a prepositions following a noun, verb or adjective
  b fixed phrases (e.g. *on purpose, apart from, as a result of/owing to*)
  c phrasal verbs

> 1 I am here as a representative of the Government.
>   **behalf**
>   I am here .... on behalf of .... the Government.
> 2 They employ extra staff at the weekends.
>   **on**
>   Extra staff .... are taken on .... at the weekends.
> 3 Prices have gone up sharply again.
>   **increase**
>   There has been ...a sharp increase in... prices.

Key word transformations

▶ Task strategy Module 1B page 20

2 **a** **Look at the task below. What language is being tested in each question?**

  b **Now do the task. Follow the task strategy and use the Help clues.**

  Complete the second sentence so that it has a similar meaning to the first sentence, using the word given. **Do not change the word given.** You must use between **two** and **five** words, including the word given. Write **only** the missing words.

  1 Phil knows how to cheat successfully at cards.
     away
     Phil knows how to .... at cards.
  2 I'll take my CD player because we might want to listen to music.
     case
     I'll take my CD player .... listen to music.
  3 It's time you started some serious work at college.
     down
     It's time you .... serious work at college.
  4 There probably won't be any more customers today.
     unlikely
     It .... be any more customers today.
  5 They had to cancel the outdoor exhibition because of the bad weather.
     called
     The outdoor exhibition .... because of the bad weather.
  6 I failed to persuade Tom to take up stamp collecting.
     succeed
     I .... Tom to take up stamp collecting.
  7 We found it difficult to write the story. **trouble**
     We .... the story.
  8 Don't worry! I'll make him tell the truth.
     out
     Don't worry! I'll .... him.

  c **Compare and discuss your answers. Which question did you find the most difficult?**

HELP
➤ **Question 1**
  You need to use a phrasal verb.
➤ **Question 5**
  You need a phrasal verb and the passive!
➤ **Question 6**
  What preposition follows *succeed*?

The consumer society

Overview

- **Reading:** multiple matching: (Paper 1 Part 3)
- **Language development 1:** conditionals
- **Writing:** email (Paper 2 Part 1)
- **Speaking:** individual long turn (Paper 5 Part 2)
- **Listening:** extracts (multiple choice) (Paper 4 Part 1)
- **Use of English 1:** open cloze (Paper 3 Part 2)
- **Language development 2:** number and concord
- **Use of English 2:** word formation (Paper 3 Part 3)
- **Language development 3:** money and banks; forming verbs

Lead-in

- What are the benefits and drawbacks of the consumer society?
- 'The people who do all the work don't get their fair share of the profits.'
  How far do you agree with this?

A matter of conscience?

Reading (Paper 1 Part 3)

Before you read

1 a Which of these charities would you be most and least likely to give to, and why?

- the homeless
- children
- the developing world
- medical research
- animals
- disaster relief
- the elderly
- the environment
- the disabled

b Do you think helping the needy should be the responsibility of individuals or of the Government?

Skimming

2 You are going to read interviews with five people about contributing to charity. Skim the article to find out if you share the same views as anyone.

Multiple matching: questions

▶ Task strategy Module 5A page 66

3 a For questions 1–15 choose from the people (A–E). The people may be chosen more than once. The first question is done for you.

Which person

- admires people that collect money for charity? `1` `C`
- thinks some people support charities out of self-interest? `2`
- believes that giving money directly to individuals in need is not the best solution? `3` `4`
- resents feeling pressured into giving money? `5`
- suspects that some charities don't make the best use of their money? `6`
- has mixed feelings about giving to street collectors? `7`
- contributes to society in non-financial ways? `8`
- is impressed by the general public's generosity after a disaster? `9`
- prefers to support less 'fashionable' charities? `10`
- intends to make a charitable donation on his/her death? `11`
- used to feel guilty about not giving money to charity? `12`
- thinks the Government should be doing what some charities do? `13`
- is of the view that the average person doesn't give enough? `14`
- admits they have given money out of a feeling of guilt? `15`

b Compare and give reasons for your answers.

Discussion

4 Which person do you agree and disagree with most?

Vocabulary: informal expressions

5 Match these definitions with the underlined expressions in the text.

1 assist
2 admire
3 (do something) on purpose
4 homeless people, living on the streets
5 impressed
6 makes you realise
7 give money
8 feel guilty

Could you spare some change, please?

What motivates you to give or deny money to people in need? We hit the streets of Manchester to find out your views.

A Tom (30)

'Whenever I see a fundraising event on TV to raise money for a tsunami or an earthquake or whatever, I am always <u>moved</u> at how generous people are,
5 particularly those who are worse off. The phone lines are constantly jammed with people <u>making donations</u>. I do think the amount of coverage world disasters are given on TV really helps – it really <u>brings it all home to you</u> and allows you to empathise with what the victims
10 are going through. But of course it's not only about giving money, although obviously that is a key part of it; I've often wished that I had medical or engineering skills to offer, so that I could actually go and do what I can to help the relief effort. I'm more unwilling though
15 to just give money to <u>beggars</u> and people on the streets because I don't think this helps solve the problem long-term, and in fact could encourage more people to sleep rough.

B Yvette (26)

20 'I can never pass anyone in the street holding a collection tin without asking myself whether or not I should give. I sometimes feel reluctant if it's for medical research or the homeless – isn't that what I pay my taxes for, why should I pay extra? But on the other hand
25 £1.00 isn't that much and if everyone gave just a little, then we wouldn't have all these problems. I read in a magazine that the average person only gives 1% of what they earn to charity, which means they spend 99% on themselves! However, I do worry that some charities
30 have become so big that they are perhaps spending too much on bureaucracy instead of sending it directly to those who need it.'

C Jeanette (57)

'I really <u>applaud</u> those people who <u>actively do</u>
35 <u>something</u> for charity, you know, like a car boot sale or a sponsored walk. Sometimes I think about taking part in something like that, but thinking is all I do – I never seem to find the time to actually do it! To tell the truth, I think that most of us need to have a personal reason
40 for getting involved in raising money for a good cause, such as knowing someone who has a certain disease or something. I do give money to charity collectors on the street whenever I have change, but if I'm honest, that's because I <u>feel ashamed</u> walking on past them when the
45 rain is pouring down and they've given up their own time. What I really must do, though, is amend my will so that when I die I can leave some of my money to a charity. I've been putting off doing this as I just can't decide which charity to leave it to.'

D Graham (45)

50 Rather than just giving change to homeless people on the street from time to time, I think it is much better and far more useful to make a regular monthly donation to one particular charity of your preference. I
55 get really annoyed with the charity collectors who stand outside shops and swoop on you, asking you for money for this cause and that cause, trying to make you feel guilty if you say no. I also disapprove of all those junk letters you get, you know, with photos of starving
60 children or animals in pain or whatever. I feel that they are almost trying to exploit you – it's a kind of emotional blackmail. It's up to me after all who I donate money to and I actually make a point of giving to organisations that get less publicity rather than the
65 trendy ones that are linked to celebrities.'

E Laura (35)

'I wouldn't have any money at all if I gave money to every charity collector on every street corner! Where does it stop? That's why I don't do it. And I've stopped
70 feeling guilty and giving myself a hard time about it because I do feel that I <u>do my fair share</u> to help the community in other ways. I'm on the board of governors at my daughter's school, I donate blood three times a year and I work as a volunteer in a retirement
75 home. I also give our old clothes and toys to the local charity shop. I think that some people only give money to charity simply to ease their conscience rather than really wanting to help those they are giving it to. The same goes for those celebrities who get a lot of publicity
80 because they are associated with a charity. Who benefits more – the celebrity or the charity?'

123

Language development 1
Conditionals

1 a Would you give your money away like Warren Buffet? Read this headline.

Warren Buffet gives his money away

Warren Buffet, the world's second richest man, now worth $44 billion, gives 85% of his wealth to five charitable foundations. Most of the money will go to the Bill and Melinda Gates Foundation …

b Read the extracts below and answer the questions.

1 Does Keith give money to charity?
2 Is it possible that Scarlett will give money to a busker tonight?
3 Is Jake as rich as Warren Buffet?
4 Did Libby give money to an animal sanctuary?

Keith

If someone from a charity comes to my door, I nearly always give them money.

Scarlett

If I see a street musician on my way home tonight, I'll probably give him or her something.

Jake

If I had Warren Buffet's money, I'd leave most of it to my children.

Libby

If I had been the old lady, I wouldn't have left my fortune to my cat but I would have given a large sum to an animal sanctuary!

"One day, this will all be yours."

c Complete the Example column in the table with the clauses in italics from the conversation.

Explanation	Example	Form
Always true. (*if = when*)		
Possible and likely.		
Unlikely or imaginary.		
Unreal in the past.		

d Now complete the Form column in the table with these forms:

- *If* + past + *would*
- *If* + past perfect + *would have*
- *If* + present + present
- *If* + present + future

2 a Make questions with *if* about the present or future using the ideas below. Choose conditionals depending on how likely you think the situation is.
1 you / win a lot of money / what / you / spend it on?
2 a classmate / ask / lend / small amount of money / what / you / do?
3 a classmate / ask / lend / large amount of money / what / you / do?
4 what / you / do / you / need change for the phone?
5 you / find a lot of money / what / you / do?
6 what / you / do / lose / wallet or purse?
7 what / you say / you / receive / a present you / not / like?
8 what / you / buy / you / go / shopping at the weekend?

b Ask each other the questions.

3 Write a sentence with *if* about each sentence in the story below.
1 James forgot to set his alarm, so he overslept.
   If James had remembered to set his alarm, … .
2 Because he was late for work, he got the sack.
3 He couldn't find another job, so he started his own business.
4 The business was a great success because it was such a good idea.
5 James worked very hard and became a millionaire.
6 So, he became very rich because he didn't set his alarm!

▶ Grammar reference page 192

'Mixed' conditionals

4 a Underline the correct alternative.

1
If I weren't so poor *yesterday / at the moment*, I would have given some money to the busker *now / yesterday*.

2
If Warren Buffet had left me his money *last week / at present*, I would be very rich *last week / now*.

b Match the examples above to these explanations.
A If I had done something different in the past, the present would be different.
B If the present were different, I would have done something different in the past.

5 Mark the correct form in each pair.
1 If I *earned / had earned* more money in my present job, I *wouldn't have gone / wouldn't go* for a job interview last week.
2 Sheila *would be able / would have been able* to go out now if she *hadn't spent / didn't spend* so much on clothes yesterday.
3 If the company *had invested / invested* more when they started, their profits *would be / would have been* bigger now.
4 If I *were / had been* the President, I *would reduce / would have reduced* taxes as soon as I was elected.
5 She *would be / would have been* at home now if she *didn't miss / hadn't missed* her train.
6 Paul *couldn't have bought / couldn't buy* that new car last week if he *weren't / hadn't been* so well-off.

Conjunctions

6 Mark the correct conjunction in each pair.
1 The company will be a success *even if / provided that* we all work hard.
2 *If / Unless* we get more customers, we will have to close.
3 *As long as / Even if* we get more customers, we may have to close.
4 We can move to bigger offices *as long as / unless* they're not too expensive.

▶ Grammar reference pages 191–192

7 Complete the sentences with *if, unless, even if, provided that, as long as* and put the verbs in brackets into a suitable tense.
1 .... you .... (*hurry up*) we .... (*miss*) the bargains in the sale!
2 We buy our office equipment from PenCo, who .... (*give*) us a discount .... we .... (*spend*) more than £100.
3 I'm really grateful. .... you .... (*not / lend*) me the money I .... (*have*) big problems now.
4 I .... (*come*) with you .... you .... (*pay*). What time does it start?
5 .... we .... (*not / run*) a business we .... (*have*) more free time, but we enjoy what we do.
6 .... Peter .... (*ask*) me to invest in his company, I .... (*not / be*) able to. I didn't have enough money at that time.
7 .... you .... (*not / work*) so many hours you .... (*not / feel*) so tired all the time. You really should try it.
8 .... this .... (*be*) my company, I .... (*not / spend*) so much on new computers last year.

<table><tr><td></td><td></td></tr></table>

Writing   Email (Paper 2 Part 1)

Lead-in   **1 Discuss these questions.**

1 Have you ever wanted to complain about something? Did you actually complain?
2 Why might you complain to: a shopping website? an airline? a hotel?
3 Would you phone Customer Services, write an email to the company or write a letter to the company director?

Understand the task   **2 Read and analyse the task. (See Module 3A, page 42, Exercise 2.)**

> You have just played a new game and you were very disappointed. Read this advertisement carefully and the notes you have made. Then write an email to the company complaining about the advertisement, saying that future advertisements should not be so misleading.
>
> ## TRY YOUR LUCK
> The new game that gives everyone the chance to win.
>
> *No! £5 a game!*
> - Big cash prizes —— *only one!*
> - Very low cost
> - All money goes to charity
>
> *Claims within three months through your local store.*   *but 50% goes on 'administration'!*
>
> Write an **email** of between **120–150** words in an appropriate style. Do not write any postal addresses.

Plan your email   **3 Put these paragraph topics in the best order for your email.**

A What you expect the company to do.
B Saying why you're writing.
C Not easy to play and 50 per cent goes on 'administration'.
D Only one big prize and it isn't low cost.

Language and content   **4 a Complete the phrases below with these verbs.**
object   complain   draw your attention   express

I am writing to:
1 .... about your advertisement.
2 .... to your advertisement.
3 .... my dissatisfaction.
4 .... to some incorrect statements.

b Match the inappropriate phrases in A with the more appropriate ones in B.

A

1 I was so fed up.

2 Just listen to me.

3 Get it right from now on.

4 That's what you say but it's a lie!

B

a You should be less misleading in future.

b I would just like to point out that ...

c We were assured that that is the case but it turns out not to be true.

d I was very disappointed.

c Complete some of the phrases in the box in an appropriate way for your email.

> I am writing to complain about/to say that I am not happy with ... .
> You say/said that ... . In fact, ...
> You do not seem to realise that ... .
> My first/second complaint is that ... .
> The problems do/did not stop there.
>
> To my surprise/horror/disappointment ... .
> Furthermore ... .
> Even worse, .../Even more worrying, ...
> When it comes to the question of ... .
> I must insist that/you ... .
> I must ask you to ... .

d Match the sentence halves in A and B.

A
1 If I had known
2 I think it is awful that
3 I would rather have
4 I really feel you should
5 I was very surprised

B
a when I found out there was only one prize.
b be more careful what you say in future.
c you charge so much for a single game.
d that there was only one big prize, I would not have entered.
e sent my money directly to the charity.

e Complete one of the phrases below to finish your email.
I hope that in future ... .
If I do not get a satisfactory reply, I will have no alternative but to ... .
Please can you assure me that ... .

Write your email

Check and improve your email ▶ Writing reference page 197–198/200

5 Now write your email using the ideas and some of the language above. Avoid copying whole phrases from the question.

6 Edit your work.

LANGUAGE SPOT: spelling

a Which words in English do you commonly misspell?

b Correct the incorrect spellings of these words:
surprized   seperate   recomend   unneccesary   comittee   imediately   sincerly   recieve   begining   embarassed   advertisment   writting

c Correct the spelling mistakes in these sentences. The number in brackets tells you how many mistakes there are in each sentence.
1 When I tryed the jeans on at home I found they were too lose. (2)
2 The casette does not help foriegn students with pronounciation. (3)
3 The college principle refused to give us there acomodation address. (4)
4 Unfortunatly the medecine had no affect at all. (3)
5 I am definately not going to buy your products again untill you have developped a more responsable approach. (4)

Spending money

Speaking (Paper 5 Part 2)

Vocabulary: shopping

1 a Look at the photos on the opposite page. In which of these two places (A and B) are you more likely to
- *have to pay a fortune* • *pick up a bargain in the sales* • *find a 'one-off'*
- *go to the checkout* • *get personal service* • *be spoilt for choice*
- *get good value*

b Which is the stressed syllable in these words: *supermarket, department store* and *shopping mall*? What's the difference between the three places?

c In which place would you expect to find these? There might be more than one answer.

organic food   an aisle   trolley   escalators   changing rooms

d A boutique is a smaller shop where you buy fashionable clothes. What is a smaller shop called where you buy these?
- meat • medicine • flowers • newspapers • vegetables
- stationery • shoes

2 Write the correct form of *cost* or *price* in the gaps.
1 'Where's the .... tag on this dress?' 'Here. Oh, it .... a fortune!'
2 I think this sofa is a very fair .... Very reasonable.
3 What's the total .... of the computer? It seems very .... !
4 We install the satellite dish at no extra .... to the customer.
5 Look! These shoes are half .... Great!

3 Complete the gaps with a word or phrase from the box and say what you think the context is.

| just   pay   keep   out of   return   offer   put   hang on |

1 I'm sorry. We're .... stock.
2 Do I have to .... at the till?
3 Is this TV on special .... ?
4 Could you .... me through to your sales department?
5 Just .... a moment. I'll go and have a look.
6 No, thanks. I'm .... looking.
7 Sorry to .... you waiting.
8 If it's faulty, you can .... it and we'll exchange it for you.

Discussion

4 Tell each other
- what your favourite and least favourite kind of shopping is.
- about a memorable shopping experience.

5 a Look at the photos. What do they show?
  b What are the advantages and disadvantages of each type of shopping?

Paraphrasing

6 Talk about things you can see in the photos using these expressions.

> *It's/They're like (a) ... .*
> *It's a kind of ... .*
> *You use it/them to ... .*
> *It's something you wear when ... .*
> *It's when you ... .*

Individual long turn

▶ Task strategy Module 3B page 45

7 a **Work in groups of three.**
  Task 1

  STUDENT 1: You are the examiner. Follow the instructions for Task 1 on page 211.

  STUDENTS 2 AND 3: You are Candidates A and B. Look at the photos on this page. Follow the examiner's instructions. Candidate A: pretend you don't really understand the task, and ask the examiner to repeat the instructions.

  b **Work in groups of three again.**
  Task 2

  STUDENT 2: You are the examiner. Follow the instructions for Task 2 on page 212.

  STUDENTS 1 AND 3: You are Candidates A and B. Look at the photos on page 211. Follow the examiner's instructions. Candidate B: pretend you don't understand the question, and ask the examiner to repeat it.

  c **Discuss the two tasks you have done.**
    1 Were you able to keep going without too many hesitations, and paraphrase when necessary?
    2 Were you reasonably accurate? Could you be understood easily?
    3 Did you complete the task according to the instructions?

Listening (Paper 4 Part 1)

Before you listen

1 **Look at the listening task below. Decide what you have to listen for in each case. Mark key words. Question 1 is done for you.**

Extracts (multiple choice)

▶ Task strategy Module 6B page 88

2 🎧 **You will hear people talking in eight different situations. For questions 1–8, choose the best answer A, B or C.**

1 You hear an advertisement on the radio. What is being advertised?
   A a television game show
   B a computer game
   C a board game   1

2 You overhear a man talking to a shop assistant.
   What is the man doing?
   A returning faulty goods
   B asking for his money back
   C trying to get some goods delivered   2

3 You hear a radio phone-in programme on the subject of cars.
   What is the caller doing?
   A blaming someone for something
   B asking for advice about something
   C making a suggestion about something   3

4 You hear part of a radio play. Where is this scene taking place?
   A in a bus station
   B in a shop
   C in a library   4

5 You overhear a woman talking in a travel agency.
   What is she complaining about?
   A the attitude of the staff towards her
   B the accuracy of the information she was given
   C the fact that her holiday arrangements were changed   5

6 You overhear a man talking on his mobile phone.
   Who is he talking to?
   A a hotel receptionist
   B a conference organiser
   C his secretary   6

7 You hear a radio announcement about a new service that's being offered in London.
   In which sector has the service been most successful so far?
   A travel
   B health
   C entertainment   7

8 You hear the beginning of a radio programme on shopping.
   What is the programme going to be about?
   A the disadvantages of e-commerce
   B a new idea that will help e-commerce
   C research into the success of e-commerce   8

Discussion

3 **Answer these questions.**

1 Have you taken *faulty goods* back to a shop? What was the problem? Did you get a *cash refund* or *credit note* for goods?

2 Have you ever felt you were being *ripped off* by a shop or service provider?

3 In what sort of situations should travel agents or airlines *pay compensation* to travellers?

4 Do you ever make purchases from *mail-order catalogues*? Do you think it's a useful service?

Use of English 1 (Paper 3 Part 2)

Lead-in

1 **Discuss these questions.**

1 Do you prefer to buy your food and other necessities in a street market or a supermarket?
2 What are the advantages and disadvantages of shopping at the same places every time?

Open cloze

▶ Task strategy Module 2B page 33

2 a **What advice would you give someone doing the exam task below? Check your answer with the task strategy on page 33.**

b **Read the title and text below quickly and correct the information in these statements.**

1 What items individual shoppers choose is important information for a supermarket but they have no effective way of collecting it.
2 It is illegal for companies to share information about their customers.
3 At the moment in the UK not many customers have 'loyalty' cards and until recently those that do have not been worried about how they are used by the supermarkets.
4 There is nothing we can do about supermarkets collecting information about us.

HELP

➤ Questions 5, 6, 7, 10
Singular or plural?

➤ Question 11
They or *there*?

c **Do the task. Follow the task strategy and use the Help clues if necessary.**
Read the text below and think of a word which best fits each space. Use only **one** word in each space. There is an example at the beginning (0).

Customer tracking

When you're stacking up grocery items at the checkout, you're probably not worried that your supermarket might **(0)** ..be.. building a profile of the kind of shopper you are. After all, who cares whether you buy **(1)** .... brand of biscuits over another? Well, supermarkets care. So much so that they issue 'loyalty' cards to offer what seem **(2)** .... great bargains. They then use these cards to keep track **(3)** .... how often you shop and **(4)** .... your buying preferences are. Often, this information **(5)** .... then 'shared' with other companies.

According to one survey, 85% of UK consumers have a loyalty card and the majority **(6)** .... so far been fairly indifferent to the practice.

However, a number of shoppers **(7)** .... becoming increasingly worried that 'loyalty' cards are **(8)** .... used to compile detailed profiles of their lifestyles. Do you realise that if you **(9)** .... just had a baby, your supermarket will be one of the first to know? No one **(10)** .... sure where this practice will lead. Already in some countries, customer profiling is used to track criminals. Will **(11)** .... be increases in insurance premiums for unhealthy eaters? What can we do if we are concerned? Basically, as always, shop somewhere **(12)** .... Retailers will always 'listen to' a drop in profits!

Discussion

3 **Discuss these questions.**

1 Do you care what information shops hold about you?
2 Do you mind receiving unsolicited advertising and offers?

Language development 2
Number and concord

> Verbs and their subjects should always 'agree':
> *She hates shopping.* (singular subject, singular verb)
> *They think she's rich.* (plural subject, plural verb)
> But it's not always easy to know whether to use a singular or plural verb form!
>
> A Nouns which are followed by a singular verb form:
> **The news** *is boring.* (athletics, politics, the United States)
> **Ninety dollars** *is a lot of money.* (two weeks, thirty miles)
> **Neither of** *these shops sells what I want.* (each of, none of)
> **Hardly anyone** *goes to the market now.* (almost nobody)
> **Everyone** *uses the supermarket.* (everybody, every + noun)
> **More than one** *small shop has closed.* (one of, every one of, a total of)
>
> B Nouns which are followed by a plural verb form:
> **People** *do their shopping on the Internet. (the police, the military)*
> **Glasses** *are becoming cheaper. (scissors, trousers, jeans)*
> **A number of** *chain stores have opened. (both of, all of, the majority of, a couple of, a group of)*
>
> **(LOOK)** at Questions 5, 6, 7, 9, 10 in the Use of English text on page 131. How many answers did you get right?
>
> C Some nouns can be followed by a singular **or** plural verb:
> *the bank, the Government, the family, the team, the school, the public*
> *The staff* **is getting** *bigger. (the staff as a single body.)*
> *The staff* **are** *not very happy with their pay. (the staff as a collection of individuals)*

1 Tick (✓) the correct sentences. Correct the incorrect ones.

1 Everyone think it's a good idea.
2 The majority of us agrees.
3 The police are coming.
4 Neither of them know what to buy.
5 These jeans doesn't fit.
6 The news about the market wasn't good.
7 Ten euros aren't very many.
8 The company has a great future.
9 This scissors doesn't cut very well.
10 The United States have a new President.

2 Complete the text with the correct present simple form of the verbs in brackets.

> **VARIETY – THE SPICE OF LIFE?**
> Every supermarket **(1)**.............. (sell) up to 40,000 products but, according to recent research, many people **(2)**.............. (feel) that greater choice **(3)**.............. (cause) unnecessary stress. Hardly anyone **(4)**.............. (want) 600 kinds of coffee! Both men and women **(5)**.............. (seem) to want less choice when shopping.
>   And none of us **(6)**.............. (be) happy to have more choice in other aspects of our lives; a significant number of people **(7)**.............. (say) they find it hard to decide what to eat. But whereas only ten per cent of men **(8)**.............. (admit) that deciding what to wear is difficult, nearly all of the women **(9)**.............. (confess) that this is a major problem for them.
>   However, none of those interviewed really **(10)**.............. (want) to change things. Too much choice is better than no choice at all!

it/there

> A *There + be = something exists:*
> **There are** *many more important jobs than hers.*
> B *It replaces a noun:*
> *What's her job like?* **It's** *quite interesting.*
> C *It is also used as an 'empty' subject to talk about time, weather and distance:*
> *It's nine o'clock. It's warm today. It's 24 km. to L.A.*

3 Complete the sentences with *it* or *there* and the correct form of *be*.

> **MONEY-SAVING TIPS**
> **(1)**.......................... lots of easy ways to save money. Here are just a few.
> • When you go food shopping, **(2)**.......................... important to write a list, and only buy what you nee
> • When choosing a restaurant, see if **(3)**.......................... 'set meal'. **(4)**.......................... usually a lot cheaper.
> • These days **(5)**.......................... many phone companie which offer cheap calls, so **(6)**.......................... a good idea to compare different companies.

4 Answer these questions with *it* or *there*.

1 What's the date today?
2 How far is it from your house to where you work or study?
3 What shopping tips can you think of for your town?
   EXAMPLE: *There's a great market ... .*

Use of English 2 (Paper 3 Part 3)

Lead-in

1 Discuss these questions.

1 What features and facilities do you appreciate most in a shop?

2 What things frustrate you when shopping?

Word formation (A)

▶ Task strategy Module 2B page 35

HELP

➤ Question 3

Do you need a prefix, suffix or both?

➤ Question 5

Be careful with your spelling!

➤ Question 9

Is this an adjective or a noun?

2 Do the task. Follow the task strategy and use the Help clues if necessary.

Read the text below. Use the word given in capitals at the end of some of the lines to form a word that fits the space **in the same line.** There is an example at the beginning (**0**).

Keeping customers happy

For years, there has been a (**0**) ...disturbing... trend in stores to cut	DISTURB
costs, by reducing staff to the (**1**).............. possible number. Many	SMALL
stores, however, now realise that when employees are (**2**)..............	EXHAUST
from overwork they become (**3**).............. with their customers.	PATIENCE
Nordstrom, an (**4**).............. well-respected US department store,	EXTREME
knows that customers find poor service (**5**).............. . The	STRESS
company believes that the helpfulness and (**6**).............. of its	FRIEND
staff contribute to customer (**7**).............. . One of Nordstrom's	SATISFY
customers was about to take a (**8**).............. recently and left her	FLY
ticket on the counter. The assistant was so worried when he	
caught (**9**).............. of it that he took a taxi to the airport and,	SEE
to the woman's (**10**).............. , delivered the ticket himself. Now	AMAZE
that's service!	

Discussion

3 Do you think service in stores is getting better or worse these days?

Word formation (B)

HELP

➤ Question 6

Do you need a prefix, suffix or both?

➤ Question 7

Is this an adjective or an adverb?

4 Do the task. (See the instructions above.)

Save or spend?

According to a recent (**0**) ...investigation... the British are poor savers	INVESTIGATE
in (**1**) .... with other nations in Europe, putting aside only 5.5%	COMPARE
of their income for 'a rainy day'. Even more (**2**) .... , only 13%	WORRY
are saving towards (**3**) .... One of the reasons for this is that the	RETIRE
British spend a (**4**) .... 16% of everything they earn on luxuries	SURPRISE
and (**5**) .... out and another 5% on their cars. As a result, in	EAT
recent years personal debt has increased (**6**) .... However, one	DRAMA
long-term (**7**) .... that the British do take seriously is in	INVEST
property. In contrast with many other nations the British seem	
obsessed with (**8**) .... their own home, and prices are so high	OWN
that houses are simply (**9**) .... for many young people starting	AFFORD
out. However, at the other end of the scale over 800,000	
households now own a second home abroad, with Spain the	
(**10**) .... location.	PREFER

5 Discuss these questions.

1 Are you a saver or a spender?

2 Do you think people should save more than they do?

3 What are the consequences of living on credit?

Language development 3
Money and banks

1 Work with another student and complete this quiz. You might want to use a dictionary to help you.

Money Vocabulary Quiz

1 Write A (= have money) or B (= not have money) next to each of these expressions.

1 I'm *a bit short of* cash today.
2 The Jacksons *live from hand to mouth*. They simply *can't make ends meet*.
3 Lucinda's very *well off*.
4 Peter *can't afford* to pay the rent this month. He's very *hard up*.
5 We're *quite comfortable*.
6 Are you *in debt*?
7 Mr and Mrs Johnson are very *wealthy*.

2 Mark the correct preposition in each pair.

1 Asha borrowed a camera to / from Alex.
2 Will you lend the car to / from us for the weekend?
3 The company owes its success to / from its excellent training programme.
4 You're spending too much money to / on food.
5 Mike's wasting most of his money on / into clothes.
6 Ella paid some money on / into her bank account.
7 Carl changed his money in / into Euros.
8 We've made a lot of money from / by computer games.
9 I've got no money by / on me.
10 When Sue died, she left her money at / to her brother.

3 a In each of these groups, three of the noun phrases do not combine with the verb given. Cross them out.

1 pay:
by cheque   the tickets   a deposit   you back   in cash
by credit card   a fine   a big profit   a bill   a discount

2 earn:
a fortune   a living   a refund   your keep   a receipt
a good salary   interest   a loan

b Replace the incorrect word in italics with a word from question 3a.
1 You get a huge *account* if you book in advance so you'll save a lot of money.
2 Investors made a big *salary* of ten per cent when their shares went up in value.
3 Don't worry! You'll get a full *withdrawal* if you cancel the holiday.
4 I see from my bank statement that rates of *investment* are very low at the moment.
5 We've just had a huge electricity *receipt*; I don't know how we're going to pay it.
6 Tara may earn a good *profit* every month but she's always in the red.
7 Mike got a £60 *cost* when the police caught him speeding.
8 How soon do you have to pay back that *lend* that you got from the bank?

2 How do you record topic vocabulary? For example, you could record money expressions in your vocabulary book under different 'money' headings, such as: *Banks   Shopping   Money Problems*.

3 Discuss whether these statements are true for you.
1 I like shopping for bargains.
2 I think credit cards are dangerous.
3 I'm happy to lend people money.
4 I believe in living – and spending – for today.
5 I think online banking is convenient but not secure.

Forming verbs

4 a Look at the four ways of forming verbs shown in the table.

No change
clean (adj.) → clean (v.)
'record (n.) → rec'ord (v.)

Internal change
hot (adj.) → heat (v.)

Prefix
large (adj.) → enlarge (v.)

Suffix
modern (adj.) → modernise (v.)

b Decide what changes, if any, to make to these words to form verbs, and complete the table above. Use a dictionary if necessary.
critic (n.)   dry (adj.)   strength (n.)
fat (adj.)   import (n.)   wide (adj.)
choice (n.)   danger (n.)   calm (adj.)
length (n.)   name (n.)   blood (n.)

5 a Match these definitions with verbs in Exercise 4.
1 ....: to talk about someone's faults
2 ....: to bring goods into a country
3 ....: to make someone unsafe
4 ....: to decide which thing

b Which of the verbs in Exercise 4 would you use to talk about:
• *making* a road *bigger*?
• *renovating* an old house?
• *making* a class *quieter*?
• *making* a bridge *stronger*?

Overview

- **Reading:** multiple choice (Paper 1 Part 1)
- **Language development 1:** passives
- **Writing:** report (Paper 2 Part 2)
- **Speaking:** individual long turn (Paper 5 Part 2)
- **Listening:** multiple matching (Paper 4 Part 3)
- **Language development 2:** past tenses and other expressions for hypothetical situations
- **Use of English 1:** key word transformations (Paper 3 Part 4)
- **Use of English 2:** open cloze (Paper 3 Part 2)
- **Language development 3:** verbs and participles + prepositions; verbs with similar meanings

Lead-in

- How far do you have to travel to your place of work/study to take part in leisure activities?
- What method of transport do you use to get there?
- How often do you travel abroad? How do you travel?
- Read this quote by the contemporary travel writer, Paul Theroux. How far do you agree or disagree? 'Travel is only glamorous in retrospect.'

Reading (Paper 1 Part 1)

Before you read

1 Read the headline and introduction opposite. Do you think the writer's experiences of the USA will be good or bad?

Skimming

2 Read the article once. Look at the map. Which places does the writer go to?

Multiple choice

▶ Task strategy Module 4A page 52

3 a For questions 1–8, choose the answer (A, B, C or D) which you think fits best according to the text. Follow the task strategy.

b Compare and give reasons for your answers.

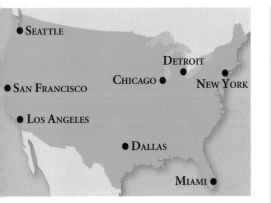

1 What was the writer's main impression of arriving in New York as a teenager?
A a sensation of loneliness
B the intense activity all around
C how beautiful the weather was
D immediately feeling 'at home' there

2 What does the writer remember about his early visits to America?
A He found New York frightening.
B It didn't live up to his high expectations.
C He didn't get to know the country very well.
D He regrets wasting so much time in the cities.

3 The writer found Miami
A unusual.   B elegant.   C depressing.   D disappointing.

4 What does the writer say about his first trip to LA?
A He disliked its artificiality.
B He ended up finding work there.
C He felt as if he had been there before.
D He didn't have a positive experience.

5 What does the writer mean by the expression *pushed the boat out* in lines 71–72?
A took strong action
B spent a lot of money
C made a lot of progress
D left him to find his own way around

6 When the writer visited the south he found that
A the people he met were positive.
B the general lifestyle was very old-fashioned.
C the place was exactly as he'd imagined as a child.
D the people had been largely unaffected by the hurricane.

7 *this* in line 115 refers to
A insulting Americans.
B travelling in the US.
C not having a passport.
D the population of the US.

8 What does the writer say about the US in the last paragraph?
A He loves the kind of food you get there.
B His ambition is to live there permanently.
C He thinks he will eventually run out of exciting places to travel to.
D He can understand Americans' reluctance to travel outside their own country.

Welcome to the USA

Television comedian and writer Dom Joly explains why he's happiest across the water.

I can still picture every trembling step of my first moments in the United States. It was the summer of 1987 and I'd taken a train from Toronto to New York. I'd just left school and this was my first big solo adventure. I was almost dizzy with excitement as the train slowly pulled into Grand Central station, very early on a clear-skied New York morning. I can still remember hesitantly pulling my little black suitcase through the breathtaking central hall of the station; it was like stepping on to the set of a thousand familiar movies. There was something unique about the place – an energy that you could almost touch. All around me New Yorkers rushed from destination to destination as though their lives depended on it. I remember feeling out of place, as if I wasn't really there, that I was floating high above the city.

I drifted out of the station into the metropolis that is New York. It was a world of huge shadows – the sun blanked out by the sheer enormousness of the Manhattan skyline. I rode the Staten Island ferry boat, conquered the Empire State building, roller-skated in Central Park. It was like meeting one of your childhood heroes and finding out that not only did they not disappoint, but they were far, far cooler than you'd

40 ever dared hoped. From that moment on, I've been obsessed, but to begin with I, like most visitors, only really flirted with the US – just visiting the cosmopolitan cities around her edges

45 I first went to Miami by chance. I had to film there and I wasn't really looking forward to it. To me, Florida was all about tasteless neon lights and hideous theme parks. In a way I was right. That's part of its appeal.

50 This is, after all, the only city in the world where a yellow Ferrari makes sense. The gorgeous combination of fabulous climate, art-deco architecture and Cuban-Hispanic

55 influence instantly made it one of my favourite cities in the world. Nothing quite beats sitting on the terrace of the Tides hotel, watching the beautiful people glide by. One

60 breakfast, I was joined by the rapper Ja Rule and his pet lion: only in Miami, only in America.

People warned me about Los Angeles. 'Nobody walks anywhere,

65 it's not a real city, it's all so fake.' Once again, they were right. It is those things, and you need to embrace them wholeheartedly to enjoy the place. My first time in LA, I

70 was there for meetings with a film company and they really pushed the boat out. I got sent a stretch limousine which whisked me in air conditioned splendour to a famous

75 hotel where Johnny Depp was having a drink in the garden. It really was a fairytale. Hollywood, Beverly Hills, Malibu – such familiar places to me through a thousand and one films

80 and TV shows. Every sharp-suited executive at every meeting promised me the earth was mine - it was a merry-go-round of broad smiles and green lights. Of course, nothing came

85 of any of this, but I was living the

cliché – the American dream.

For an upcoming television series I recently drove from Atlanta through the southern states to New Orleans.

90 Growing up, this part of the USA had always felt a slightly scary place. But crossing into Alabama, rather than the fields and fields of cotton I had expected, I found beautifully hilly

95 country peppered with golden lakes and shady wooden homes. Driving further south, we were constantly confronted with traditional southern hospitality and tables groaning with

100 fattening food. Arriving in New Orleans eight months after the devastating hurricane found a population struggling but not quite broken. Most of the things you expect

105 in a modern American city were still not functioning – traffic lights, air conditioning – but the can-do American attitude to life was in full-swing.

110 One of the most common insults thrown at Americans of late is that they are insular, disconnected from the world, with apparently only 20% of the population in possession of a

115 passport. To us this seems unthinkable. When you travel in the States it all makes sense. There's not that European need to travel 'abroad' when it'll take you a lifetime to

120 discover your own country. To me, the US is like a candy-store and I'm the sweet-toothed kid waiting at the door eager to sample new treats. I want to go to Hawaii and learn to

125 surf, go to Texas and become a cowboy and then there's ... STOP. ENOUGH. I can't take any more. Well I can actually. I've been there more times than to any other country and

130 I've only scratched the surface. Every time I look out of a window ... outside is America.

Discussion

4 Discuss these questions.

1 Which of the places in the article would you most and least like to go to?
2 Which country in the world have you most loved visiting? Why?
3 If you could visit anywhere in the world, where would you go?

Vocabulary: adjectives and nouns

5 Match the adjectives in column A with the nouns in B they go with in the article.

A		B	
1	sweet	A	smiles
2	sharp	B	steps
3	tasteless	C	tooth
4	clear	D	sky
5	trembling	E	suits
6	broad	F	neon lights

Language development 1

Passives

1 **a** What type of holiday accommodation do you prefer? For example, a hotel, a self-catering apartment or a campsite? Why?

b Read the text and answer the questions.
1 What are the advantages of these self-catering apartments?
2 What possible disadvantages are there?

These high-quality self-catering apartments are grouped around a central garden. They were built in traditional Ottoman style by a team of highly skilled workers and have been designed to stay cool in summer. The rooms have all been decorated to a very high standard. A buffet breakfast is served around the pool for a small charge, and a patio barbecue area is now being constructed. This will soon be completed and available for use by guests. Shops can be found within ten minutes' walk. We are sure you will have a wonderful holiday.

c Mark examples of the passive in the text. Why is the passive used here?

d Complete the table with examples from the text.

Passive form	Examples
Present simple	1 ....
	2 ....
Present perfect	3 ....
	4 ....
Past simple	5 ....
Present continuous	6 ....
will future	7 ....
Modal	8 ....

▶ Grammar reference page 193.

2 **a** Correct the mistakes in the text below.

Our apartments **(1)** *be situated* on the Bosphorus and have excellent views. Last winter they **(2)** *was redecorated*. Internet facilities **(3)** *can been supplied* by our local representative on request and fire safety equipment **(4)** *have be installed* by the time you arrive.

Smaller apartments **(5)** *are been built* at the moment and will be available next year. Also, permission **(6)** *has be given* to build two all-weather tennis courts.

Availability **(7)** *must checked* with our Booking Service before making a reservation and guests **(8)** *will asked* to pay a deposit.

b Rewrite the sentences below to make them more formal, beginning with the words and phrases in italics.
1 We are always improving *our facilities.*
2 We have modernised *all our flats* in the last two years.
3 We have equipped *our kitchens* to the highest standards.
4 Maids will make *the beds* daily.
5 You can find *the holiday village* 2 kilometres outside the town.
6 The village offers *a full programme of sports activities.*
7 We received *very few complaints* last year.
8 Guests may accommodate *extra people* on the sofa beds.
9 Our brochure indicates *the maximum number of people allowed in each caravan.*
10 You must return *keys* to reception on departure.

3 Read the information in the box and answer the questions.

A The passive is sometimes used to put new information at the end of the sentence for emphasis. Mark the correct form:
*The telescope is very useful. It was invented **by / from** Galileo.*

B Some verbs (e.g. *give, lend, send, show, promise*) can have two objects – a person and a thing.
Active: *The rest of the class gave **Tania a present**.*
Which passive structure below do you think is more common, 1 or 2?
Passive:
1 ***Tania was given a present*** by the rest of the class.
2 ***A present was given to Tania*** by the rest of the class.

C In news reports, passive structures are often used with *say/believe/consider/think*, etc. Complete these sentences with an appropriate verb.
1 *We think Filton is planning ten new hotels.* (active)
Filton is .... *to be planning* ten new hotels. (passive + infinitive)
2 *Analysts say that SkyFly's profits are up.* (active)
It is .... *that* SkyFly's profits are up. (passive + *that* clause)

D Some verbs are followed by an infinitive without *to* when active but an infinitive with *to* when passive. Mark the correct forms.
Active: *They heard the crowd cheer a long way away.*
Passive: *The crowd was heard **cheer / to cheer** a long way away.*
Active: *They made me empty all my bags at Customs.*
Passive: *I was made **empty / to empty** all my bags at Customs.*

▶ Grammar reference page 193

4 Complete the responses. Put the verbs in the most appropriate passive form.
1 A: Did Mozart compose the *Unfinished Symphony*?
   B: No, I think (*Schubert / compose*)
   ....
2 A: Why was there so much confusion?
   B: Some people (*give / two tickets*)
   .... by mistake.
3 A: Why has that man been arrested?
   B: I think he (*see / steal*) ....
   some things.
4 A: When's the next election?
   B: It (*believe / Prime Minister / call*)
   .... one soon.

5 A: What's Megan doing next year?
   B: She (*promise / place*) ....
   at university.
6 A: Didn't Marie Curie discover penicillin?
   B: No, I'm pretty sure (*Fleming / discover*)
   ....
7 A: Do the police know how the burglar got in?
   B: Yes, he (*think / hide*) ....
   in the museum during the day.
8 A: What a lovely antique shop. Oh, no, I've broken a vase!
   B: Oh dear, I think you (*make / pay*)
   .... for that!

5 a Rewrite the text below to make it more formal, in the style of a report, using passives where appropriate.

> The town has changed a lot in the last 30 years. They have pulled down all the old factories and replaced them with hi-tech science parks. Many of the residents feel it's unfortunate that they have also demolished one of the older schools, as they will have to send their children by bus to the next town. Some people say that they will build a brand new school in the town in the next few years when the Government provides extra funding. The newer residents in particular will appreciate that.

b What changes have happened in your town? What changes are planned for the future?

Golders Green Parade, London, circa 1920

Golders Green Parade, London, 2001

Writing   Report (Paper 2 Part 2)

Lead-in

1 Discuss these questions.

1 Have you ever travelled abroad as part of a group? What are the advantages and disadvantages?

2 What problems do group organisers have?

Understand the task

2 Read the task below and answer the questions.

1 How many PARTS are there to the task?

2 Decide how personal or formal your STYLE should be. (Remember your ROLE and who you are reporting to.)

▶ Writing reference page 204

3 What will make the reader think it is a GOOD report?

> Students in your college have just returned from a ski trip abroad. There were a number of problems about the location and the organisation. You were on the organising committee and the Principal has asked you to highlight the problems and make recommendations for next year.
>
> You have been asked to write a **report** for the Principal.
>
> Write your **report** in **120–180** words in an appropriate style.

Plan your report

3 a Make notes under these headings. Then choose the two most important points under each heading.

<u>Location</u>	<u>Organisation</u>	<u>Next year</u>
no snow lower down	only one-hour ski lessons	change location

b Match these pieces of advice to the paragraphs below. Some go with more than one paragraph.

Paragraph 1: Introducing the report
Paragraph 2: Describing the first problem
Paragraph 3: Describing the second problem
Paragraph 4: Summarising and recommending

a Focus on a maximum of two points.
b State the purpose of the report.
c Give a clear summary of the situation.
d Describe how you got the information.
e Only give relevant information.
f Give just one or two recommendations.
g Give the facts briefly and clearly without strong opinions.

c Match your notes in Exercise 3a to the paragraphs (1–4).

d Choose the best subject heading for your report from the ones below.

A Problems and Solutions

B Half-term Horrors

C College Ski Trip

e Think of a suitable heading for each paragraph (1–4).
Note: You could number (1, 2, 3, etc.) or use bullet points (•) within a paragraph to make your points clearer.

Language and content

4 a Complete these possible topic sentences for each paragraph.

Paragraph 1: The report describes … .
Paragraph 2: Students said that … .
Paragraph 3: Another problem was that … .
Paragraph 4: On balance it is recommended that … .

b Use these phrases to complete the sentences in the table below.

1 … some students were unhappy with the arrangements.
2 … lessons need to be learnt for the future.
3 … highlight the problems that occurred during the half-term ski trip.
4 … only one-hour ski-lessons were included in the price.
5 … that a handbook is produced for group leaders, listing their duties.
6 … more interested in skiing than looking after students.
7 … I sent out questionnaires to all participants.
8 … there weren't enough beds in the cabins.
9 … sleep on the floor.
10 … were excellent, there weren't enough beginners' slopes.

Introduction	*The aim of this report is to …* *In order to prepare this report …*
Reporting findings	*It appears that …* *The main problem was that …* *Some students had to …* *Not surprisingly …* *Although the advanced slopes …* *Some group leaders were …*
Concluding and making recommendations	*All things considered, …* *We have no hesitation in recommending …*

c Mark the best word in each pair to complete this advice:

Use *active / passive* verb forms in a report to make it *more / less* formal and *more / less* personal.

Write your report

5 Now write your report using some of the language above. Avoid copying whole phrases from the task. Use passive forms where appropriate.

Check and improve your report

6 Edit your report using this list.
- Is the information relevant? (Have I included everything, but not too much?)
- Is the style clear and neutral?
- Does the report feel balanced? (Are different viewpoints presented fairly?)

▶ Writing reference page 204

LANGUAGE SPOT: passive report structures ▶ Grammar reference page 193

a Complete the second sentence so that it has a similar meaning to the first.

1 The Principal is thought to be in favour.
  It is thought ....
2 About 50 students are expected to attend.
  It is expected ....
3 Many of the students are reported to have had difficulties getting a visa.
  It is reported ....
4 Some of them are said to have left early.
  It is said ....

b Now do the same with these sentences, using *supposed to.*

1 People say that air travel is becoming easier and cheaper.
  Air travel ....
2 People say that we travel further on holiday these days.
  We ....
3 People say that travel broadens the mind.
  Travel ....
4 People say that good public transport reduces the number of private cars.
  Good public transport ....

Getting around

Speaking (Paper 5 Part 2)

Vocabulary: transport

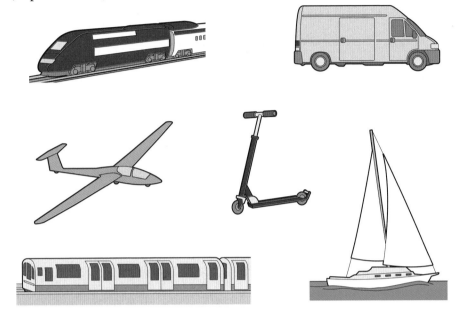

1 a **Which of the forms of transport in the pictures have you used?**

 b **Which is the odd one out in each of these and why?**
   1 canoe, yacht, the tube, rowing boat
   2 moped, scooter, motorbike, delivery van
   3 tram, helicopter, glider, spaceship
   4 clutch, handlebars, accelerator, steering wheel
   5 deck, oars, carriage, mast
   6 hatchback, saloon, sidecar, estate

 c **Mark the stress on the words and phrases with more than one syllable.**

2 a **Match these expressions with different forms of transport. There might be more than one answer.**
   take a driving test   be forced to land   get clamped
   it's two stops on the Northern Line   take on as hand luggage
   stop in a lay-by   apologise for the late running 9.00 a.m. to …
   confirm your flight   fasten your seatbelt   go for a cruise
   get points on your licence   disembark   get low on petrol

 b **Correct the mistakes.**
   1 I'm tired. Let's *get onto* a taxi.
   2 I think we *get out of* the bus at the next stop.
   3 Oh, no. We've *lost* the last train. How are we going to get home?
   4 'Have you ever *driven* a horse?' 'Yes, I did when I was young.'
   5 Our ship *parks* in Cairo for a day. Let's go sightseeing when we get there.
   6 What's the *fare* of the ticket? I don't think I've got enough money on me.
   7 It's a long *travel* there and back. We can't do it in a day.
   8 Wonderful! The train's exactly *in time*!

3 **What are the best/worst things about modern transport?**

4 a Look at the statements below about Paper 5 Part 2 and discuss whether they are *True* or *False*.

1 You each have a minute to talk about the photos.
2 The task has two parts.
3 You should describe each photo separately.
4 You will be asked for your opinion.
5 You can interrupt while the other candidate is speaking.
6 You each give a short response after the other candidate's long turn.

b Look at the list of things (1–7) you might have to do in the exam. Match them to the expressions (a–g) below.

1 talk about similarities
2 talk about differences
3 speculate about a picture
4 give opinions on something
5 ask for clarification/check information
6 paraphrase
7 correct what you say

> a *It could be a … . It looks … .*
> b *So, do you want me to … ?*
> c *The one on the left looks … while the other one … .*
> d *It's like a … .*
> e *What I meant was … .*
> f *As far as I'm concerned, … .*
> g *Both of these … .*

c Add any other expressions you can think of.

Individual long turn

▶ Task strategy Module 3B page 45

5 a Work in groups of three.

Task 1

STUDENT 1: You are the examiner. Follow the instructions for Task 1 on page 212.

STUDENTS 2 AND 3: You are Candidates A and B. Look at the photos on this page. Follow the examiner's instructions.

b Work in groups of three again.

Task 2

STUDENT 2: You are the examiner. Follow the instructions for Task 2 on page 211.

STUDENTS 1 AND 3: You are Candidates A and B. Look at the photos on page 212. Follow the examiner's instructions.

c Discuss and compare your answers. Did you:

- follow the instructions?
- speak clearly and accurately?
- use appropriate vocabulary?
- communicate what you wanted to say?
- use the full minute?

Listening (Paper 4 Part 3)

Before you listen

1 How do you prefer to get from place to place? Which of these factors are the most and least important for you?
- expense
- reliability
- convenience
- comfort
- environmental issues
- fun
- style

Multiple matching

▶ Task strategy Module 4B page 60

2 a 🎧 You will hear five different people giving reasons why they use different kinds of bikes to get to work. For questions 1–5, choose from the list A–F what each speaker says. Use the letters only once. There is one extra letter which you do not need to use.

A I'm helping to keep the environment clean   Speaker 1 …

B I bought it to save me money   Speaker 2 …

C I wanted to avoid being in large crowds   Speaker 3 …

D It's a reliable form of transport   Speaker 4 …

E I like surprising the people I work with   Speaker 5 …

F It helps me to get more work done

b Compare and give reasons for your answers. Listen to the recording again if necessary.

Discussion

3 Discuss these questions.
1 Do you agree that people 'look down on' certain forms of transport?
2 How important are cars in your country as a status symbol? Which are the most prestigious cars to own?
3 Do you think it is the responsibility of the Government to make public transport so cheap that it will persuade people to stop using their cars in urban areas?

Vocabulary: transport

4 Answer the following questions about yourself or your country. They include expressions from the text.
1 Do any forms of transport regularly go *on strike*?
2 When is *rush hour*?
3 Do you prefer to drive *second hand* or *flash* cars?
4 Which public transport system is the most *reliable*?
5 Are motorists generally *considerate* to cyclists?
6 Which form of transport do you think is the most *convenient*?

Language development 2
Past tenses for hypothetical situations

1 Read the comments in the thought bubbles and answer the questions below.

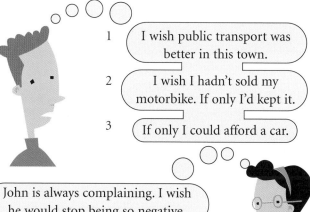

1 I wish public transport was better in this town.

2 I wish I hadn't sold my motorbike. If only I'd kept it.

3 If only I could afford a car.

John is always complaining. I wish he would stop being so negative.

If only the Town Council would set up a park-and-ride scheme.

1 Which comments refer to a situation in:
   • the present   • the past   • the future?
2 What verb form is used in each case?
3 What's the difference between *wish* and *if only*?

---

wish **+ past versus** *wish* **+** *would*

A We use *wish* + past when we want our own situation to be different.
   I wish I ~~would have~~ *a fast car.* ✗
   I wish I **had** *a fast car.* ✓

B We use *wish* + *would* when we want another person or thing to be different.
   I wish you ~~changed~~ *your mind about moving.* ✗
   I wish you **would change** *your mind about moving.* ✓

▶ Grammar reference page 195

2 What would you say in these situations? Use *I wish* or *If only.*

EXAMPLE: Your friend has invited you to go out tonight, but you have too much work to do.
I wish I could go out tonight. If only I didn't have so much work to do.

1 You regret dyeing your hair bright red. Blonde suits you better.
2 Your brother is always borrowing your car without asking. You want him to stop.
3 It's late, but you can't afford to get a taxi home, so you'll have to take the bus.
4 You're watching a film at the cinema but you don't like it at all.
5 Your flatmate has been in the bathroom for a long time and you want to use it yourself.

3 Complete these sentences about yourself.
EXAMPLE: I wish ..I was taller... but I'm not.
1 I wish .... but I'm not.
2 I wish .... but I haven't.
3 If only .... but I can't.
4 I wish .... but I didn't.
5 If only .... but he/she won't.
6 I wish I could ....

Other expressions for hypothetical situations

A *It's (about/high) time* + subject + past
  It's (about) time we **went** *home.* (we should go now)
  Don't you think it's time you **got** *a job?* (implies criticism)

B *would rather* + subject + past or past perfect
  I'd rather you **didn't smoke** *in the house.* (I don't want you to)
  I'd rather you **hadn't gone out** *last night.* (but you did)

C *as though/as if* + past or past perfect
  You're looking at me as if/as though I **was/were** *crazy.* (but I'm not)
  You look as if you **had seen** *a ghost.* (but you haven't)

---

4 Decide which option A or B best shows the meaning of each sentence.
1 It's time you learned how to drive.
   A You haven't learned yet.
   B You don't have time to learn.
2 I'd rather you hadn't invited him to the party.
   A You didn't invite him.
   B You invited him and I'm annoyed.
3 You talk as if you had done all the work yourself.
   A You did all the work.
   B You didn't do all the work.

5 Complete the sentences with an appropriate verb in the correct form.
1 It's about time you .... how to use that computer properly. You've had it long enough.
2 My brother treats me as if I .... a child, even though I'm only two years younger than him!
3 No, I don't want to phone her. I'd rather you .... her.
4 He talks as though he .... her but he hasn't. He's only seen her on TV.
5 Why did you buy me such an expensive gift? I'd rather you .... something cheaper.

6 Complete the sentences in an appropriate way.
1 The film was awful, wasn't it? I wish ... .
2 My room's in a complete mess. It's about time ... .
3 My best friend sometimes acts as if ... .
4 I don't have any money left! If only ... .
5 My brother has gone to work abroad. I'd rather ... .

Use of English 1 (Paper 3 Part 4)

Lead-in

1 What advice would you give to these two candidates?

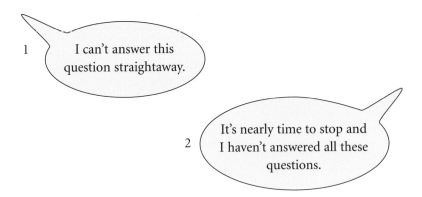

1 I can't answer this question straightaway.

2 It's nearly time to stop and I haven't answered all these questions.

Key word transformations

▸ Task strategy Module 1B page 20

2 a Do the task below. Remember – you usually have to make more than one change to the original sentence.

Complete the second sentence so that it has a similar meaning to the first sentence, using the word given. **Do not change the word given.** You must use between two and five words, including the word given. Write **only** the missing words.

1 I'm sorry I didn't go to the party last night.
wish
I .... to the party last night.

2 I would prefer you to phone Jane.
rather
I .... Jane.

3 Tim advised Sarah to book a table at the Indian restaurant.
you
'If I .... a table at the Indian restaurant,' Tim said to Sarah.

4 I regret lying to my brother.
had
I .... my brother the truth.

5 The theatre was practically empty.
hardly
There .... the theatre.

6 People say that dancing is good for your health.
supposed
Dancing .... good for your health.

7 You should stop going to late night concerts.
time
It's .... to late night concerts.

8 I'd rather you didn't use my car.
mind
Would .... my car?

b Answer these questions about the task.
1 Which questions test language from page 145?
2 How does question 8 require you to make more than one change?

Use of English 2 (Paper 3 Part 2)

Lead-in **1 Discuss these questions.**
  1 What is your most memorable car journey?
  2 Was it a happy experience or frightening?

Open cloze

▶ Task strategy Module 2B page 33

2 a Mark the correct alternative in each pair to complete this advice on the open cloze.
  1 Fill in the spaces *before/after* you have read the whole text.
  2 Spend a *short/long* time on each space.
  3 Put *one/more* than one word in each space.

b Read the title and text and find out:
  1 what seems to have happened to the man.
  2 why he was arrested.

c Do the task.
Read the text below and think of a word which best fits each space. Use only **one** word in each space. There is an example at the beginning (**0**).

THE
RUNAWAY CAR

It seemed like a freak accident. John Adams, 27, a taxi driver, was trapped in his automatic Mercedes driving (**0**) ....**at**.... 210 kph for 100 kilometres along a road crowded (**1**) .... rush-hour traffic after his accelerator jammed. 'I took my foot (**2**) .... but the car wouldn't slow down. Of course I thought (**3**) .... turning off the engine but I was frightened that the steering would lock. At first, with my foot on the brake I kept (**4**) .... a steady 110 kpm. I even managed to get (**5**) .... to the police on my mobile, but then I (**6**) .... see smoke coming from the brakes. At that point, my speed went right up and I had to concentrate (**7**) ...... trying not to crash. I remember bursting (**8**) .... tears, thinking I was going to die.' Adams was followed (**9**) ...... several police cars and a helicopter as he swerved (**10**) .... and off the hard shoulder trying to avoid other traffic. His journey only ended when he crashed into a barrier and turned the car over. Amazingly, he managed to escape unhurt. However, after extensive tests on the car (**11**) ...... mechanical defects have been found and Adams was suspected (**12**) .... dangerous driving and arrested. The case has yet to come to court.

d Which questions test verb + preposition combinations?

e Which questions test phrasal verbs?

Discussion **3 Discuss these questions.**
  1 Do you think Adams was telling the truth?
  2 How could driving be made safer?

Language development 3
Verbs and participles + prepositions

LOOK at these examples from the Use of English text on page 147.

A Verb + preposition
*Adams was driving **at** 210 kph.*
*He was followed **by** several police cars.*

B Participle + preposition
*He was driving along a road crowded **with** rush-hour traffic.*

1 Mark the correct prepositions in each sentence. Use your dictionary if necessary.

Have you heard (1) *for/about/at* our Neighbourhood Watch scheme? It aims to prevent local people (2) *from/at/to* becoming victims of crime. It's no good simply complaining to the police (3) *of/by/about* the criminals who damage our cars in the street or who steal things that don't belong (4) *at/to/on* them.

They can't cope (5) *by/at/with* the problem on their own. Since we set up the scheme, people have reported suspicious behaviour to the police and we have succeeded (6) *on/for/in* making our area a much safer place to live.

2 Complete the sentences with the correct prepositions.

1 *for/on*
We had to wait half an hour .... a table, but it was nice to eat out and be waited ....

2 *about/of*
We're thinking seriously .... starting a band. I suppose we'll have to think .... a name for it!

3 *from/to*
The manager seems resigned .... the fact that the leisure centre is losing money; I expect he'll resign .... the job quite soon.

4 *as/for*
He's always been known .... a singer more than an actor. He's best known .... his love songs.

5 *of/from*
I turned down Andy's invitation to the cinema last week, because I hadn't heard .... the film. I haven't heard .... him since then.

6 *for/to*
It was a great party, but I'll have to apologise .... the neighbours .... making so much noise.

3 Complete the text with the correct prepositions.

SPACE TOURISM:
DREAM OR REALITY

When I want a change (1) .... my usual routine, instead of dreaming (2) .... a perfect cruise on the open seas, I sometimes wonder (3) .... putting my name down for a trip aboard a spacecraft. Of course for the next few years recruitment for the very few places available is only aimed (4) .... the mega-rich since you have to pay huge sums (5) .... the privilege – from $20–$100 million, depending (6) .... how long you go for. However, compared (7) ...... a few years ago, when space tourism was just a fantasy, a number of companies are now seriously considering building hotels located (8) .... space and before long space travel will be something we can all look forward (9) .... They believe that low cost options taking us 100–160 km into the earth's atmosphere will be available, maybe for as little as $20,000 a trip. Not surprisingly, though some scientists object (10) .... the idea that space will become crowded (11) .... tourists. Nevertheless, when you stuck in a traffic jam staring (12) ...... the stationary cars in front of you, it's not hard to see the attractions of travelling weightlessly through space at over 25,000 km an hour!

Verbs with similar meanings

Some verbs of perception have similar meanings, but are easily confused:
*It is not just about **listening to** music.*
*… it may be difficult to **hear** each other.*

4 Complete the sentences with the verbs in the correct form.

1 *look/see/watch*
a I've .... everywhere for my sunglasses. Have you .... them?
b Do you want to dance? No, I'd rather just sit and ....

2 *gaze/peer/stare*
a You shouldn't .... at people. It's rude.
b I .... at the stage, but I was too far away to see much.
c We stood and .... at the wonderful view.

3 *hear/listen*
a I .... hard but I couldn't .... what she was saying.
b I could .... to his songs all day – he's got a beautiful voice.
c We're going to .... that new band at the weekend.

4 *feel/touch*
a I could .... something .... my shoulder.
b .... how soft the material is.
c My brother doesn't let anyone .... his CDs.

MODULE 11
Well-being

Overview

- **Reading:** gapped text (Paper 1 Part 2)
- **Language development 1:** clauses of reason, purpose and contrast
- **Writing:** letter (Paper 2 Part 1)
- **Listening:** sentence completion (Paper 4 Part 2)
- **Speaking:** collaborative task, discussion (Paper 5 Parts 3 and 4)
- **Language development 2:** *so/such*; *too/enough/very*; *as/like*
- **Use of English 1:** key word transformations (Paper 3 Part 3)
- **Use of English 2:** multiple-choice cloze (Paper 3 Part 1)
- **Language development 3:** idiomatic expressions and phrasal verbs to do with health

Lead-in

- How do you think the photos illustrate the theme of well-being?
- Choose two or three photos which you think go together, and explain how they are related.
- What is most important to **your** well-being?

11A Happiness

Reading (Paper 1 Part 2)

Before you read

1 a **Look at the photo.**
   1 Would you say this glass is half empty or half full?
   2 Do you think your answer reflects your character? How?

   b **Look at the title of the article opposite and discuss the questions.**
   1 What do **you** think are 'the secrets of true happiness'?
   2 Is it possible to learn how to be happy?

Skimming

2 **Skim the text. (Ignore the gaps at this stage.) What answers does the article give to the questions in Exercise 1b?**

Gapped text

▶ Task strategy Module 3A page 38

3 **Seven sentences have been removed from the article. Choose from the sentences A–H the one which fits each gap (1–7). There is one extra sentence, which you do not need to use.**
   a **Do the task, following the task strategy if necessary.**
   b **Compare and justify your answers. What grammatical and lexical links helped you?**

Discussion

4 **Discuss these questions.**
   1 What did you find most interesting about the article? From your own experience, is there anything you strongly agree or disagree with?
   2 What advice in the article do you think you would like to try?

Vocabulary: word formation

5 a **Change the nouns below into adjectives using one of the suffixes in the list. Check the spelling in your dictionary if necessary.**
   -able   -(i)ous   -(i)ed
   1 contentment   2 satisfaction   3 frustration   4 anxiety
   5 depression   6 stress   7 misery

   b **When and why have you experienced any of these feelings?**

A That's why being part of a social group, such as a family, a community or a club adds to their overall sense of well-being.

B Such people, for example, seem to find satisfaction in activities which are meaningful and give a feeling of personal achievement.

C The latter develops in response to the experiences a person has during his or her life.

D There will always be someone else with more than you, so trying to compete can often lead to frustration and anxiety.

E To avoid this, it is important to pick a sport or activity you enjoy and which you do when you want to, rather than when you think you should.

F In other words, no matter how happy or unhappy an individual event may make us, this is just a temporary state.

G The key, apparently, is not taking your feelings for granted, but rather learning to celebrate them.

H Other scientists, however, maintain that happiness is not so difficult to achieve.

The Secrets of True Happiness

Lollie Barr reviews some recent research.

A happy nature is a gift we all wish we'd been born with. Everybody knows someone with this gift: the cheerful type of person with a positive attitude who will always say a glass is half full rather than half empty. It's the person who is not easily put off when things go wrong and who appears to lead a happier life as a result. Such people may be healthier too, since there seems to be a link between happiness and good health. But what is the secret of happiness? And how can we achieve it?

Psychologists define this feeling of well-being as 'when thoughts and feelings about one's life are mainly positive'. The key seems to be contentment with what you already have, emotionally, materially and professionally. The more people try to keep up with others, for example, the more likely they are to be dissatisfied with life. 1

David Lykken, Professor of Psychology at the University of Minnesota, is a leading specialist in happiness. As a result of studying 300 sets of twins, he now believes that happiness is more than 50 per cent genetically determined. He also believes that we each have our own fixed 'happiness point', a level we always return to, whatever happens to us in life. 2

But does this mean we are stuck with the level of happiness we were born with? Dr Michael Isaac, a psychiatrist, believes this is not necessarily the case. This is because although a person's temperament is not easily changed, their character can be. The former determines what kind of things will make someone happy, but not how much pleasure that person obtains from them. 3 This is why Dr Isaac believes we need to study happy people and learn how to be like them.

4 They also tend to be interested in things other than themselves. This could be through their day-to-day work, for example, or by caring for others less fortunate, or by having some kind of spiritual focus to their life.

Happy individuals also tend to relate to other people and are able to give and receive affection. 5 They are, therefore, more likely to belong to things like sports teams, choirs and political parties. Researchers at Harvard University have found that people involved in such activities were happier than those who were not, and that this had nothing to do with how well-off people were financially.

Another factor in happiness appears to be physical activity. Exercise improves a person's mood and gets rid of tension. But there must be a balance between activity and rest, because stress results in unhappiness. 6

But mental activity can be just as important. Psychologists believe it's possible to train yourself to recognise happiness and, therefore, feel the benefits of it more often. 7 One way of doing this is to set yourself the task of noticing, say, five different happy moments in the day. The more you recognise when there's a decision to be made about how you feel, the better you'll become at choosing happiness over misery, it is claimed.

151

Language development 1

Clauses of reason

1 a What do you do to relax?

b Read extracts from an article about Queen Elizabeth, the Queen Mother, and answer the questions.
1 What can make us healthier?
2 What did the Queen Mother do to relax?

A
Some scientists claim that happy people are healthier *owing to* the influence of happy emotions on our immune system.

B
Many people are convinced that the Queen Mother's long life was *due to* her positive, optimistic outlook and her strong will.

C
Because of her many interests, such as corgis, horse-racing, salmon-fishing, Scotland, bagpipe music and gardening, she was never bored.

D
She was popular with the nation, *as* she was charming and had a warm personality.

E
Since she was passionate about horse-racing, in the 1950s she decided to become an owner. In all, her horses won over 400 races.

F
The younger royals loved her *because* she had a good sense of humour and gave them a lot of personal support.

c The expressions in italics in the text extracts introduce an answer to the question *Why?* Which expressions can go in each sentence below?
1 Mark left his job .... it was stressful. (+ subject + verb)
2 Mark left his job .... the stress. (+ noun)
3 Mark left his job .... the fact that it was stressful. (+ *the fact that* + subject + verb)

2 a Complete these sentences about Joe with the words or expressions from Exercise 1b.
1 Joe put on some music .... he wanted to relax.
2 He had lost his job .... his age.
3 The club had reduced its staff .... the fact it was losing money.
4 But .... he was a talented trainer, he knew he'd get another job.
5 .... his many interests, he was never bored.
6 A lot of unhappiness is .... boredom.

b Complete the sentences in three different ways, using the words in brackets.
1 Dave was late for the meeting … (*snow*)
a because it ....
b because of ....
c due to ....
2 Marta decided to drive to work … (*rain*)
a as it ....
b because of ....
c since ....

Clauses of purpose

The expressions in **bold** all express purpose. They introduce an answer to the question *what for?*

| *The office closes early on Fridays* | **in order that** **so that** | *we can have a longer weekend.* |

| *I like to go away* | **in order to** **so as to** **to** | *have a break.* |

I take my mobile phone **in case** *anyone needs to contact me.*

3 a Which expressions in the box above can go in each sentence below?

1   I have a sauna once a week .... relax. (+ verb)

2   The fitness centre stays open late .... people can go after work. (+ subject + verb)

3   I usually call before I go, ... they're closed for any reason. (+ subject + verb: precaution)

b Mark the correct alternative in each pair.

1 Get regular exercise *to / so that* keep yourself fit.

2 Take food and drink to work *in order that / in case* you can't stop for lunch.

3 Breathe deeply *in case / so that* your whole body relaxes.

4 Read an amusing book *in order to / in order that* reduce tension.

5 *In order to / In order that* you can see a problem clearly, change your routine.

6 Allow plenty of time for journeys, *in case / so that* there are delays.

7 Leave work on time *so as to / so that* spend time with your friends and family.

8 Only drink one cup of coffee a day *so as not to / not to* overstimulate your body.

Clauses of contrast

The expressions in **bold** connect contrasting ideas:

| *I ran all the way* | **despite** **in spite of** | *being exhausted. (+ -ing)* *my exhaustion. (+ noun)* *the fact that I was exhausted. (+ the fact that)* |

| *I ran all the way* | **even though** **although** **though** | *it was very cold. (+ subject + verb)* |

| *Tom loves judo,* | **whereas** | *Mary prefers swimming. (+ subject + verb: contrasting but not contradicting ideas)* |

4 Look at the examples in the box above and match the sentence halves.

1   My mother goes out to work whereas
2   He's still out of work despite
3   Jo is very active although
4   David isn't getting better even though
5   They always seem happy despite
6   He's unhappy in spite of the fact that
7   Sam gets a huge salary while
8   I'm feeling really tired in spite of

a   his appetite has returned.
b   he makes a lot of money.
c   going for three interviews a week.
d   having slept well last night.
e   my father stays at home.
f   his assistant hardly earns anything.
g   their poverty.
h   she hasn't been feeling well lately.

5 Complete these sentences in a logical way.

1   Unfortunately, I can't give up smoking even though … .
2   She couldn't sleep last night because of … .
3   I must call Mike so that … .
4   Despite … , she was wearing a heavy coat.
5   Sheila phoned the restaurant to … .
6   He left his mobile phone behind in spite of … .

▶ Grammar reference page 186

Writing   Letter (Paper 2 Part 1)

Lead-in   **1** **Discuss this question, giving examples.**

Do you think people nowadays are more or less polite than they used to be?

Understand the task   **2** **Read and analyse the task below. Was the letter written by an older or a younger person?**

You read this letter in a local newspaper and you think that some of the things the person says in it are untrue. Read the letter and the notes you made beside it. Then, using all your notes, write a letter to the editor of the newspaper giving your opinion and correcting the information.

Children have always been noisy – they have to play.

Not true! Most young people are polite.

Why is it that these days young people in our city are so noisy and aggressive? Every time you get on a bus or go shopping, they seem to be having an argument with someone or trying to push past you. You walk down the street and even young children are shouting at each other, making an awful noise.

Older people, particularly those over 50, are much calmer and quieter. When we were young, we were patient and polite. That's why life was much more pleasant then.

I've seen old people get aggressive and impatient in shops.

Write a **letter** of between **120–150** words in an appropriate style. Do not write any postal addresses.

Plan your letter   **3** **a** Decide on the best order for the points discussed in the letter. Can any of them be grouped together?

b Make a paragraph plan for the letter.

Language and content

4 Replace the underlined phrases in this student's letter with more appropriate ones from the table below.

> Dear Sir or Madam,
>
> <u>About that letter</u> about young people's behaviour in last week's Courier. <u>I just can't get on with</u> the points the writer makes.
>
> <u>It's total rubbish</u> that all young people are noisy and aggressive. Round my way, <u>most young people are polite</u>.
>
> <u>And I can't go along with</u> the generalisations about younger and older people. Children are no noisier today than they used to be. They have always had to play. <u>And you'd say</u> older people are more polite? I have seen older people being aggressive and impatient in shops, for example.
>
> <u>In the end,</u> while we should all have consideration for others, <u>I reckon</u> we should all try to be more patient and tolerant of each other. We were all young once!

Opening	*I am writing in response to the letter … .*
Disagreeing	*I have to disagree with … .* *It is simply not true that … .* *I also disagree with … .* *And do you really think … ?*
Tentatively agreeing	*And whereas it may be true that … .* *We have to accept that … .*
Describing your experience	*In my experience, … .*
Summarising	*In conclusion, … .* *I think … .*

Write your letter

5 Now write your letter using the ideas and some of the language above. Avoid copying whole phrases from the question.

Check and improve your letter

6 Edit your work.

▶ Writing reference pages 197–198

LANGUAGE SPOT: attitude phrases

Mark the correct alternative in each sentence.

1 *To be honest / As far as I know*, I think young people are more polite than older people.
2 *Actually / Presumably*, the person who wrote the letter doesn't meet many young people.
3 *As a matter of fact / Clearly / Naturally*, last Saturday there was a fight between a group of youths in the town.
4 *Frankly / Certainly / Surely*, some young people create a lot of trouble, that's true, but … .
5 *Strictly speaking / Roughly speaking / Generally speaking*, the writer has a point. Young people seem to shout at each other, even when they're joking.
6 *In my opinion / Admittedly / At least*, I don't meet many young people, but I see them on TV.
7 *As far as I'm concerned / According to me*, older people can be just as aggressive.
8 *In person / Personally / Truly*, I think we should be more tolerant of each other.

Health and fitness

Listening (Paper 4 Part 2)

Vocabulary: health and fitness

1 Do you try and keep fit? Do you take regular exercise?

2 a Work with another student and complete this quiz.

HEALTH QUIZ

1 In your view, what's the best way of improving each of these: *strength, stamina, flexibility, co-ordination?* (Examples: *weight-lifting, aerobics, sit-ups, press-ups, yoga*)

2 What advice would you give someone who wants to do each of these?
- burn *calories* and lose *weight*
- decrease *cholesterol* (to help prevent *a heart attack*)
- strengthen their *immune system* (to protect them against *infection* and *disease*)
- lower their *blood pressure* (to help prevent a *stroke*)
- improve their *circulation*
- get more *fibre* in their diet
- *look after* their skin

3 a What are the *symptoms* of
- *flu?*
- *food poisoning?*
b Which part(s) of your body is affected by these?
- *arthritis*
- *migraine*
- *bronchitis*
- *tonsillitis*

4 Are these *True* or *False?*
1 Bread and potatoes are a good source of *carbohydrates.*
2 There are no *calories* in lettuce.
3 A lot of *processed* food lacks the *vitamins* and *minerals* found in fresh vegetables.
4 Eggs and nuts are low in *protein.*
5 Pasta is a good source of *iron.*

b Compare your answers with other students and keep a record of any words you want to remember.

3 Complete the gaps with the correct preposition.
1 *Polyunsaturated fats* are much better .... you than *saturated fats.*
2 Tania is *allergic* .... house dust. It makes her sneeze and her eyes itch.
3 Jack went .... water for several hours and in the heat he got very *dehydrated.*
4 It took me ages to recover .... a terrible *virus* that was going around. *Antibiotics* made no difference at all.

4 In your view, which is more important: exercise or a balanced diet?

Before you listen

5 **a** **What do you know about health around the world?**

  1 Which nationalities do you think have particularly healthy or unhealthy lifestyles? What are the reasons for this?

  2 What are the most common diseases in the world today? Are some more common in specific countries?

  b **Look at the task in Exercise 6 below. Can you guess whether the word(s) will be a noun, verb or adjective? Can you guess what the missing information might be? Remember you can use between one and three words.**

Sentence completion

6 🎧 **You will hear an interview about health and diet in some countries around the world. For questions 1–10, complete the sentences. Follow the task strategy. The first one is done for you.**

Task strategy

- Read through the notes. The missing information is usually factual.
- Listen and complete the gaps with a word, number or short phrase from the recording (no more than three or four words).
- The notes must make sense, but you don't have to create correct grammatical sentences.
- Check your answers during the second listening. Guess if necessary.

  1 A growing problem in Britain today is the number of overweight children.

  2 Penny believes that improving the quality of _____ will have a big effect on the nation's health.

  3 At the moment, the British spend four times as much on food for _____ than for schoolchildren.

  4 In a traditional Japanese diet, _____ of their calories come from carbohydrates.

  5 The Inuit of Greenland are an extremely _____ population.

  6 A link between omega-3 oils and better _____ has only just been found.

  7 Eating curries could be the reason why many elderly Indians still have good _____.

  8 It is now thought that drinking _____ could be good for the health.

  9 Penny says the French tend to eat fewer _____ than the British.

  10 Penny points out that French people may stay slim because of the timing of their _____.

  Now listen again.

Discussion

7 **Discuss these questions.**

  1 Were you surprised by anything you heard in the interview?

  2 How does your country compare to the ones you heard about?

Vocabulary: food

8 **Think of as many examples as you can of food which comes under the following headings. Which is unhealthy and which is good for you, or alright in moderation?**

Carbohydrates	Fat	Protein
pasta	*olive oil*	*eggs*

Speaking (Paper 5 Parts 3 and 4)

Lead-in

1 a Read the statements below about Paper 5 Parts 3 and 4, and discuss whether they are *True* or *False*.

Part 3:

1 Candidates speak for three minutes each.
2 The task has two parts.
3 You are not allowed to disagree with your partner.

Part 4:

4 You may be asked more than one question.
5 You should give short answers.
6 You should listen carefully to the other candidate.

b Look at the list of things (1–6) you might have to do in the exam. Match them to the expressions (a–f) below.

1 begin a discussion
2 involve the other candidate
3 disagree politely
4 ask for clarification
5 come to a conclusion
6 develop ideas

> a *I'm not quite sure what we have to do first.*
> b *Why don't we start by ...?*
> c *Do you think we should ...?*
> d *Yes, but ... .*
> e *I hadn't thought of that! We could also ... .*
> f *So are we agreed that ...?*

c Add any other expressions you can think of.

Collaborative task

▶ Task strategy Module 4B page 59

2 Work in groups of three.

STUDENT 1: You are the examiner. Turn to page 214 and read the instructions.
STUDENTS 2 AND 3: You are Candidates A and B. Look at the pictures A and B on page 157. Follow the examiner's instructions.

Three-way discussion

▶ Task strategy Module 5B page 73

3 a Work in groups of three. Take turns at being the examiner and candidates.

EXAMINER: Ask some of the questions below.

1 What kind of food do you like?
2 What kind of 'convenience food' would you really hate to give up?
3 Whose responsibility should it be to educate children about health issues?
4 What do you do to stay healthy?
5 Do you think that people these days are healthier than they used to be?
6 Do you think we worry too much about our health?

b Discuss and compare your answers. Did you:

- put your ideas across clearly?
- keep closely to the task?
- work well with your partner to complete the task?
- use a range of vocabulary?
- use correct grammar and pronunciation?

Language development 2

so/such; too/enough/very

1 a Read the examples in the box and complete the rules.

- *so/such*
  *Why is it **so difficult** to lose weight?*
  *You shouldn't eat **so many** sweets – they're bad for you!*
  *He walks **so fast** (that) I can hardly keep up with him.*
  ***Such bad behaviour** is not acceptable.*
  *He's **such a nice person** – everyone likes him.*
  *There was **such a lot** of salt in the food (that) I couldn't eat it.*

  1 We use .... before adjectives, adverbs and quantifiers.
  2 We use .... before a noun phrase with an uncountable noun.
  3 We use .... + ... before singular countable nouns.

---

b Read the examples in the box and answer the questions below.

- *enough/too/very*
  *Five hours a night isn't **enough sleep**.*
  *There aren't **enough facilities** for young people.*
  *It **isn't warm enough** (for us) to go swimming.*
  ***Too much** red meat isn't good for you.*
  *That health club is so expensive! It's much **too expensive** (for me) **to** join.*
  *I'm **very tired** – but not **too** tired to go out!*

  1 *enough* goes in front of a/an .... and after an
     ....
  2 Match the words to the definitions below.
     1 *too* (+ adjective/quantifier)
     2 *very* (+ adjective)
     3 *enough* (+ noun/adjective)

     a a lot
     b as much as we want/need
     c more than is good, reasonable or acceptable

---

2 Correct the mistakes in the sentences.

1 Jim's a so good doctor that everybody likes him.
2 My yoga class is great; I'm always too relaxed afterwards.
3 Paul has bought such an expensive fitness equipment!
4 The food is too spicy for me to eat it.
5 The vegetables in your diet aren't enough.
6 I'm very tired to go jogging now.
7 John is so unfit so he can't even run for a bus.
8 The money isn't enough for us to buy a drink.
9 You should be pleased with yourself for losing so weight.
10 I'm not enough old for to join that club.

as/like

A Comparison: *like* + noun, *as if/though* + clause
   *He's just **like** his father.*
   *I wish I could sing **like** Pavarotti (did).*
   *This looks/seems **like** a nice place.*
   *It seems **as if/like** (informal) he's going to be late.* (likely situation)
   *They treat me **like** their daughter/**as though I was** their daughter.* (imaginary situation)
   The following verbs are often followed by *like* + noun or *as if* + clause: *feel, look, seem, smell, sound, taste.*
   *It **looks like** rain/**as if** it is going to rain.*
   *He looks **as if** he had seen a ghost.* (See Module 10B, page 145.)

B Role, function: *as* + noun; manner: *as* + clause
   *He's found a job **as** a barman.*
   *Please think of me **as** a friend.*
   *He arrived late, **as** he had warned us.*
   *Please do **as** I tell you.*
   Other verbs followed by *as*: *describe, be known, recognise, regard, treat*

C Examples: *like/such as* + noun
   *Foods **like/such as** beans are a rich source of protein.*

---

3 Look at the information in the box above and complete the sentences with *as, like, such as* or *as if/as though*.

1 I love sweet things .... chocolates.
2 My friend Anna is looking for a job ....
   an au pair.
3 Taking up yoga sounds .... a good idea.
4 Foods .... oranges are full of Vitamin C.
5 He looks .... he hadn't slept for a week.
6 .... you can see, I've lost ten kilos!

4 Complete this extract from a letter with *as, like* or *such as*.

I'm working (1)........................... a nurse in a clinic in the Himalayas and, since I live next to the clinic, people expect me to behave (2)........................... a nurse all the time. (3)........................... with any nursing job, my main task is to look after patients, but here I also do other things, (4)........................... help prepare the food and take it to the homes of sick people. The views from my bedroom are spectacular – it looks (5)........................... paradise! – and (6)........................... you predicted, sometimes I feel I never want to go back home.

Use of English 1 (Paper 3 Part 4)

Lead-in

1 a What advice would you give someone doing the exam task below? Check your answers by looking back at the task strategy on page 20.

b Look at the completed transformations below. Can you correct this candidate's mistakes?

> 1 I remember the first time I met my wife.
> **meeting**
> I remember _meeting my wife for_ first time.
> 2 The tickets may be expensive so take plenty of money.
> **case**
> Take plenty of money _in case of the tickets are_ expensive.
> 3 By eight o'clock, Tom was very tired so he went back to bed.
> **that**
> By eight o'clock, Tom _was too tired that he_ went back to bed.
> 4 We'll get into the stadium if we arrive by eight.
> **long**
> We'll get into the stadium _as long as we will arrive_ by eight.

Key word transformations

▶ Task strategy Module 1B page 20

2 a Do the task below.

Complete the second sentence so that it has a similar meaning to the first sentence, using the word given. **Do not change the word given.** You must use between **two** and **five** words, including the word given. Write **only** the missing words.

1 I'm just eating my dinner – do you mind if I phone you later?
 get
 I'm just eating my dinner – can .... later?
2 You could stay with us next time you're in town.
 put
 We could .... next time you're in town.
3 If it were cooler, we could go for a walk.
 hot
 If it .... could go for a walk.
4 Jane had never eaten a meal that was as delicious as that one.
 such
 Jane had never eaten .... meal.
5 'Do you want to buy my car or not?' Alan asked Judy.
 whether
 Alan asked .... to buy his car or not.
6 This car is too small for any more luggage.
 enough
 There .... in this car for any more luggage.
7 Tom is not usually so bad-tempered.
 like
 It is .... so bad-tempered.
8 Jazz is less popular now than it was 50 years ago.
 not
 Jazz .... it was 50 years ago.

b Compare and discuss your answers.

Use of English 2 (Paper 3 Part 1)

Lead-in

1 Discuss these questions.

1 How do you cheer yourself up when you're feeling low?

2 How does shopping affect your mood?

Multiple-choice cloze

▶ Task strategy Module 1B page 21

2 a Read the title and text quickly and answer the questions.

1 What is 'retail therapy'?

2 When can it be bad for your health?

3 In what way can it be good for your health?

b Do the task.

Read the text below and decide which answer **A**, **B**, **C** or **D** best fits each space. There is an example at the beginning (**0**).

0 A clouds   **B** mood   **C** weather   **D** humour

'Retail therapy'

Some people like to go shopping for fun when they're feeling a bit under the (**0**) .....C...... . They claim that indulging in some 'retail therapy' (**1**) .... them up and they start to feel better. However, while buying things we don't really need can give a temporary 'buzz', in the long- (**2**) .... it can increase personal dissatisfaction. Also, 'comfort buying' is the first (**3**) .... towards shopping addiction, causing many a shopper to get into debt, which is (**4**) .... good for their health.

However, some recent research has (**5**) .... that shopping can lighten more than our wallets.

Walking is (**6**) .... as a good way of reducing the risk of coronary heart disease and it is (**7**) .... that on average British women cover 214 km a year by going to the shops. This (**8**) .... at about 4.45 km and 193 calories burnt for every two-hour trip. Going with a friend was found to be even more (**9**) .... than solo shopping, because people (**10**) .... to stay out longer and cover more distance in pairs. So while unnecessary consumption may not be the (**11**) .... of all happiness it can offer other health benefits – (**12**) .... of course we don't do it online!

1	**A** comforts	**B** cheers	**C** takes	**D** relieves
2	**A** time	**B** period	**C** moment	**D** term
3	**A** step	**B** position	**C** point	**D** direction
4	**A** barely	**B** hardly	**C** unnecessarily	**D** unusually
5	**A** shown	**B** said	**C** explained	**D** allowed
6	**A** admitted	**B** stated	**C** declared	**D** recognised
7	**A** valued	**B** estimated	**C** formed	**D** reviewed
8	**A** gets round	**B** gives over	**C** works out	**D** makes up
9	**A** strong	**B** active	**C** beneficial	**D** able
10	**A** tended	**B** turned	**C** took	**D** held
11	**A** branch	**B** heart	**C** plant	**D** root
12	**A** however	**B** provided	**C** nevertheless	**D** although

Discussion

3 Discuss these questions.

1 Do you think shopping is good for your health?

2 Which domestic activities:

• help keep people fit?

• are bad for you?

Language development 3
Idiomatic expressions: health

LOOK at the sentence from the Use of English text on page 161 and choose the correct meaning for the expression in bold.

*Some people like to go shopping for fun when they're feeling **under the weather**.*

1   unhappy because it is cold
2   not very well

1 a   Read the following text, then mark the correct alternative in each pair in the sentences below.

George was **(1)** *feeling his age*. He hadn't **(2)** *felt himself* for a while and he was **(3)** *off his food*, which was unusual for him. He went to see his doctor, who said he was **(4)** *run-down* and needed a rest. The doctor told George to take a holiday and **(5)** *recharge his batteries*. He also said George needed to change his lifestyle, stop smoking and take more exercise. So George went to the south of France for three months, and when he got back, he was **(6)** *in good shape*. His doctor gave him **(7)** *a clean bill of health*. That was 20 years ago. George is **(8)** *still going strong* today.

1   George was *middle-aged / very old* when he went to the doctor's.
2   He went to the doctor's because he felt *different / unwell.*
3   Also, he *had no more food / didn't want to eat.*
4   The doctor said he *was very tired / had run too much.*
5   The doctor told George to *get back his energy / get a new battery.*
6   When George got back from holiday, he *had a good figure / was physically fit.*
7   His doctor said he was *clean / healthy.*
8   Today George is *fit and healthy / strong.*

b   Check your answers in the *Longman Exams Dictionary*. When you look up an idiomatic expression, look for the first noun, verb, adjective, adverb or preposition.

> **feel¹** /fiːl/ *v past tense and past participle* **felt** /felt/ **15 feel your age** to realize that you are not as young or active as you used to be: *Looking at his grandson made him really feel his age.*

Phrasal verbs: health

2 a   Complete the sentences with the correct form of a phrasal verb from the list. Use each verb once only.

cut down on   get over   take up   give up
come down with   cut out   pick up   put on

1   I think you need to .... some weight after so long without food.
2   You ought to .... sweet things, and .... chocolate completely.
3   You've probably .... a bug – there's something going round.
4   Why don't you .... smoking altogether? You know it's bad for your health.
5   You must be .... a cold. You'll soon .... it though.
6   You should .... yoga to strengthen your muscles.

b   Complete the dialogues with the sentences from Exercise 2a.

1   A: I've got backache.
     B: ....
2   A: How many cigarettes do you smoke a day?
     B: About 20.
     A: ....
3   A: I can't stop sneezing.
     B: ....
4   A: Do you think I'm overweight?
     B: Yes, I do. ....
5   A: I feel very weak and thin after my illness.
     B: ....
6   A: I've got a terrible stomachache.
     B: ....

3   Ask a partner these questions.

1   Have you taken up a sport recently, or in the past?
2   When did you last come down with something? Did you get over it quickly?
3   What do you think you should cut down on, or cut out?

MODULE 12
Getting your message across

Overview

- **Reading:** multiple choice (Paper 1 Part 1)
- **Language development 1:** connecting ideas; participle clauses
- **Writing:** set book (Paper 2 Part 2)
- **Speaking:** complete paper (Paper 5 Parts 1–4)
- **Listening:** multiple-choice questions (Paper 4 Part 4)
- **Use of English 1:** multiple-choice cloze (Paper 3 Part 1)
- **Language development 2:** *needs + -ing/to be done*;
  causative: *have/get something done*
- **Use of English 2:** word formation (Paper 3 Part 3)
- **Language development 3:** word formation: review

Lead-in

- Which different methods of communicating information
  and ideas are shown in the photos?
- What is the main purpose of each medium?
- What positive and negative effects have they had on our lives?

The Talented Mr Ripley

PATRICIA HIGHSMITH

PENGUIN READERS

Reading (Paper 1 Part 1)

Before you read

1 a What do you read most/least often? For example: newspapers, magazines, fiction books, non-fiction books, technical manuals? Why?

 b You are going to read an extract from a novel by Patricia Highsmith, which was made into a film in 1999. Look at the cover and a still from the film above. What kind of novel do you think it is: romance, historical, crime thriller, science fiction, etc.?

Reading

2 Read the extract once fairly quickly. Do you think your answer in Exercise 1b was right? Give reasons.

Multiple choice
▶ Task strategy Module 4A page 52

3 a Read the extract again. For Questions 1–7, choose the answer A, B, C or D which you think fits best according to the text. Follow the task strategy. Question 1 has been done for you. The highlighted words show how the answer was found.

 b Compare and justify your answers.

Discussion

4 a Discuss the story.
    1 What do you think will happen next?
    2 Which character do you sympathise with most? Which one would you like to meet?
    3 Having read this extract, would you like to read the novel or see the film? Why?/Why not?

 b What are the advantages and disadvantages of making a film based on a novel? Give examples of films you have seen.

Vocabulary: feelings; idiomatic expressions

5 a Find nouns and adjectives in the text that express feelings, emotions and reactions. Then explain why Dickie or Tom experienced these feelings.
    EXAMPLES: nouns: *hate, affection*
    adjectives: *enthusiastic*

 b Look at the numbered expressions 1–4 in the text. Can you explain what they mean?

Dickie said absolutely nothing on the train. Under a pretence of being sleepy, he folded his arms and closed his eyes. Tom sat opposite him, staring at his bony, arrogant, handsome face, at his hands with the green
5 ring and the gold signet ring. **It crossed Tom's mind**[1] to steal the green ring when he left. It would be easy: Dickie took it off when he swam. Sometimes he took it off even when he showered at the house. He would do it the very last day, Tom thought. Tom
10 stared at Dickie's closed eyelids. A crazy emotion of hate, of affection, of impatience and frustration was swelling in him, hampering his breathing.

He wanted to kill Dickie. It was not the first time he had thought of it. Before, once, twice or three
15 times, it had been an impulse caused by anger or disappointment, an impulse that vanished immediately and left him with a feeling of shame. Now, he thought about it for an entire minute, two minutes, because he was leaving Dickie anyway and what was there to be
20 ashamed of any more? He had failed Dickie in every way. He hated Dickie because, however he looked at what had happened, his failing had not been his own fault, not due to anything he had done, but due to Dickie's rudeness! He had offered Dickie friendship,
25 companionship and respect, everything he had to offer, and Dickie had replied with ingratitude and now hostility. Dickie was just **shoving him out in the cold**[2].

If he killed him on this trip, Tom thought, he
30 could simply say that some accident had happened. He could – he had just thought of something brilliant: he could become Dickie Greenleaf himself.

He could do everything that Dickie did. He could go back to Mongibello first and collect Dickie's things,
35 tell Marge any story, then set up an apartment in Rome or Paris, receive Dickie's cheque every month and forge Dickie's signature on it. He **could step right into Dickie's shoes**[3]. He could have Mr Greenleaf Senior **eating out of his hand**[4].
40 The danger of it, even the inevitable temporariness of it, which he vaguely realised, only made him more enthusiastic. He began to think of how. The water. But Dickie was such a good swimmer. The cliffs. It would be easy to push Dickie off some cliff when they took
45 a walk, but he imagined Dickie grabbing at him and pulling him off with him and he tensed in his seat until his thighs ached and his nails cut red into his thumbs. He would have to get the other ring off, too. He would have to tint his hair a little lighter. But he
50 wouldn't live in a place, of course, where anybody who knew Dickie lived. He had only to look enough like Dickie to be able to use his passport. Well, he did, if he –

Dickie opened his eyes, looking right at him, and
55 Tom relaxed, slumped into the corner with his head back and his eyes shut, as quickly as if he had passed out. 'Tom, are you OK?' Dickie asked, shaking Tom's knee. 'OK,' Tom said, smiling a little. He saw Dickie sit back, with an air of irritation, and Tom knew why;
60 because Dickie had hated giving him even that much attention. Tom smiled to himself, amused at his own quick reflex in pretending to collapse, because that had been the only way to keep Dickie from seeing what must have been a very strange expression on his face.

1 What do we learn about Tom in the first paragraph?
  A He has already tried to steal Dickie's ring.
  B He is familiar with the details of Dickie's life.
  C He has just had an argument with Dickie.
  D He is unsure whether Dickie is asleep or not.

2 Why does Tom decide that he wants to kill Dickie?
  A He feels unfairly treated by Dickie.
  B He wants to get away from Dickie.
  C He thinks that Dickie has failed him.
  D He feels ashamed of Dickie's behaviour.

3 In the third paragraph, Tom plans how he will
  A cause Dickie to have an accident.
  B go and live in Dickie's apartment.
  C leave Dickie and return to Rome.
  D receive money intended for Dickie.

4 How does Tom feel at the thought of actually killing Dickie?
  A terrified of the consequences
  B unsure of what to do with the body
  C thrilled by the risks involved
  D confident of his ability to do it

5 The word *grabbing* (line 45) describes a way of
  A holding somebody.
  B looking at somebody.
  C speaking to somebody.
  D understanding somebody.

6 Why did Tom pretend to faint?
  A to annoy Dickie and start an argument
  B to distract attention from how he looked
  C to make a boring journey more interesting
  D to make Dickie more sympathetic towards him

7 What does the phrase *Tom knew why* (line 59) refer to?
  A Tom's smile
  B Dickie's attention
  C Dickie's irritation
  D Tom's expression

a I read this book in order to find out more about the American way of life.

b As it was written by an American, it gives an accurate picture of life there.

c I had to read a lot of it before fully understanding the humour.

d If I'd known more about the USA before I started, I would have understood the book better.

e It's about two people who decide to drive across the USA.

f While they are driving along, they meet all kinds of people.

g Each night they arrive in a different town and feel exhausted.

h Because they don't know anyone, they have to find somewhere to stay.

i When they have found a hotel, they usually go out to eat.

j Sometimes they are so tired that they sleep in the car.

k However, they don't realise that they are being followed.

Language development 1

Connecting ideas

1 a **Read the student's sentences, which describe a book he/she has read. Answer the questions.**

   1 Why did the student read the book?
   2 What made it more difficult to understand?
   3 Why do the characters sometimes sleep in the car?

   b **Mark the words in the student's sentences which are used to connect ideas, and use them to complete the table.**

Type	Example	Example from Exercise 1a
Relative pronoun	*which, that*	1 ....
Conjunction + clause	*when*	2 ....
		3 ....
Conjunction + -ing	*after*	4 ....
Clause of result	*such a ... that*	5 ....
Conditional	*unless*	6 ....
Linking conjunction	*but*	7 ....
	Nevertheless, ...	8 ....
Clause of purpose	*... to ...*	9 ....
Clause of reason	*since*	10 ....
		11 ....

▶ Grammar reference page 186

2 **Correct the mistakes in these sentences.**

1 The part what I liked best was the ending.
2 The main character is an old man who he has never left his home town.
3 It was a such good book that I couldn't stop reading it.
4 During the police look for the main suspect, Holmes makes other enquiries.
5 It is set in a town where there are a lot of factories in.
6 It can be helpful to see the film before to read the book in English.
7 If you will like science fiction, you'll probably like this book.
8 It is a good story despite the main character is not very realistic.
9 The police are called in for investigate the theft of a painting.
10 I didn't like the ending because of I thought it was disappointing.

Participle clauses

Participle clauses can be used in writing to make sentences shorter.

Look at these examples of shortened sentences from Exercise 1a:

A Present and perfect participles (actions/situations at the same time or in sequence)
While they are driving along, they meet all kinds of people.
→ ***Driving*** *along, they meet all kinds of people.*
Because they don't know anyone, they have to find somewhere to stay.
→ ***Not knowing*** *anyone, they have to find somewhere to stay.*
When they have found a hotel, they usually go out to eat.
→ ***Having found*** *a hotel, they usually go out to eat.*

B Past participles (for passives)
As it was written by an American, it gives an accurate picture of life there.
→ ***Written*** *by an American, it gives an accurate picture of life there.*

C Past participles used as adjectives.
Each night they arrive in a different town and feel exhausted.
→ *Each night they arrive in a different town,* ***exhausted***.

3 **Look at the information in the box and complete the second sentence with a participle so that it means the same as the first.**

1 Since Jackson is an immigrant, he decided to write about immigrants.
.... an immigrant, Jackson decided to write about immigrants.

2 As he writes in the first person, he brings the story to life.
.... in the first person, he brings the story to life.

3 Because he has experienced problems himself, he writes very realistically.
.... problems himself, he writes very realistically.

4 Although the book was criticised at first, it was a huge success.
Although .... at first, his book was a huge success.

5 Despite the fact that she has had many problems, the protagonist never gives up.
Despite .... many problems, the protagonist never gives up.

6 Now that I've read this one, I can't wait for his next novel!
.... this one, I can't wait for his next novel!

7 I got to the end of the book and felt completely satisfied.
I got to the end of the book, ...

4 **Look at the cover of the book *Heat and Dust*. The sentences below explain what the book is about. Use language from Exercises 1–3 to connect the ideas in the sentences as suggested. In each case, combine the sentences to make one long sentence.**

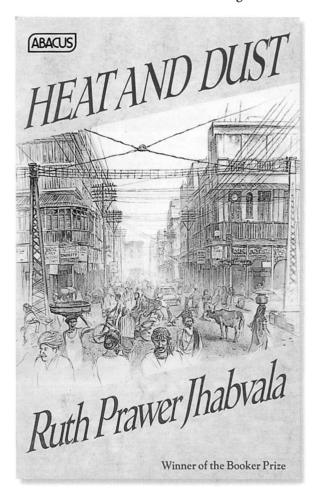

Winner of the Booker Prize

1 The book was written by a woman. She has lived in India for many years. It tells us a lot about life there. *(participle; relative)*
Written by a woman who has lived in India for many years, the book tells us a lot about life there.

2 It is about a young English woman. She goes to India with her child. She wants to find out the true story of her grandmother. *(relative; reason)*

3 Her English grandparents lived in India together. Her grandmother fell in love with an Indian man. *(contrast)*

4 She arrives there. Then she starts to follow the same life path as her grandmother. She falls in love with an Indian. *(perfect participle; conjunction + clause)*

5 It is set in two periods and tells two women's similar stories. It shows that lifestyles and attitudes change a lot over two generations. Love and relationships never change. *(participle; contrast)*

Writing Essay: set book (Paper 2 Part 2)

Lead-in   1   **Discuss these questions.**
1   What book have you read?
2   What kind of book is it?
3   What did you like most/least about it?

Understand the task   2   Read and analyse the task. What sort of writing are you being asked for in each task (e.g. a letter? a report?)?

> Answer **one** of the following two questions based on your reading of one of the set books.
>
> **Either a)** Your teacher has asked you to write a composition, giving your opinions on the following statement:
>
> *A good story should have a good beginning, a good middle and a good end.*
>
> Write your **composition**, explaining your views with reference to the book you have read.
>
> **Or b)** Your pen friend wants to buy a book in English for her father's birthday. He likes books with either interesting characters or an exciting story line. Your pen friend has written to ask whether you would recommend the book you have read. Write a letter in reply, giving your opinion and explaining the reasons.
>
> Write your **letter** in **120–180** words in an appropriate style.

Plan your answer   3   a   **Choose exam task a) or b) above, and answer these questions.**
1   What kind of story is your book?
2   Which aspects of the book are you going to focus on: plot, characters, general setting, a particular place?

b   **Make notes under these headings. Make sure they relate to the question only.**

Characters	Events	Setting (place)

c   **Number the events you have listed (1, 2, 3, etc.) in the order they occur.**

d   **Choose the most important points for your answer.**

e   **Can you match your points from Exercise 3d to the paragraph plan below?**
Paragraph 1: Reason for writing
Paragraph 2: General statements about the book + reasons
Paragraph 3: Statement(s) (about the story line) + reason + example
Paragraph 4: Statement(s) (about the characters) + reason + example
Paragraph 5: Conclusion + recommendation.

Language and content

4 a Put each of these adjectives under one of the headings for your notes in Exercise 3b. (There may be more than one possibility.) In context, would they be *Positive* (P) or *Negative* (N)?

lifelike   weak   unexpected   passionate   predictable   imaginative
brave   disappointing   lovely   successful   interesting   convincing
funny   clever   attractive   boring   sensitive   awful

b Can you think of any other adjectives you could use?

c How would you complete these expressions for your answer?

This is a story about … .
It is set in … .
The character(s) I like most/least … .
The reason I feel that … is … .
I think it is (written quite cleverly/extremely well-written) … because … .
It's full of … .
The best part of the book is when … .
I like/don't like the beginning/ending because … .

Write your answer

5 Write your answer using some of the language above.

Check and improve your answer

6 Edit your draft using this list.
Have you …
- expressed yourself clearly?
- given reasons for your opinions?
- included enough detail, but not too much detail?
- used a range of words, expressions and structures?
- used appropriate linking expressions?

▶ Writing reference page 206

LANGUAGE SPOT: avoiding repetition

a The words in bold below have been used to avoid repetition. What do they refer to?

*No one writes better stories than Mike **does**, and **he's done so** for years. I like his early **ones**. Have you read any of **them**? If **so**, what do you think of **them**?*
*If **not**, why don't I lend you **some**?*

b Replace the phrases in italics in the sentences with one or more of these words in the correct form.

so   not   one(s)   some   do

1 I think this is the first novel he has written. If *it is the first novel he has written*, it is an extraordinary achievement.
2 Most people who write novels *write novels* because they feel they have something to say.
3 They're very well-drawn characters, particularly the evil *characters*.
4 No one has written as many great plays as Shakespeare *wrote great plays*.
5 Have you got his latest book? If *you haven't got his latest book*, I'll lend it to you.
6 I like Chekhov plays. There's a good *Chekhov play* on at the Arts Theatre.
7 Have you got any good ideas? I need *good ideas* quickly.

Speaking   (Paper 5 Parts 1–4)

Vocabulary: press and advertising

1 a **Look at the pictures. Which of these is:**
- a local paper?
- an online newspaper?
- a national newspaper?
- a tabloid?
- a broadsheet?

b **Find an example of these:**
- a headline
- a column
- a 'breaking news' item
- a sports section
- a colour supplement.

c **What do these people do on a newspaper?**
- a foreign correspondent
- a crime reporter
- a columnist

d **Which is the correct word?**
1. News of the couple's separation *beat/hit* the headlines the next day.
2. The star decided to issue a *press/newspaper* release.
3. The journalist rushed to *find/meet* his deadline before the newspaper went to *publication/press*.
4. Most newspapers have regular *qualities/features* such as TV guides, classified ads. and weather *forecasts/predictions*.
5. There are so many *shiny/glossy* fashion magazines nowadays and they are full of advertisements for all the well-known brand *companies/names*. Whether they want to *promote/support* an older design or *take off/launch* a new one, they all have to try and *seize/grab* the attention of the reader.

e **What kind of newspaper do you read and why? Do you read the ads?**

2 a **Write the correct form of the word in the gaps. Use a dictionary to help you if necessary.**

1. *The Sun* is a best-selling tabloid .... newspaper published in the UK. It has the highest .... of any newspaper in the world with a current .... estimated at over 7 million.

    DAY
    CIRCULA▮
    READER

2. Some people say that standards in .... are declining and that the .... content of all newspapers has gone downmarket, with too many items revolving around celebrities.

    JOURNAL▮
    EDITOR

3. In most public service broadcasting there are no .... The only form of .... that is allowed is of its own programmes.

    COMMER▮
    ADVERTI▮

b **Make a note of any words you want to remember and mark the stress.**
Example:

PERSON   ACTIVITY
(who collects and writes news stories)

JOURnalist   JOURnalism

3 **Discuss these statements.**
1   There are so many sources of news nowadays that newspapers are no longer important.
2   All adverts are dishonest. They do not give us a true picture of a product.
3   Adverts have very little influence on what we buy.

Part 1: Interview
▶ Task strategy Module 8B page 115

4 a **Work in groups of three. One student is the examiner, the other two are Candidates A and B.**
STUDENT 1: You are the examiner. Turn to page 214 for a list of questions to choose from. Stop after three minutes.
STUDENTS 2 AND 3: You are candidates. Look back at the task strategy for points to remember.

b **Change roles so that everyone has a turn at answering the questions.**

Part 2: Individual long turn
▶ Task strategy Module 3B page 45

5 a **Work in pairs. One student is Candidate A and the other is Candidate B. Respond to the examiner's instructions below.**
Task 1
To Candidate A: Here are your two photos. They show people finding out about the news. Compare and contrast the photos, and say whether you prefer reading or listening to the news. You have one minute.
To Candidate B: Do you buy a newspaper?

b **Work in pairs again. Respond to these instructions.**
Task 2
To Candidate B: Look at the photographs on page 213. They show two different kinds of radio interview. Compare and contrast the photos, and say which you think makes the most interesting interview.
To Candidate A: Do you listen to the radio?

Part 3: Collaborative task
▶ Task strategy Module 4B page 59

6 a **Work in pairs. Look back at the task strategy for points to remember.**

b **Read the examiner's instructions below and do the exam task.**
Look at the photos on page 213. They show different types of cars. First, talk to each other about what kind of people you think would buy each car. Then decide which car would be most suitable for a small family. You have about three minutes for this.

Part 4: Discussion
▶ Task strategy Module 5B page 73

7 **Now ask each other these questions. You have three or four minutes for this.**
1   What do you think of car advertisements?
2   Do you drive a car?
3   If you could choose, what kind of car would you have?
4   Should governments do more to encourage people to use public transport?
5   What is the best way to travel around your country?
6   Which form of transport do you like least?

Listening (Paper 4 Part 4)

Before you listen **1 a** Which newspaper do you usually read? What do you like about it? How does it compare with other papers?

b Look at the listening task below. Read the questions but not the answers A–C.

1 What personal qualities do you think are necessary to be a journalist?

2 Discuss possible answers which you might hear.

Multiple choice

▶ Task strategy Module 6B page 88

2 🎧 You will hear an interview with a journalist. For Questions 1–7, choose the best answer A, B or C.

1 What convinced Mike to follow a career in journalism?
  A a course he took
  B his lack of success in business
  C the advice of a family member

2 What type of training did Mike have once he started work?
  A He studied for formal qualifications.
  B He worked closely with a more experienced colleague.
  C He received feedback on his work from newspaper readers.

3 When Mike first started working with the police, they
  A were unsure whether to trust him.
  B had little time to spend with him.
  C refused to accept drinks from him.

4 Why didn't Mike use the information he gained about Prince Charles?
  A It was against the law to do so.
  B He had promised that he wouldn't.
  C It was felt to be unfair to do so.

5 According to Mike, what is a journalist's most important quality?
  A being committed to the job
  B having good writing skills
  C feeling sure of your abilities

6 What does Mike say about modern journalism?
  A It's not as exciting as it used to be.
  B It's no longer as sociable as it was.
  C It's less demanding than in the past.

7 What disadvantage of journalism does Mike warn young people about?
  A the financial insecurity
  B the disruption of domestic life
  C the competitive atmosphere

Discussion **3** Now that you have heard Mike talking about his job, discuss these questions.

1 Do you have the right qualities to be a journalist?

2 What aspects of the job would you like/dislike?

Use of English 1 (Paper 3 Part 1)

Lead-in

1 a Are these statements *True* or *False*?

In Paper 3 Part 1
- you need to know the meaning of the 'missing' word
- what the whole text is about is not important
- you need to know whether the 'missing word' would go with other words in the context.

b What advice would you give a candidate for this part of the paper?

Multiple-choice cloze

▶ Task strategy Module 1B page 21

2 a Read the title quickly and answer the questions.

1 What image do advertisers of men's fragrances usually try and create?
2 Where is the brand name usually placed?
3 What is unusual about the advert in the picture?

b Do the task.

Read the text below and decide which answer **A**, **B**, **C** or **D** best fits the space. There is an example at the beginning (**0**).

0 A sensed   **B** remarked   **C** noticed   **D** witnessed

WHAT ARE THEY TRYING TO TELL US?

Advertisers aim to get their product (0) ...C.... and, in the competitive (1) .... of men's fragrances, image and brand name are all-important. Their advertisements assume that all young men want to be attractive to women and that an image needs to be (2) .... of a young man who becomes more confident and masculine after using the fragrance. Therefore, (3) .... all glossy lifestyle magazine adverts feature a glamorous male model in his early twenties and try to (4) .... an emotional impact. Interestingly, a picture of the product, the brand name and sometimes a (5) .... memorable phrase are often on the right-hand side of the image and play a (6) .... role.

In one (7) .... advert, the word 'story' is added to the brand name and the bottle of fragrance is in the (8) .... of a book. Unusually, the male model looks very serious, is rather unmasculine and wearing (9) .... glasses. The image of his head is (10) .... with words from a story typed on an old-fashioned typewriter. (11) .... the image is very stylish and is obviously intended to (12) .... to more serious, less sporty men or perhaps to women who would like their men to be like that!

1 A position	**B** world	**C** home	**D** spot
2 A created	**B** told	**C** changed	**D** had
3 A really	**B** largely	**C** above	**D** nearly
4 A take	**B** feel	**C** make	**D** occur
5 A quick	**B** short	**C** keen	**D** intense
6 A supporting	**B** holding	**C** following	**D** carrying
7 A just	**B** latest	**C** recent	**D** late
8 A size	**B** picture	**C** character	**D** shape
9 A humourless	**B** thick	**C** dense	**D** severe
10 A added	**B** counted	**C** joined	**D** merged
11 A Nevertheless	**B** For instance	**C** Personally	**D** Eventually
12 A attract	**B** charm	**C** appeal	**D** call

Discussion

3 Discuss these questions.

1 Do you think adverts are dishonest?
2 What things do you think should not be allowed in TV adverts, and why?

Language development 2

> A *need + -ing/to be done*
> Active: *Someone **needs to** check the adverts.*
> Passive: *The adverts **need checking*** ⎤
>   *The adverts **need to be checked*** ⎦ *to make sure they're legal.*
>
> B *have/get something done*
> • We can use *have/get something done* when we arrange
>   for someone to do something for us.
>   *We think of the ideas ourselves, but we **have/get the adverts**
>   **made for us.***
> • We can also use *have/get something done* when someone
>   else does something to us that we don't want.
>   *We **had** our office **broken into** last night.* (had = not my fault)
>   *I **got** my nose **broken** in a fight.* (got = my fault)

needs + -ing/to be(done)

1 a Correct the mistakes in these sentences in two different ways.
1 The advert's too long. It needs shorten.
2 Those posters are out of date. They need to replace.

**b What needs doing? Respond to these sentences using *need*
+-ing and a verb from the list.**

rebuild   water   tidy up   cut   repaint   clean
1 This garden's a mess.
2 The grass is long.
3 The plants all round the house are very dry.
4 That wall's fallen down.
5 Those windows over there are filthy.
6 The paint on the doors is coming off.

**c Look at these notes. Explain how to make a TV advert
using *needs to be*.**

> ### How to make a TV advert
> 1 First raise money.
> 2 Then write advert.
> 3 Prepare script and bring to life.
> 4 Find good production company.
> 5 Hire experienced director.
> 6 Recruit well-known actors.
> 7 Shoot advert in studio you can afford.

have/get something done

**2 a Respond to the sentences using *have/get
(done)* and any other language which is
necessary.**
1 A: Let's copy those pictures. Have you
     got a photocopier?
   B: No, I'll get them copied at the office.
2 A: Where's your DVD player?
   B: I .... (*steal*).
3 A: Let's repair your computer
     ourselves.
   B: No, ...
4 A: Have you checked the tyres on the
     jeep?
   B: No, ...
5 A: Shall we install the washing
     machine ourselves?
   B: No, ...
6 A: These knives are very blunt.
   B: Yes, ... (*sharpen*).

**b Why do we go to these places? Use
have/get (done).**
1 a dentist's
2 an optician's
3 a dry cleaner's
4 a hairdresser's
5 a manicurist's
6 a photographer
7 a picture framer's
8 a supermarket on the Internet

**c Which of these things do you do
yourself? Which do you have done for
you?**
• paint your room when it needs
  decorating
• mend your TV when it's broken
• tidy the house/apartment where
  you live
• clean your car
• service your car
• clean your coat when it's very dirty
• do the gardening

3 Discuss these questions.
1 If you could have some of your clothes
   made especially for you by a
   tailor/shoemaker, etc. which ones would
   they be and what would you have done?
2 If you could have a house built for you,
   where would you have it built and how
   would you have it designed?

Use of English 2 (Paper 3 Part 3)

Lead-in

1 Discuss these questions about Paper 3 Part 3.

1 Is it better to read the text line by line or sentence by sentence?
2 Should you answer the questions in order, or leave any you can't do and come back to them?

Word formation (A)

2 a Read the text below and answer the questions.

1 What do some paparazzi do to get photographs?
2 How do they defend what they do?

▶ Task strategy Module 2B page 35

b Do the task. Follow the task strategy.

Read the text below. Use the word given in capitals at the end of some of the lines to form a word that fits the space **in the same line**. There is an example at the beginning (**0**).

The paparazzi

Our interest in the private lives of celebrities seems (**0**) endless.	END
This has caused a (**1**)............... in the number of 'paparazzi',	GROW
those photojournalists who follow (**2**)............... celebrities around	GLAMOUR
to get (**3**)............... pictures of them, which they then sell to	EMBARRASS
popular magazines. There is a (**4**)............... large number of	FRIGHTEN
them, and some go to (**5**)............... lengths to get a picture. For	BELIEF
example, they will hire a helicopter in order to fly (**6**)...............	DANGER
close to the home of a celebrity and, much to his or her	
(**7**)............... , peer into the bedroom. But the paparazzi say that	ANNOY
stars do not deserve (**8**)............... , since they're only too happy	PRIVATE
to have their (**9**)............... weddings and the inside of their	ROMANCE
(**10**)............... homes photographed for huge fees.	ORDINARY

Word formation (B)

3 a Read the text below and answer the questions.

1 What are special advisers?
2 Why are some people in the UK concerned about them?

b Do the task. (See the instructions above.)

Special advisers

Every (**0**) government likes to get its message across	GOVERN
in the best possible light. However, in the UK there	
has been a (**1**)............... increase in the number of	WORRY
advisers whose (**2**)............... it is to get the public's	RESPONSIBLE
(**3**)............... and to make sure that all news is good news.	ATTEND
These people tell (**4**)............... how they want a story to	REPORT
appear and have therefore become very (**5**)............... in	POWER
politics. They also write (**6**)............... sentences for	MEMORY
speeches, which then get broadcast on radio or TV.	
Nowadays, there is a (**7**)............... of ways of getting	VARY
news to people and (**8**)............... parties feel that the	POLITICS
public don't want to listen to long, careful (**9**)...............	ARGUE
from their leaders. However, some people think this	
reduces (**10**)............... of the press.	FREE

Language development 3

Word formation: review

1 a Look at the Use of English texts on page 175 and complete the table.

Adjective	Negative adjective	Noun	Adverb
responsible	....	....	....

b Complete the table, using a dictionary if necessary.

Adjective	Adverb	Noun	Verb
....	....	belief	....
....	worryingly	....	....
embarrassing	....	....	....
....	....	....	recognise
amazing	....	....	....
....	....	decision	....
....	....	....	think
legal	....	....	....
....	satisfactorily	....	....
....	....	....	astonish

c Use prefixes to make the opposites of these words.

legal *(adj.)*   satisfactorily *(adv.)*   romantic *(adj.)*
appear *(v.)*   accurate *(adj.)*   moral *(adj.)*
probable *(adj.)*   logical *(adj.)*   regular *(adj.)*
perfectly *(adv.)*

d Complete each sentence with a word from Exercises 1a, b or c above that has a similar meaning to the words in brackets. There may be more than one possibility.

1 The newspaper was .... to reveal secret information about the Queen. (*not thinking about the effects of their actions*)

2 It was an .... to the company that so many people complained about their adverts. (*something uncomfortable*)

3 Greenco says it is an environmentally friendly company, so it seems .... that its leaflets are not made of recycled paper. (*not based on careful thought*)

4 It is .... to make a false claim in an advert. (*against the law*)

5 To everyone's .... , our low cost advertising campaign was a big success. (*great surprise*)

6 The victim thanked the press for being so .... during the case. (*kind and considerate*)

7 News editors mustn't hesitate. They have to be .... (*able to make up their mind clearly and quickly*)

8 Many of the figures quoted in the newspaper were .... (*not correct*)

2 Complete the second sentence so that it is similar in meaning to the first sentence. Use the words in brackets, and the correct form of one of the words below.

use   fashion   relation   survive

1 The police and the media are getting on well these days. (*better*)
The police and the media have a .... these days.

2 This bag is no good at all – it's got a hole in it. (*absolutely*)
This bag is .... – it's got a hole in it.

3 I used to buy that music magazine long before everyone else bought it. (*became*)
I used to buy that music magazine long before it ....

4 The doctors said he would probably live. (*chance*)
The doctors said he had a good ....

3 a Complete these extracts from people talking about magazines with the correct form of the words in brackets.

1 I read a couple of great computer magazines each month. They're very .... (*profession*) produced.

2 Some men's magazines are quite .... (*entertain*) but I find others completely .... (*read*).

3 If I had to .... (*general*), I suppose I prefer magazines with .... (*stimulate*) articles about things that are happening in the world.

4 I have great .... (*admire*) for magazines about cooking. They are so .... (*create*) and I don't really like to .... (*critic*) them. However, sometimes I find their recipes a bit .... (*rely*).

5 I hate magazines that insult my .... (*intelligent*). So many of them are just about the .... (*relation*) of famous people. Not only are such articles extremely .... (*bore*), I find them rather .... (*offend*).

b Discuss these questions.

1 What kind of magazines do you read and why?

2 What kind of magazines do you dislike?

Reference material

Exam reference

▶ See page 3 for Exam overview

Paper 1: Reading (1 hour)

There are three parts to this paper and a total of 30 questions. Questions in Parts 1, 2 and 3 carry two marks each. In Part 4 there are more questions, which carry one mark each.

Each part of the paper contains a text. One part may contain two or more shorter related texts. These come from a variety of sources, including newspaper and magazine articles, stories and brochures.

Each text has a different type of task, which tests specific aspects of reading (e.g. understanding gist or finding specific information).

You can make notes on your question paper but the answers must be transferred to the answer paper before the end of the exam.

Part 1: multiple choice

▶ See pages 52–53 for an example.

There are questions on the text followed by four possible answers (A D). You have to decide which answer is correct. The questions are in the same order as the information in the text.

This part tests detailed understanding of the text. Questions may include asking about opinions and attitudes expressed in the text, working out the meaning of vocabulary in context and understanding the relation between words and phrases (e.g. *What does 'it' refer to?*). There may also be a question which tests general understanding of the whole text (e.g. *Who was the text written for? Where does the text come from?*).

Part 2: gapped text

▶ See pages 38–39 for an example.

Sentences have been taken out of the text, jumbled and put in a box after the text. The task is to decide where in the text each sentence comes from. There is an extra sentence which doesn't fit anywhere.

This task tests your understanding of how the text is structured. To do the task you have to be aware of the logical sequence of the text by looking for key words and ideas, and understand how grammatical and lexical devices are used to link sentences and paragraphs *(e.g. Having done that, she left).*

Part 3: multiple matching

▶ See pages 66–67 for an example.

The task is to match statements or questions to paragraphs (a group of different paragraphs related in theme, or a single text divided into paragraphs). Sometimes the information may be found in more than one section and you will be asked to provide two answers (in any order).

This part of the paper focuses on your ability to scan texts quickly in order to find specific information. Although the text may seem long, you do not need to read it in detail and the information required can usually be located quickly.

Paper 2: Writing (1 hour 20 minutes)

For this paper you have to write two texts of between 120 and 150 words (Part 1) and 120 and 180 words (Part 2). Both questions carry equal marks.

You are tested on your ability to achieve the task set. You must include all the necessary information, use a range of vocabulary and structures, organise your writing clearly, and use language which is appropriate for the person you are writing to. Any errors you make in grammar, spelling, punctuation, or paragraphing must not prevent adequate communication. Your handwriting must be legible.

Part 1: letter or email

▶ See the Writing reference on pages 197–198 for an example. In Part 1 the task is compulsory. You are given a situation and some information to read (notes, illustrations, adverts, letters, notices, leaflets, etc.) and you have to write a letter or email in response. Marks are based on a general impression in conjunction with how well you have achieved the task set, using the information given.

In order to achieve the task you must do the following.

- Carry out the instructions, using the information given.
- Include the information required from the input material, leaving out what is not relevant.
- Plan and organise your letter or email carefully, using suitable paragraphing and cohesive devices.
- Write in an appropriate style for whoever will be reading the letter or email.
- Use a variety of language to do whatever is required (e.g. complain, ask for or give information, etc.).

Part 2: writing task

▶ See the Writing reference on pages 199–206 for examples. You choose one of five options. Questions 2–4 always consist of three of these: an article, a letter, a report, an essay, a review or a story. Question 5, which has two options, is always based on a 'set book' – the reading texts decided by the examination board.

You are told what kind of text to write (e.g. a story, a report, etc.) and given a context (e.g. who you are writing to and why you are writing). You have to decide what to include, how to organise your text and what kind of language to use.

Questions 2–5

Informal letter or email: this will be to a known reader, such as a pen friend. You are expected to write in a suitable informal style, and share your opinions, feelings or experiences, according to what the task requires.

Formal letter of application: this will be written to an individual or an organisation. You are expected to organise your letter and write in a suitable formal style.

Article: the context will be clear from the question or visual input. You are often expected to include a description of something/somebody or an anecdote. You should write in an appropriate style and engage the reader's interest.

Short story: this is usually for a magazine, anthology or competition. You are given a sentence which you have to use, either at the beginning or the end. The aim is to interest the reader and write in a lively or dramatic style.

Report: you are expected to provide the reader (e.g. your boss, your teacher) with factual information in a neutral style and possibly to make suggestions or recommendations. You should organise your report clearly and include headings.

Review: you are expected to write a report for an English-language magazine or newspaper. You need to express a personal opinion about something which you have experienced, e.g. a film or a holiday.

Essay: this is usually written for a teacher. You usually need to discuss the good and bad points of a topic, and give your opinions and suggestions.

Set book: the questions are general enough for any of the set texts, and you may have to tell details of part of the story, describe the characters or a particular scene. The question might ask you to write a composition, a letter, an article, or a report and you are expected to discuss the question and not simply summarise the plot. You should imagine that your reader may be someone who has not read the book.

Paper 3: Use of English (45 minutes)

There are four parts to this paper and a total of 42 questions. Questions in Parts 1, 2 and 3 carry one mark each. Part 4 carries up to two marks for each question. In this part of the exam, words must be spelt correctly. The question paper can be used for rough work but answers must be transferred to the answer sheet.

Part 1: multiple-choice cloze

▶ See page 63 for an example.

To choose the correct word or phrase to fill the spaces in the text you have to:
- understand the context
- know the meaning of the 'missing' word
- know whether the 'missing' word would go with the other words in the context (e.g. Is it part of a fixed phrase? Which preposition follows it?).

You are tested on vocabulary: words and prepositions (e.g. *love of, succeed in*); prepositions and words/fixed phrases (e.g. *above average, do without*); phrasal verbs (e.g. *take after someone*); linking words (e.g. *although, in case*); adverbs (e.g. *particularly, nearly*); and sets of words with similar meanings (e.g. *travel, voyage, journey, excursion*).

Part 2: open cloze

▶ See page 47 for an example.

You have to fill in the spaces in a text with one appropriate word of your own choice so that it makes sense.

You are tested mainly on grammar, but you can also be tested on words and prepositions (e.g. *interested in, a way of*); fixed phrases (e.g. *on his way home, at least*); and phrasal verbs (e.g. *get on with someone*).

Grammar areas include: verb forms (e.g. auxiliaries, passives); pronouns (e.g. relatives – *who, which*, etc.); comparative forms (e.g. *more, less, than, as*); articles (*a, the*); determiners (e.g. *this, these*); possessives (e.g. *of*); conditionals; quantifiers (e.g. *one of*), time conjunctions (e.g. *before, while*); linking expressions (e.g. *because, but*); *neither/nor; it/there; make/do; whether or not; let/allow; as/like*, etc.

Part 3: word formation

▶ See page 91 for an example.

You are given a short text with ten gaps and you have to change the form of a word at the end of some of the lines to make it fit a space in the same line. For the word to make sense in context you may need to add a prefix (e.g. *un-*) or a suffix (e.g. *-able*), or both, to change it into a noun, adjective, verb form or adverb. You may need to make some words negative or plural according to the context; some verbs into participles (e.g. *write – written*);

and some adjectives into superlatives (e.g. *big – biggest*). You might have to make internal changes (e.g. *strong – strength*) or compounds (e.g. *rain – raindrop*). You don't need to make more than two changes to the original word.

Part 4: key word transformations

▶ See page 62 for an example.

You are given the beginning and end of a sentence and you have to complete it so that it has a similar meaning to the sentence above it. There is a 'key' word, which you must use, and which you must not change in any way. Using the key word involves making more than one change to the original sentence. You have to use between two and five words including the key word. Contracted forms (e.g. *I'll*) count as two words.

You are tested on both grammar and vocabulary. Each question receives two marks; one mark may be given if there is a small error.

Grammar areas include: active and passive verb forms; comparatives and superlatives; indirect and reported speech; clauses of purpose and result (e.g. *so … that*); verbs + *-ing/to*; modals; *wish/it's time* + past; conditionals; verb + two objects; quantity (e.g. *hardly any*); adverbs; *it/there*; *make/let/allow*; *despite/in spite of*; *since/for*; *prefer/rather/had better*; *remember/forget*; *lend/borrow*; *in case*; *too/enough*; *so/such*.

Vocabulary areas include: words and preposition (e.g. *be good at*); phrasal verbs (e.g. *look forward to*); changing nouns to verbs; and expressions (e.g. *out of work*).

Paper 4: Listening
(approximately 40 minutes)

This paper has four parts. Each part has one or more recorded texts and comprehension questions. There are a total of 30 questions. Each question carries one mark. Recordings can include interviews, conversations, talks and announcements, etc. The recordings might be a series of short extracts (of approximately 30 seconds) or longer extracts (of approximately 3 minutes). Each recording is played twice.

Each task focuses on a different aspect of listening (e.g. understanding the gist or main points, or identifying specific information).

You can make notes on your question sheet during the exam but at the end you are given 5 minutes to transfer your answers to the answer sheet provided.

Part 1: multiple choice (extracts)

▶ See page 88 for an example.
You will hear eight short unconnected recordings of one or two people speaking in different situations. Each extract lasts approximately 30 seconds and you hear each extract twice before you go on to the next one. In this part of the paper both the questions and the three options which go with each question are recorded, as well as being in your answer booklet, so that you have time to think about the recording coming up.

Each question requires you to 'tune in' and listen out for clues, so that you can understand a general situation (e.g. *What are the people talking about? How does the teacher feel? Who is speaking? Where are the children?* etc.). You are not being tested on the detail.

Part 2: sentence completion

▶ See page 74 for an example.

This is always a longer extract (approximately 3 minutes) with one or more people speaking. The questions require you to complete sentences, normally with a maximum of three words. The questions are in the same order as the text and all the words you have to write are on the recording. However, the words are not in the same order as on the recording – it is not a dictation.

The key is to listen for the information you need and ignore the rest. Your spelling must be understandable, though not necessarily perfect, and your handwriting must be clear.

Part 3: multiple matching

▶ See page 60 for an example.

You will hear five short related monolgues. You hear all the extracts together once, before you hear them all again a second time. The task is to match each extract to one of the six options on a list. One of the options is not used. As in Part 1, this part of the paper tests your ability to listen for the general meaning; to pick up clues and get information about the context, ignoring irrelevant information.

Part 4: multiple choice

▶ See page 116 for an example.

This is always a longer extract (approximately 3 minutes) involving a monologue or a text with two or more interacting speakers. It is often an interview, where people give their opinions. The task requires you to choose answers from three options (e.g. matching statements to three speakers).

As in Part 2, this part of the paper requires you to listen for specific information or detail.

Paper 5: Speaking
(approximately 14 minutes)

This paper is divided into four parts. Assessment is based on performance in the whole of the speaking test, based on the following criteria:
- how accurate and appropriate your vocabulary and grammar is
- the fluency and range of your language
- how comprehensible your pronunciation is
- how well you work with your partner or examiner to carry out the task.

There are always two examiners present. One of the examiners (the interlocutor) explains the tasks and asks the candidates questions, while the other (the assessor) assesses the candidates and gives marks. In Parts 1 and 2 the candidates speak mainly to the interlocutor and in Parts 3 and 4 with a partner (another candidate). You may or may not know your partner. You should speak as clearly and naturally as possible.

Part 1: interview

▶ See page 115 for an example.

The examiner will ask you personal information in an interview (approximately 3 minutes). You will have to use a range of social language and verb forms in order to talk about such things as: where you live, your family, what you do in your spare time and your future plans.

Part 2: individual long turn

▶ See page 45 for an example.

You have to speak without interruption for about a minute to compare and contrast two photos on a similar theme, and give your personal reaction to them. The examiner will tell you the subject of the photos and give you the task, which requires you to:
- talk about differences and similarities between the photos, and speculate on what they are about
- give your opinions on and reactions to something connected to the photos.

You also have to answer a question after your partner has spoken, so you need to look at his/her photos and listen to what he/she says, so that you can be prepared to comment.

Part 3: collaborative task

▶ See page 59 for an example.

You work with your partner for 3–4 minutes to complete a task, using the pictures or diagrams which the examiner gives you. The task may involve solving a problem, making a plan, putting things in order of priority or making a decision. There are no right or wrong answers and it is not necessary to agree with each other.

You are tested on your ability to cooperate and work together on a task: you are expected to take turns at speaking, sometimes lead the conversation, involve your partner and come to a conclusion. However, it is more important how you work towards the completion of a task than actually completing it.

Some of the language you need to use includes: asking for, giving and reacting to opinions and suggestions, speculating, interrupting, opening and closing the discussion.

Part 4: discussion

▶ See page 73 for an example.

You will be asked questions which develop ideas related to the topic in Part 3. The discussion will open up into more general areas.

This is an opportunity to show how much language you know. Although this part of the exam is led by the examiner, there must be a balance between giving your own opinions and listening to and involving your partner. The examiner will stop you after approximately 4 minutes.

Grammar reference

Contents

1 Articles

A The indefinite article

a/an: with singular countable nouns
(but *some* with plural or uncountable nouns and *one* when we want to emphasise the number)

1 When we introduce something new, unfamiliar or unexpected to another person:
*I need **a** new car.*
*It's **a** good opportunity to travel.*
*There's **an** old woman in the street.*

2 In descriptions and classifications (to say what kind of thing):
*It's **a** lovely day, isn't it? It's **a** big hotel. What **a** nice town!* (descriptions)
*My sister is **a** doctor.* (jobs)
*The play was **a** comedy.* (classifications)

3 Meaning all:
***An** orange has a lot of vitamin C.* (= all oranges)
(We also say: ***Oranges** have a lot of vitamin C.*)

4 Meaning *every* in expressions of time/quantity/speed:
*twice **a** week*
*two euros **a** kilo*

B The definite article

the: for singular and plural nouns.

1 When the other person knows who or what we are referring to:
*Where's **the** car?* (you know which car I mean)
*Do you know **the** people at that table?* (you can see them)
*There's a man and a woman outside. **The** woman says she's your sister.* (I have already mentioned the woman.)
***The** earth goes round **the** sun.* (it's the only one)

2 In certain fixed expressions:
*He joined **the** police/ **the** army/ **the** navy.*
*Let's go to **the** shops/**the** cinema/**the** theatre/**the** bank.*
*She plays **the** piano/**the** violin.*
*I went to **the** airport/**the** bus station.*

3 In some general statements:
*Who invented **the** telephone?* (inventions)
***The** tiger is in danger of extinction.* (species – but *Tigers are … is more common*)

4 The definite article is used with these proper nouns:
- oceans and seas (***the** Pacific ocean*)
- rivers (***the** Amazon*)
- groups of islands (***the** Bahamas*)
- mountain ranges (***the** Alps* but not individual mountains: ***Mount** Fuji*)
- deserts (***the** Sahara*)
- countries with plural nouns and political terms (***the** USA, **the** Netherlands, **the** Czech Republic*)
- groups of people (***the** Germans, **the** rich*)
- hotels/cinemas/theatres (***the** Ritz, **the** Variety Theatre*)
- newspapers (***the** Times*)
- political bodies (***the** Government, **the** Labour Party*)

C Zero (no article Ø)

Zero article before plural and uncountable nouns.

1 When we refer to something general or abstract:
*Ø **Houses** are getting much more expensive.*
*He's making Ø good **progress**.*
*He's got a lot of Ø **courage**.*
*He's studying Ø **French history**.* (but ***the** history **of** France*)

2 Before institutions, when someone is part of the institution:
*He's at Ø **university/school/church**.*
*She's in Ø **prison/hospital**.*
*I got to Ø **college** at 8:30.* (I'm a student there – part of the college)
BUT *I got to **the** college at 8:30.* (the building I was visiting)

3 Before:
- people: *My name's Ø **Brad Pitt**.*
- most countries: *He lives in Ø **Germany**.*
- continents: *Have you been to Ø **Asia**?*
- counties: *They come from Ø **Yorkshire**.*
- villages/towns/cities: *She works in Ø **London**.*

- parks: *We went for a walk in Ø* **Hyde Park**.
- streets: *I did some shopping in Ø* **Oxford Street**.
  BUT **the** *High Street*.
- languages: *I speak Ø* **French**.
- sports: *He plays Ø* **golf**.
- plural parts of the body: *He's got Ø big* **ears**.
- illnesses: *Bob's had Ø* **appendicitis**.
- gerunds: *We often go Ø* **skating**.

4 Before meals and in most expressions of time/dates/seasons:
at Ø **breakfast**, *Ø* **last week**, *at Ø* **5:30**, *in Ø* **June**, *on Ø* **time**, *in Ø* **autumn**

5 In certain fixed expressions:
watch Ø **television** (but *listen to* **the** *radio*)
go to Ø **work/bed**, *go Ø* **home**
go by Ø **bus/train/car**

2 Countable and uncountable

A Countable nouns

Most common nouns are countable. Countable nouns can be singular or plural. They refer to things we can count (e.g. *one car, two cars*). We can use *a/an* with singular countable nouns:
I took **an** *umbrella and* **a** *coat with me.*

B Uncountable nouns

Uncountable nouns (usually) have no plural. We can't count liquids (*water*), materials (*wool*) or abstract qualities (*progress, behaviour*). We use *some/any* (or no article) with uncountable nouns, not *a/an*:
some/any progress (NOT ~~a progress/two progresses~~)
Some common uncountable nouns are:
accommodation, advice, behaviour, bread, butter, electricity, fun, food, furniture, health, information, knowledge, luggage, money, music, news, research, salt, scenery, spaghetti, traffic, travel, trouble, weather, work

C Countable and uncountable nouns

Some nouns can be either countable or uncountable:

Countable	Uncountable
a chicken (the animal)	*some chicken* (the meat)
chocolate (a sweet or a drink)	*chocolate* (the substance)
two coffees (two cups of coffee)	*some coffee* (the substance)
a glass (of milk)	*glass* (the substance)
a hair (a single hair)	*my hair* (the hair on my head)
have a good time (experience)	*I haven't any time.*
a good cheese (a variety of cheese)	*I like cheese.* (in general)
a paper (a newspaper)	*Have you got any paper?* (the material)
There are four rooms/spaces.	*Is there any room/space?* (it's crowded)
He's got two businesses.	*do business* (buy and sell)

2 Some uncountable nouns can be limited by using a countable expression:
a piece/bit of (bread, news, information, advice)
a drop of (water/milk)
a slice of (bread/toast/cake)
an item of (news)

3 Some determiners go with countable nouns (e.g. *many*), some with uncountable (e.g. *much*) and some can go with both (e.g. *a lot of*).
Note: there is a difference in meaning between *few/a few* and *little/a little*:
Countable:
There are a few (= some) *people.*
There are few (= not many) *people.*
Uncountable:
There's a little (= some) *time.*
There's little (= not much) *time.*

▶ page 61 for examples of determiners that go with countable and uncountable nouns.
▶ page 192 for articles with countable and uncountable nouns.

3 Adjectives

A Form of adjectives

1 Most common adjectives have no special endings (e.g. *large, rich*).

2 Sometimes we add a suffix to a noun or verb to form an adjective, e.g.:
comfort (n.) > *comfort**able*** (adj.)
live (v.) > *live**ly*** (adj.)
Some common adjective suffixes include:
noun > adjective: *wood**en**, sens**ible**, child**ish**, fam**ous**, music**al***
verb > adjective: *act**ive**, care**ful**, help**less**, sleep**y***

3 A number of adjectives end in *-ly* and look like adverbs e.g.: *live**ly**, friend**ly**, love**ly**, lone**ly**, dead**ly***

4 Some adjectives have the form of the past or present participle.
- *-ed* (past participle) adjectives describe our reaction to something/someone:
  I was very **bored** *with/by the play.*
- *-ing* (present participle) adjectives describe the thing/person/event/experience that causes the reaction:
  The play was very **boring**.
Other common pairs of participle adjectives include:
amused/amusing, annoyed/annoying, depressed/depressing, disappointed/disappointing, excited/exciting, interested/interesting, terrified/terrifying, tired/tiring

5 In two-part adjectives the second part is often a participle, e.g.:
well-known, beautifully-dressed, time-consuming

B Gradable and ungradable adjectives

1 An adjective which is gradable can be used in the comparative and superlative forms (e.g. *cold, colder, the coldest*). We can use an adverb of degree to make it stronger (e.g. **very** *cold*) or weaker (e.g. **fairly** *cold*).

2 Ungradable adjectives are extreme (e.g. *furious, awful*) or absolute e.g. (*dead, correct*). We can use an adverb which emphasises them, but not an adverb which makes them stronger or weaker:
absolutely *furious* (**very** *furious*)
completely *wrong* (**fairly** *wrong*)
totally *exhausted* (**rather** *exhausted*)

3 Adjective word order
Normally, no more than three adjectives go before the noun. Adjectives go in a particular order according to what type of adjective they are.
The order of adjectives is:
opinion/judgement + size + age + shape + colour + pattern + nationality + material (+noun):

a	**small**,	**red**,	**silk**	scarf
	(size)	(colour)	(material)	
a	**lovely**,	**old**,	**Italian**	car
	(opinion)	(age)	(nationality)	
a	**big**,	**round**,	**wooden**	table
	(size)	(shape)	(material)	

4 Adverbs

A Form of adverbs

1 In most cases, we add *-ly* to the adjective to form the adverb (e.g. *careful* > *careful**ly***).
If an adjective ends in *-ll*, we add *-y*, (e.g. *full* > *full**y***).
If an adjective ends in *-y*, the *-y* changes to *-i*, (e.g. *happy* > *happ**ily***).
In some cases other changes are needed:
fantastic > *fantastic**ally***, *remarkable* > *remarkab**ly***,
true > *tru**ly***

2 *Good* is an exception and is irregular: *good* > *well*

3 Some adjectives have *-ly* endings (e.g. *friend**ly**, live**ly**, lone**ly**, sil**ly***). We cannot add *-ly* to make these into adverbs. Instead we use *in a … way/manner/fashion*:
*He smiled **in a friendly way**.*

4 Some adverbs have the same form as adjectives (e.g. *fast, hard, straight, far, early*):
*He works **hard**.* (adv.) *He's a **hard** worker.* (adj.)

5 Some adverbs have two forms with different meanings:
*I worked **hard** all morning.*
*He has **hardly** changed at all.* (almost not)

*The bus came ten minutes **late**.*
*I've been feeling ill **lately**.* (recently)

B Position of adverbs

1 Different types of adverbs and adverb phrases can be used in different positions in a sentence, but not always in every position. The most 'neutral' position for adverbs is at the end of the sentence, but they can go in front/mid position for emphasis:
Front: **Occasionally** *he misses the bus.*
Middle: *He **occasionally** misses the bus.*
End: *He misses the bus **occasionally**.*
But NOT: *He misses ~~occasionally~~ the bus.* (between verb and object)

2 Most frequency adverbs (e.g. *always, often, never*) go before the main verb, but after the verb *be*:
*He **always walks** to work.*
*He **is always** late.*

3 Frequency adverbials (e.g. *every week, twice a year*) can't go in mid position:
Front: **Every summer** *we go there.*
End: *We go there **every summer**.*
But NOT: *We ~~every summer~~ go there.*
We go ~~every summer~~ there.

C Adverbs of degree

We use adverbs of degree to make adjectives and adverbs stronger or weaker.

1 The adverbs *very* and *extremely* collocate with most gradable adjectives:
very/extremely *impressive, lively, beautiful*

2 The adverb *absolutely* collocates with most ungradable adjectives:
absolutely *wonderful, gorgeous, exhausted*

3 Other adverbs often tend to collocate with certain adjectives although these collocations are not exclusive:
utterly *useless, delightful, miserable*
highly *skilled, educated*
totally *crazy, exhausted*
completely *different, relaxed*

4 The adverbs *quite* and *rather* can have more than one meaning, depending on the adjective/adverb they are used with.
- *quite* + adjective (= *moderately, fairly*)
  *The book was **quite** good. It was **quite** a good book.*
  *I like him. He's **quite** nice.*
  (This use is not common in American English.)
- *quite* + ungradable adjective/adverb (= *completely/absolutely*)
  *The news was **quite** extraordinary.*
  *He was **quite** right to make a complaint.*
- *rather* + negative adjective (= *moderately*)
  *He's **rather** a lazy student./He's **a rather** lazy student.*
- *rather* + positive adjective (= *very*)
  *She's **rather** good at maths.*

5 Comparatives and superlatives

A Types of comparison

1 We use the comparative form + *than*, or *as … as* to compare two or more things:
*Chloe is a **better** swimmer **than** Hannah.* (to a higher degree)
*Harry is **as** good a mathematician **as** Ryan.* (to the same degree)
*Amy is **less** confident **than** Katie.* (to a lower degree)
*Amy is **not as** confident **as** Katie.* (to a lower degree)

2 We use the superlative form when we want to pick out one thing from all the others:
*Mount Everest is **the highest mountain** in the world.*

B Adjectives

1 Regular adjectives

		Comparative	Superlative
One syllable	old	old**er**	*(the)* old**est**
	large	larg**er**	*(the)* larg**est**
One syllable with one vowel + one consonant at the end	big	big**ger**	*(the)* big**gest**
One or two syllables with -*y* at the end	happy	happ**ier**	*(the)* happ**iest**
Two or more syllables	careful	**more** careful	*(the)* **most** careful

2 Exceptions
- one syllable adjectives:
*I feel **more ill** today than I did yesterday.*
*I feel **colder** OR **more cold** today than I did yesterday.*
*We got more and **more lost**.* (adjectives formed from past participles)
- some common two-syllable adjectives (e.g. *clever, gentle, simple, shallow, narrow, pleasant, cruel, polite, quiet, stupid*):
*clever – clever**er** (OR **more** clever) – **(the)** clever**est** (OR **(the) most** clever)*
- two-syllable adjectives ending with -*y*:
*He looks much **happier** (OR **more happy**) these days.*
- ungradable adjectives (e.g. *superior, unique, fundamental*) do not have a comparative form.

C Adverbs

1 We don't use *more/(the)most* with adverbs which have the same form as adjectives (e.g. *hard, fast, early, long, quick*):
*fast – fast**er** – (the) fast**est***
*early – earl**ier** – (the)earl**iest***

2 With most other adverbs we use *more/(the)most*:
***more** carefully/(the) **most** carefully*
Note: in informal English you will sometimes hear -*er*/-*est* adjectives instead of the more 'correct' *more/most* adverbs:
*He drove much **slower** than usual.* (instead of *much more slowly*)

D Irregular adjectives/adverbs

	Comparative	Superlative
good/well	better	*(the)* best
bad/badly	worse	*(the)* worst
much	more	*(the)* most
little	less	*(the)* least
far	farther/further	*(the)* farthest/furthest
old	elder/older	*(the)* oldest/eldest

E Sentence patterns

1 Comparative + *than*:
*The meat is more expensive **than** the fish.*
*He's taller **than me**.* (*than* + object pronoun)
*He's taller **than I am**.* (*than* + subject pronoun + verb)
Note: the *than* clause is sometimes not stated:
Fish is getting more expensive these days. (i.e. than it was before.)

2 *the* + superlative + *in/of*:
*The bathroom is **the** biggest room **in** the house.*
*She's **the** brightest student **in** the class.*
*Today is **the** shortest day **of** the year.*
Note: *the* is not always used with the superlative form:
Try your hardest!
Jack and Jessica were best.

3 *the* + superlative + clause:
*It's **the** fastest car **(that) I've ever driven**.*

4 *less/(the) least* (the opposite of *more/(the) most*):
*He's **the least intelligent person** (that) I know.*
*He's **less intelligent than** his sister.*
Note: more commonly used:
*He's **not as** intelligent **as** his sister.*

5 Comparing quantities
- We use *more/less/the most/the least* to compare quantities:
*She spends **more/less** (money) than her brother does.*
*She earns **the most/least** (money).*
- In formal style *fewer/fewest* is used before plural nouns:
*There are **more/fewer** (of us) here each year.* (plural countable noun)
*I spend **more/less** (of my) time on the golf course.* (uncountable noun)

6 Common modifiers ▶ page 12:
*The book was **a lot/much/far/a great (good) deal** more (less) interesting than I thought.* (a big difference)
*The film was **a bit/a little/slightly/rather** more (less) interesting than the book.* (a small difference)

7 Expressions:
*In the next few years the Internet will get **quicker and quicker**.* (to show an increase)
*It's getting **hotter and hotter**.*
*The **earlier** we leave, **the earlier** we get there.* (the two changes go together)
***The better** the weather, **the more crowded** the roads get.*
***The less** you earn, **the less** you have to spend.*
***The sooner, the better**.*

6 Clauses

A Identifying clauses in sentences

1 A clause has a subject and a verb, and it either forms a sentence:
I was walking home
or part of a sentence:
… when I met Pete.

2 There are many ways of joining clauses in sentences, e.g.:
words like *which* (relative clauses: ▶ page 186)
if (conditionals: ▶ pages 191–192)
than (comparatives and superlatives: ▶ page 185)
(said) that (reported speech: ▶ pages 193–194)
when (time: ▶ page 55)

B Clauses of reason, purpose, result and contrast

1 Clauses of reason (*Why?*):
*He couldn't see **because** he wasn't wearing his glasses.*
Other connecting words/expressions include:
because of/for/owing to/due to (+ noun)
as/since (+ subject + verb)
seeing/owing to the fact/due to the fact (that + subject + verb)

2 Clauses of purpose (*What for?*):
*I looked in the dictionary **to** check the meaning.*
Other connecting words/expressions include:
in order to/so as to (+ infinitive)
in order that/so that/in case, for fear (that) (+ subject + verb)
Note: we can also say:
*I looked in the dictionary **because** I wanted to check the meaning.*

3 Clauses of result:
*I feel **so** tired **that** I'm going to bed.*
Other connecting words/expressions include:
so much/so many … that and *such a … that* (+ subject + verb)

4 Clauses of contrast:
*I went to work **despite** the fact that I felt very tired.*
Other connecting words/expressions include:
• *in spite of/despite* (+ noun/present participle/perfect participle):
  She fell asleep, in spite of the cold.
  She stayed awake, despite being tired.
• *although/though/even though/even if/much as/whereas/ while/however/no matter how (much/many/badly)/in spite of the fact that* (+ subject + verb)
Note: *while* and *whereas* contrast ideas that don't contradict each other:
*Nurses' salaries have risen **while/whereas** doctors' salaries have fallen.*

C Participle clauses

▶ page 85 for participles used in reduced relative clauses.

In participle clauses the subject of the participle must be the same as the subject of the main clause.
Being a French teacher (= me), *I speak French very well.*

1 Present participles:
*I stayed awake all night, **thinking** about our life together.* (– *and thought*)
***After phoning** you, I realised my mistake.* (time: = *After I phoned*)
***In/On trying** to open the door, I broke my key.* (time: = *While I was trying*)
***Being** a pilot, I knew how to fly the plane.* (reason: = *As I was a pilot*)
***Having** a pilot's licence, I knew… .* (reason: = *As I had …*)
*I wrote **telling** her the news.* (purpose: = *in order to tell her*)
***Despite not feeling** well, I went into work* (contrast: = *Despite the fact that I didn't feel well*)
*The man **living** next door is an old friend of mine.* (relatives: = *who lives*)

2 Perfect participles:
***Having done** most of the course I want to finish it.* (reason: = *Since I've done* – active)
***Having been given** a pay rise, I decided to celebrate.* (time: = *After I had been given* – passive)

3 Past participles:
Past participles are used for passives and are found more in writing than conversation:
***Seen** from this distance, it looks quite attractive.* (= *When it is seen*)
***Although built** fairly recently, it looks quite old.* (= *Although it was built*)
*Cars **made** in Japan are very common in Europe.* (= *which are made*)

7 Relative clauses

A Relative pronouns in clauses

Relative clauses provide additional information about a noun, a clause or a sentence. They begin with a relative pronoun.

Noun	Relative pronouns
people	*who (whom, that)*
things (animals)	*that (which)*
time	*when*
place	*where (which* + preposition)
possession	*whose*

Note: the relative pronouns *what/who* can be used without a noun:
*They didn't know **what** (the thing) **I wanted/who** (the person) **I meant.***
***What** (the thing) **I saw** was amazing.*

B Defining relative clauses

1 Defining relative clauses (without commas) provide essential information:

*The man **who/that bought the jacket** is over there.* (people)
*That's the car **which/that won the race**.* (things)
*It was the moment **when I knew for sure**.* (time)
*He's the man **whose house is for sale**.* (possession)
*That's the house **where Sam lives**.* (places)

2 We usually place a preposition at the end of a relative clause:
*That's the house **which I used to live in**.* (places)
But we place a preposition before the relative pronoun in more formal English:
*The delivery date for your goods will depend on the postcode area **in which you live**.*
We also place a preposition before the relative pronoun when the relative clause is very long:
*This is the letter **in which** he said he was looking forward to coming home.*

3 The relative pronoun can be left out if is the object of the verb in the relative clause:
*The film (which/that) **we saw** was three hours long.*

4 Participle clauses (see also page 83) and infinitives can sometimes replace relative clauses.
*People **buying** this product will be disappointed.* (= who buy)
*The car **parked** outside belongs to Tara.* (= which is parked)
*The last person **to leave** the office should switch the lights off.* (= who leaves)

C Non-defining relative clauses

1 Non-defining relative clauses are more common in written English than spoken English. They provide extra information (between commas) not essential to the sentence. The sentence would make sense without the clause:
*My mother, **who lives in Scotland**, is 94.*
*She was ill, **which was very unusual for her**.* (Here *which* refers to the whole main clause, not just the subject.)

2 After numbers and words like *some, many, most, neither*:
*There were a lot of people in the house, **some of whom** I'd met before.*
*I did German and Italian at university, **neither of which** I had learnt before.*

3 *That* is not used in non-defining clauses and object pronouns cannot be omitted:
*This book, **which** my father gave me, is over 50 years old.*
(NOT *This book, ~~that~~ my father gave me, …*)

8 Verb forms: the present

A Present habit

1 The present simple is used for:
- habits:
  *I **clean** my teeth every night.*
- permanent or long-term situations:
  *I **come** from Australia.*
  *They **live** near the sea.*
- permanent facts:
  *Ice **melts** in the heat.*

Typical time expressions used with the present simple include:
usually, always, never, hardly ever, as often as I can, twice a day, whenever I can

2 Present continuous (+ *always*) and *keep* (*on*) + *-ing* are used for surprising or annoying habits. (for things which happen very often/too often):
*Kate's **always giving** me chocolates. I don't know why!*
*She's **always saying** silly things. (It's annoying.)*
*She **keeps (on) saying** silly things.*

3 We use *tend to* for things that usually happen:
*He **tends to** interfere in other people's business.*
*Men **don't tend to/tend not to** live as long as women.*

4 We use *will* for:
- the typical way a person behaves:
  *My brother **will** sit for hours just reading a book.* (with a time expression e.g. *for hours*)
- stating what you think/assume is true:
  *That'**ll** be your sister on the phone. Can you answer it?*

B Present state

The present simple is used with certain verbs which describe a state rather than an action:
*I **like** college.*
*That cake **looks** good.*
*I **believe** you.*
These are 'state' verbs, such as verbs of:
- appearing: (e.g. *appear, seem, look*)
- thinking (e.g. *doubt, feel, gather, know, mean, remember, think, understand, expect*)
- feeling (e.g. *dislike, hate, love, want, wish, prefer*)
- sensing (e.g. *hear, see, smell, taste, sound*)
- owning (e.g. *belong, need, owe, own*)

These verbs are not normally used in the continuous, except when they describe a mental or physical action or process:
*I'**m thinking** of you all the time.* (mental action)
*He's **appearing** in a new film.* (physical action)

2 Other verbs for which we usually use the present simple include:
promise, refuse, agree, deny, depend, fit, mean, involve, matter

C Present event/situation

The present continuous is used for:
- something happening now: *I'**m watching** TV at the moment.*
- a temporary situation: *She's **studying** economics.*
- a changing/developing situation: *It's **getting** dark.*

Typical time expressions used with the present continuous include:
at present, currently, at the moment, for the time being, today

9 Verb forms: present perfect

A Present perfect simple

Form: *have* + past participle.
The present perfect simple is used to talk about past actions and situations in a time period that is unfinished:
I've lived in China. (in my life, which is unfinished)
The taxi's arrived. (it's here now)
I've lived in this house for ten years. (the ten-year period until now)
Note: *gone* and *been* are both used to make the present perfect of *go*, but with different meanings:
He's gone to London (he's in London now)
He's been to London (it's a past experience; he isn't in London now)

The uses of the present perfect simple include:

1 Experience:
   Have you ever met a famous person? (= at any time)
   I've never lived abroad. (= at no time)
   He's travelled widely.
   NOT *I have ever lived*

2 Things (recently) completed in the past with a result now:
   I've hurt my leg. I can't walk. (past event – we are not thinking *when* it happened, but it's relevant now)
   Look! The aircraft's just landed. (= a short time ago)
   Note: *just* always goes before the main verb.

3 Things that have happened (or not happened) up to now:
   * *yet* (up to now – but we expect it to happen):
     Have you read the letter yet?
     I haven't read it yet. (NOT *I have read it yet.*)
     Note: *yet* comes at the end of the sentence and is used only in questions and negative sentences.
   * *still* (up to now – but we expected it to happen by now):
     They still haven't called me.
     (NOT *They have still called me.*)
   * *already* (before now)
     Have you already seen this film?
     Yes, I've already seen it.
     Note: *already* goes before the main verb or at the end of the sentence and is used in questions and positive sentences.
   Other adverbials used with the present perfect include *so far* and *up to now, recently*.

4 Unfinished actions or states which started in the past and continue now:
   I've lived in this town for five years.
   (NOT *I live in this town for…*)
   She's been a teacher since she left university.
   Note: to answer *How long…?* we use *for* and *since*:
   * *for* with a period of time: *for three weeks*
     (NOT *during three weeks*)
   * *since* with a point of time: *since 2000, since last week, since three weeks ago*

B Present perfect continuous

Form: *have* + *been* + *-ing*.
The present perfect continuous is used to talk about activities in a period of time that is unfinished. It places focus on the activity in progress, not the finished action.

1 Recent temporary activity:
   I've been reading a good book.

2 Recent repeated/extended activity:
   Your brother has been ringing.
   She's been playing tennis all morning.

3 Present perfect continuous/present perfect simple
   * the present perfect continuous focuses on the activity, not on whether the activity is finished or not. The present perfect simple can be used to focus on completion of an activity:
     'Why are you so dirty?' 'I've been cleaning my room.'
     (maybe the cleaning is finished, maybe not.)
     I've cleaned my room. Do you want to see it? (the cleaning is finished)
   * the present perfect continuous is also used for temporary situations which may change:
     I've been living in this house for two years. (I still live here but it's probably temporary.)
     I've lived in this house for two years. (I still live here and I probably won't move.)
   * *be, know* and other state verbs are not normally used in the continuous:
     She's been a teacher since 1999. (NOT *She's been being* …)
     ▶ page 187 for state verbs.

10 Verb forms: past time

A Past simple

Form: regular verb + *-ed* (*stay* > *stayed*); but there are many verbs with irregular forms (*see* > *saw*, *go* > *went*).
The past simple is usually used with a definite time expression (e.g. *last night, two years ago*) to talk about completed actions in past time.

1 Completed actions at a particular time in the past:
   I went to Rome last Thursday.

2 Completed situations over a definite period of time in the past:
   I worked in a bank when I was younger.

3 Repeated actions/situations in the past:
   We went to the beach every summer. (past habit)

4 Actions which happen quickly one after the other:
   When I arrived they turned off the television and started cooking.

Note: the past simple is also used in reported speech
(▶ page 193) and to talk about unreal situations
(▶ pages 191–192 for Conditionals and 195 for *wish*).

B Past continuous

Form: *was/were + -ing* (e.g. *was living*).
The past continuous is used in the following ways.

1 At a particular time in the past when we were in the middle of a (temporary) action/situation:
*On Friday night we **were listening** to a CD.*
Sometimes the action/situation is interrupted by a shorter event (in the past simple):
*We **were listening** to a CD when the telephone **rang**.*
Sometimes other people are doing things at the same time:
*We **were listening** to a CD while my brother **was reading** a book.*

2 Background descriptions:
*(We went out into the street.) It **was raining** hard and people **were carrying** umbrellas.*

3 Describing typical behaviour with *always*:
*She **was always smoking** in the house.*

4 To talk about planned events that did not happen:
*We **were meeting** Jane the next day but she didn't come.*
Notes:
- we use the past continuous to focus on the activity or its effect on us. We are not saying whether or not the action is completed. With the past simple, the action is always completed.
- with state verbs such as *have, seem, know*, etc. we usually use the past simple not the past continuous:
*(I **knew** him well. NOT I ~~was knowing~~ him well.)*
  ▶ page 187 for state verbs.

C Past perfect simple

Form: *had* + past participle (*had visited*).
The past perfect simple is used when we talk about actions or events before a past time:
*When we got to the airport the plane **had** already **left**.*
However, if the order of events is clear, we often prefer the past simple:
*The plane left before we **got** there.*
Note: the past perfect simple is also used in reported speech.
▶ pages 193–194 to talk about unreal situations.
▶ pages 191–192 for Conditionals and 195 for *wish*.

D Past perfect continuous

Form: *had + been + -ing* (e.g. *had been working*)
We use the past perfect continuous for an activity over a period of time up to a specific time/event in the past:
*Before I came to London I **had been working** in Paris.*
*They **had been waiting** for an hour when the bus finally arrived.*
Notes:
- we use the past perfect continuous to focus on the activity or its effect on us, not the completed action.
- with state verbs (*seem, know, understand*, etc.) we usually use the past perfect simple not the past perfect continuous (▶ page 187 for state verbs):
*It **had seemed** difficult to do. (NOT It ~~had been seeming~~…)*

E Past habit

1 Past simple + adverb of frequency can be used for past habits:
*Every day I **got up** at 7 a.m. and **went** to work by bus.*

2 *Used to* for states/habits which are no longer true:
*I **used to** live in Edinburgh.* (state)
*I **used to** go out every Friday.* (habit)

3 We can use *would* for habits – but NOT states – which are no longer true:
*When I was younger, I **would** go out every Friday.*
(but NOT When I was younger I ~~would live~~ in London.)

4 We can use *kept (on)* to suggest criticism of a habit:
*He **kept (on)** talking while I was trying to sleep.*

11 Verb forms: the future

A Future forms

A variety of forms can be used to talk about the future:
- *be going to* + infinitive
- present continuous (▶ page 187)
- *shall/will* + infinitive
- present simple (▶ page 187)
- *be to* + infinitive
- *be due to/be about to* + infinitive
- *be on the point of* + *-ing*
- future continuous (*will/shall/going to + be + -ing*)
- future perfect (*will/going to + have* + past participle)
- future perfect continuous (*will + have + been + -ing*)

B Future meanings

1 Planned events
- we use *going to* for things we've already decided/intentions:
I'm going to buy a new suitcase. My old one broke last week.
- present continuous (+ a time expression) is used for arrangements:
I'm taking my driving test tomorrow. I applied a few weeks ago.
- we use the future continuous for a planned/routine action without personal intention – polite:
Will you be going to the meeting tomorrow? If so, could you give my apologies?
Note: state verbs like *feel, know*, etc. are not normally used in the continuous. ▶ page 187 for state verbs.

2 Fixed events
- present simple (+ a time expression) is used for public timetables and programmes:
*The bus **leaves** in half an hour.*
*My French classes **finish** next week.*
- *is/are to* for formal official arrangements:
*The Queen **is to visit** Australia next year.*

3 Unplanned events
We use *will/shall* for events decided more or less at the moment of speaking (e.g. offers, promises, requests, refusals, decisions):

*That looks heavy. **Shall** I help you?/**I'll** help you.*
*It's cold in here. **Will** you close the door?* (request)
*I **won't** lend her any money. She never pays it back.*

4 Predictions
- *be going to* is used when we notice something in the present which will make something happen:
  *I feel ill. I think **I'm going to** be sick.*
  *It's very cloudy. I'm sure it's **going to** rain.*
- we use *will/'ll* when we expect something to happen – it is our opinion based on experience/knowledge:
  *We'll be there/We **won't** be there before midnight.*
  *The sun **will** rise at 6:30 a.m. tomorrow.*
- To show how sure we are about something we use phrases like:
  I expect/I'm sure/I think/I don't think (we'll be late).
  or modals (▶ page 103):
  *We **may/might/could** be there before midnight.*

5 For events close to happening we can use *about to* or *on the point of*:
  *She's **about to** burst into tears.*
  *She's **on the point of** bursting into tears*
  We can use *due to* for more planned events:
  *The bus **is due to** arrive at nine o'clock tomorrow.*

6 The future continuous is used for action in progress at a fixed time in the future:
  *I'll **be lying** on a beach when you get this card.*

7 The future perfect is used for something completed before a specific time in the future:
  *We'll **have finished** before you get back.*
  (OR *We **may** have finished … if it is less sure.*)

8 We use the future perfect continuous for something that may not be completed/may be ongoing at a specific time in the future:
  *I'll **have been learning** English for five years by the time I take the exam.*

9 Future in the past: sometimes when we are talking about the past, we want to refer to something that was in the future at that point in the past. We use the same structures that we use for talking about the future, but change the verb forms:
  *I **was going to** come but I changed my mind.*
  *We arrived at the building where the interview **was to** take place.*

10 The present simple is used in time clauses with future meaning and Type 1 conditional clauses:
   *When you **see** Tom, give him a big kiss for me.* (time clause)
   *If the Beach Café **is** full, we'll go to Maxim's instead.* (Type 1 conditional)

12 Modals

Modals express our attitudes and emotions to an event or situation. The modal auxiliary verbs are: *can, could, may, might, must, will, would, shall, should, ought to* and *need*.

There are other non-modal verbs and expressions (e.g. *be able to, have to, allow*) which we can sometimes use instead of modal verbs.

A Form

Present time:		Past time:		
modal	+ infinitive	modal	+ *have*	+ past participle
You can	go.	*You* could	have	gone.

Notes:
- *he/she/it can go* (there is no change in the third person)
- modal verbs have no infinitive form

B Permission

1 *Can, could* and *may* are used to talk about permission:
- *can*:
  ***Can** I go out? Is that all right?* (asking for permission)
  *He **can** go to the cinema on his own. That's OK.* (giving permission)
- *could*:
  ***Could** I borrow some money?* (asking for permission – more polite than *Can I…?*)
  *She said that I **could** go to the party.* (reporting permission)
- *may*:
  ***May I** leave class early today? I've got a job interview.* (asking for permission – for more formal situations)

2 Other non-modal verbs and expressions can be used to talk about permission:
- *let* + object + infinitive
  *My parents **let me go** to concerts with my friends.*
  Note: *let* does not have a passive form.
- *allow (to)*
  *They **allow her to watch** TV.* (*allow* + object + *to*-infinitive)
  *I **was allowed to leave** class early today.* (passive + *to*-infinitive)
  Note: in a sentence like this, where the permission resulted in an action, we can't use *could*
  (NOT *I ~~could~~ leave the class early today*).
- *permit (to)*
  *You **are permitted to smoke** only in the designated areas.*
  *Smoking **is permitted** only in the designated areas.* (rules made by someone else – more formal than *allow*)

C Prohibition

1 *Can't, couldn't, mustn't* and *may not* are used to talk about prohibition:
- *can't*:
  *He **can't** go to a nightclub. He's too young.* (prohibition)
- *couldn't* (past form of *can*):
  *He said I **couldn't** use it.* (he refused permission)
- *mustn't*:
  *You **mustn't** talk in the library. Please be quiet!* (direct order)
  Note: the past form of this sentence is :
  *I **wasn't allowed to** talk in the library.*

- *may not*:
  *Candidates **may not** leave the room during the exam.* (prohibition)

2 Other non-modal expressions can be used to talk about prohibition and rules that are made by someone else:
- *not supposed (to)*
  *You're **not supposed to** park here.*
- *allow (to)*
  *My manager **won't allow me to take** the day off.*
  *You're **not allowed to take** photographs here.*
- *permit (to)*
  *You **are not permitted to smoke** in here.*
  *Smoking **is not permitted** here.* (more formal than *allow*)
- *forbid/ban*
  *Cars are **forbidden/banned** in the town centre.* (prohibition – very strong)
  Note: *forbid* is more likely to be used in formal notices than when speaking.

D Obligation and necessity

1 We use *must/mustn't* to express strong obligation or necessity:
- *must* (stronger than *should/had better*):
  *I **must** post the letter straightaway.* (I, personally, feel it is necessary)
  Note: For the future of *must* we use *will/'ll have to* and for the past we use *had to*:
  *I'll **have to** hurry or I'll miss the last bus.*
  *She **had to** go home because she felt ill.*
- *mustn't* (stronger than *shouldn't*):
  *You **mustn't** forget your keys.* (an obligation NOT to do something)

2 Other non-modal verbs can be used to talk about strong obligation and necessity:
- *have (got) to* is used when the situation or someone else (not the speaker) makes it necessary:
  *I **have to** work late tonight. My boss says so.*
  *We'll **have to** invite my mother next time.* (the situation makes it necessary)
  *I **had to** go to the doctor's yesterday.* (past time – it was necessary)
- *make* is used for a strong obligation imposed by someone else:
  *Her parents **make** her wash the dishes.* (*make* + object + infinitive)
  *She **is made to** wash the dishes.* (passive + *to*-infinitive)

3 *Should/shouldn't, ought to/ought not to* are used to express a slightly less strong obligation or a duty/responsibility:
  *You **should/ought to** phone and let them know you'll be late.*
  *They **shouldn't** leave without permission.*

4 *Should have/ought to have* is used when something was the right thing to do, but you didn't do it:
  *You **should have/ought to have** had an early night last night. You look tired.* (you didn't go to bed early)
  Note: *shouldn't have* is commonly used, but *ought not to have* is rare.

5 *Supposed to* is a non-modal expression we use to talk about our responsibilities and the correct way of doing things:
  *What time **are we supposed to** be at the office?*

E Lack of obligation/necessity

1 We use *don't have to/haven't got to, needn't/don't need to, needn't have* and *didn't need to* to express lack of obligation or necessity:
- *don't have to/haven't got to*
  *You **don't have to** wash those dishes. They're clean.* (it's not necessary)
  Note: *have got to* is more informal than *have to*.
  We use *didn't have to* as the past form of both *don't have to* and *haven't got to*:
  *I **didn't have to** go to the doctor's yesterday.* (it wasn't necessary)
- *needn't/don't need to*
  *You **needn't/don't need to** wash those dishes. They're clean.* (it's not necessary)
  Note: *need* can be a modal verb (negative = *needn't*) or an ordinary verb (negative = *don't need*).
- We use both *needn't have* (modal verb) and *didn't need to* (ordinary verb) when we talk about past time, but they have different meanings:
  *There were plenty of seats on the train. We **didn't need to** stand.* (It wasn't necessary.)
  *There were plenty of seats on the train. We **needn't have** stood.* (It wasn't necessary, but we did stand.)

F Advice and recommendation

1 *Should(n't)/should have, ought to/ought to have* are used to give advice and recommendations. (*Ought to* is less commonly used than *should*.)
  *You **should** see it – it's a great film.* (recommendation)
  *You **shouldn't/ought not to** go to work today – you really don't look well.* (advice)
  Note: the past forms *should have/shouldn't have* suggest criticism:
  *You **should have** told me you weren't coming. I waited for ages.*
  *He **shouldn't have** shouted at me.*

2 The non-modal expression *had better (not)* is stronger than *should/shouldn't*:
  *It's cold. You**'d better** wear a coat.* (it's the best thing to do)
  *Hurry up! We**'d better not** be late.*

▶ page 103 for modals of speculation and deduction.
▶ page 118 for modals of ability.

13 Conditionals

We can categorise conditionals into three main groups:
- likely or real events/situations:
  If you go out later, can you please turn out the light?
- unlikely (or imaginary) events/situations:
  If I had four million euros, I'd buy a big house in Spain.
- unreal events/situations in the past
  If I'd arrived late again, my boss would have been furious.

Notes:

- the main clause can come before the *if* clause in conditional sentences, but the punctuation is different:
  If it rains, we won't have a picnic. (a comma comes after the *if* clause)
  We won't have a picnic if it rains. (there is no comma between the clauses)

A Likely/real conditionals (Type 1 and zero)

1 Type 1 conditionals are used for events/situations that are likely to happen:

- present + modal (with present/future meaning)
  If there's a good film on TV, I'll watch it. (possible/likely situation + result)

  *If you **need** a ticket,*   *I **can** get you one.* (offer)
                       I'll get you one. (promise)
                       *I **might** be able to get you one.* (possibility)

- present + *going to*
  *If there's a good film on TV, I'm definitely **going to** watch it.*
- present + imperative
  *If the phone **rings**, please **answer** it.* (instruction – for a possible event)
- other conjunctions can be used to introduce conditions (e.g. *as long as, provided that, even if, unless*):
  *I'll kill you **unless** you turn that music down!* (= if you don't)
  *She won't go, **even if** she's invited.* (= whether or not)
  *I'll cook dinner, **as long as** you do the washing-up.* (= only if)

Notes:

- If we are sure something will happen, we use *when*:
  ***When** I leave school, I'm going to become a teacher.* (NOT ~~If I leave~~ …)

2 A 'zero conditional' is used for facts that are always true. We use a zero conditional when both events happen and *if* means *when*:

- present + present:
  *If/When you **press** this switch, the television **comes** on.* (always true/normal event/fact)
- past + past:
  *If/When the weather **was** bad, we always **stayed** indoors.* (past habits)

3 There are other possible patterns for situations/events which are likely or possible:

- modal + modal/imperative:
  If you'll just wait a moment, I'll see what I can do. (request)
  *If you **should** get lost, **go** into the Tourist Office.* (less likely, but possible)
  *If it'll help you to sleep, **open** the window.* (result)
- present continuous + modal/imperative:
  *If you're **expecting** someone, I **can** leave.*
- present perfect + modal/imperative:
  *If you've **finished** your work, we **can** go.*

B Unlikely/imaginary conditionals (Type 2)

1 Type 2 conditionals are used for unlikely or imaginary events/situations in the present or future. In Type 2 conditionals:

- past + *would/could/might* + infinitive:
  *If you **went** abroad, you **might learn** something about foreign cultures.* (unlikely that you will go, but possible)
  *If you **were driving** to London, which way **would** you **go**?* (imaginary – you're not driving)
  *If he **didn't have** a car, he'd **find** it difficult to get to work.* (imaginary – he has a car)
- both *was* and *were* can be used with *If I/he/she/it …* :
  *If I **were** rich, I wouldn't work.*
  *If I **was** rich, I wouldn't work.* (not normally used in formal English)
- *were* can start the sentence and replace *if* in formal English:
  ***Were** you really ill, I'd look after you, but you're perfectly OK.*
- *should* is sometimes used instead of *would* after *I* and *we* in more formal contexts (e.g. formal letters):
  *I **should** be grateful if you would contact me … .*

2 We can use Type 2 conditionals for offers, suggestions, advice and requests:
   *I **wouldn't do** it if I **were** you.* (advice)
   ***Would** you **mind** if I **used** your phone?* (request)
   An offer can be made more or less direct, depending on the type of conditional used:
   Type 1: *If you **need** the key, I **can** probably find it.* (direct)
   Type 2: *If you **needed** the key, I **could** probably find it.* (less direct/I'm less sure you need the key)
   Type 3: *If you **were to need** the key, I **could** probably find it.* (even more tentative, polite)
   Note: polite requests can also be made using *If you would …* :
   *If you **would** take your seats, ladies and gentlemen, we'll **start** the meeting.*

C Unreal/imaginary conditionals in the past (Type 3)

1 Type 3 conditionals are used for unreal or imaginary events/situations in the past. They are often used to express regret or criticism:

- past perfect + *would/could/might* + *have* + past participle:
  *If I **had heard** the alarm, I **would have** woken up on time.* (but I didn't hear it so I overslept.)
  *I **would have** helped her if she had asked me.* (but she didn't, so I didn't help.)
- *had* at the start of the sentence can replace *if* (formal):
  ***Had** you been ill, I would have looked after you.*

2 It is possible to mix conditionals Type 2 and 3, particularly when a past event has an effect in the present:
   *I **would be married** now if I'd **had** the courage to propose to her.*
   *If you **were** more intelligent, you **would have thought** about that before.*

▶ page 195 for *wish/if only*.

14 Passives

In passive sentences, the action, event or process is more important than who or what does the action:
*Fruit **is picked** in the autumn.*
If we want to mention the 'person doing the action', we use *by*:
*I **was robbed** last night **by** a man in a dark jacket.*

A Forms

		to be	+ past participle
present simple		is	
present continuous		is being	
past simple		was	
past continuous		was being	
present perfect		has been	
past perfect	It	had been	made in Taiwan.
be going to		is going to be	
will		will be	
future perfect		will have been	
present/future modal		may be	
past modal		must have been	

Negative: *It **wasn't made** in Europe.*
Question: ***Was** it **made** in Taiwan?*
Note: verbs that do not take an object (e.g. *arrive*) do not have a passive form: (NOT *She ~~was arrived~~.*)

B Sentence structure

1 In an active sentence the subject is the person/thing that does the action. In a passive sentence the subject is the person/thing to which something happens:

Active:	subject	active verb	object
	Tracey Emin	*won*	*the prize.*
Passive:	subject	passive verb	agent
	The prize	*was won*	*by Tracey Emin.*

2 In a sentence with two objects there are two possible sentence structures, but usually we make the person the subject of the passive sentence:

Active:	subject	active verb	indirect object	+ direct object
	He	*gave*	*Sue*	*a CD.*

Passive: *Sue was given a CD.*
(*A CD was given to Sue* is possible but less likely.)

3 We can use the passive with 'reporting verbs' (e.g. *say, expect, suppose, agree, know, think, understand, claim*) to talk about an opinion held by some people/a lot of people/experts, etc. The following patterns can be used:
 • subject + passive + *to*-infinitive:
   Our team   was expected   to do well.
   It   is supposed   to be a fine day tomorrow.
 • It + passive + *that*
   It   has been agreed   that we have to make improvements.

4 Some verbs (*see, hear, make, help, know*) are followed by an infinitive (without *to*) when they are active, but a *to*-infinitive when passive:
*They **heard** him **shout**. > He **was heard to shout**.*

C Use of passives

1 Passives are more often used in written language (e.g. newspapers, reports, scientific writing, notices and announcements). They can often sound formal and impersonal:
*Customers **are requested** not to leave their bags unattended.*

2 Passives can be used to take personal responsibility away from the speaker:
*Income tax **will be increased** next year.*

3 We sometimes use passives to continue the theme of what is being talked about. In the following sentence the new information – *Beethoven* – is put at the end for emphasis:
*This is a marvellous symphony. It **was written** by Beethoven.*

4 Passives are also used when information about who does something is expressed in a long phrase:
*He **was given** a box of chocolates by a woman wearing a dark coat and black boots.*

5 In informal English we can sometimes use *get* + past participle with a passive meaning, for things that happen by accident or unexpectedly:
*The postman **got bitten** by a dog. (= was bitten)*
*How **did** your car **get damaged**? (= who/what was it damaged by?)*

15 Reported speech

'I want to give you something,' he said. (direct speech)
*He **said** (that) he **wanted** to give me something.* (reported speech.)

A Reporting statements

1 To report something said in the past, we normally change forms one step back in time. This is sometimes called 'backshift':

Direct speech	Reported speech
Present:	
*I **don't like** you.*	> *She said she **didn't like** me.*
*What **are** you **doing**?*	> *He wanted to know what I **was doing**.*
Present perfect:	
*I've never **been** to China.*	> *He said he **had** never **been** to China.*
Past:	
*I **saw** him.*	> *He said he **had seen** him.*
*I **was having** lunch.*	> *He said he'**d been having** lunch.*
Future:	
*I'**ll help** you.*	> *She said she **would help** me.*
*We'**re going** out.*	> *They said they **were** going out.*
Some modals:	
*I **can't** read it.*	> *He said he **couldn't** read it.*
*We **must** go.*	> *They said they **had to** go.*
*I **may** be late.*	> *She said she **might** be late.*

2 No backshift is needed with:
- past perfect:
  *I **had seen** him.* > *He said he **had seen** him.*
- modals: *would, should, might, could, ought to*:
  *We **might** go out for meal.* > *They said they **might** go out for a meal.*

3 Sometimes backshift is needed with other forms, depending on the context:
*He **said** he **wanted** to give me something.* (reporting the past)
*He **said** he **wants** to give me something.* (we are emphasising it is still true)
*He **said** he **had wanted** to give me something.* (to emphasise one thing happened before the other)
*He **had said** he **had wanted** to give me something but he changed his mind.* (*said/wanted* happened before *changed his mind*)

4 Some changes in common time and place words are:

Direct speech		Reported speech
today	>	that day
tomorrow	>	the next day/the following day
next (week)	>	the following (week)
yesterday	>	the day before, the previous day
last (year)	>	the (year) before/the previous (year)
this	>	that
here	>	there
come	>	go
bring	>	take

B Reporting questions

To report questions:
- we use a reporting verb (e.g. *ask, want to know, wonder*) and the same word order as in statements:
  'Do you like science fiction films?' > *He asked **if I liked** science fiction films.*
- Yes/No questions – use *if* or *whether*:
  'Are you coming with us?' > *He asked **if** I was going with them.*
  'Do you want tea or coffee?' > *She asked me **whether** I wanted tea or coffee.*
- Wh- questions – use the *wh-* question word:
  'When is she leaving?' > *He wanted to know **when she was leaving**.*
- in questions with modals, only *can* and *may* change:
  *'**Can** you tell me the way?'* > *She asked if I **could** tell her the way.*
  *'**Could** you tell me the way?'* > *She asked if I **could** tell her the way.*
  *'**May** I interrupt for a moment?'* > *I asked if I **might** interrupt for a moment.*

C Reporting requests/commands

To report requests/commands we use the reporting verbs: *ask, tell*:
- verb + object + *to*-infinitive:
  'Come here, please!' > *He **asked me to go** there.*
- for negative requests/commands use *not* + *to*-infinitive:
  'Please don't speak so quickly.' > *He **told me not to speak** so quickly.*

D Reporting verbs

Some reporting verbs simply report the speaker's words (e.g. *say, tell, state, answer, reply*). Other reporting verbs tell us something about the speaker's intention. The choice of verb sometimes depends on how we interpret what the person was saying:
*He **persuaded** me that he wanted to give me something.*
This group of verbs includes:
admit, advise, claim, convince, feel, insist, persuade, suggest, think, urge, warn

E Verb patterns

1 Verb + *to*-infinitive:
agree/ask/offer/promise/refuse/threaten (+ **to see her**):
*He **refused to see** her.*

2 Verb + object + *to*-infinitive:
tell/advise/ask/invite/order/persuade/remind (+ **her to come**):
*I **told her to come**.* (NOT *I told to her to come.*)

3 Verb + *-ing*:
admit/deny/report (+ **being/having been there**)
*He **denied having been** there.*
suggest/recommend (+ **doing something**):
*They **suggested trying** the new Chinese restaurant.*

4 Verb + object + *that*:
tell/advise/convince/persuade/promise/remind + **me that** …
*They **told me that** I should come back later.*
(NOT *They told to me that* …)

5 Verb + object + preposition + *-ing*:
congratulate + **him on passing** the exam
accuse + **her of cheating**
blame + **us for breaking** it
discourage + **you from going** to the concert
Note also:
- *apologise **to** + object + **for** + -ing*:
  *I **apologised to her for being** late.*
- *insist **on** + -ing*:
  *We **insisted on seeing** the manager.*

6 Verb (+ preposition + object) + *that*:
say/admit/complain/explain/mention/suggest + **(to him) that** …
With these verbs the hearer is not the direct object:
*Ann **said (to him) that** she felt tired.*
(NOT *Ann said him that* …)

▶ pages 194–195 for verbs + *-ing* forms and infinitives.

16 Verbs + *-ing* forms and infinitives

*I haven't **finished reading** the newspaper.* (verb + *-ing*)
*I **hope to see** you soon.* (verb + *to*-infinitive)
*I saw him **leave**.* (verb + infinitive)

A Verbs followed by *-ing*:

admit, adore, appreciate, avoid, can't face, can't help, can't stand, can't resist, carry on, consider, delay, deny, detest, dislike, don't mind, enjoy, fancy, feel like, finish, give up, imagine, involve, keep (= continue), mention, mind, miss, postpone, practise, put off, resent, risk, suggest, understand

B Verbs followed by *to*-infinitive

afford, agree, aim, appear, arrange, ask, attempt, can't afford, can't wait, choose, claim, decide, demand, deserve, expect, fail, guarantee, happen, help, hope, learn, manage, mean, offer, plan, prefer, prepare, pretend, promise, refuse, seem, swear, tend, threaten, turn out, want, wish

Note: many verbs followed by *to*-infinitive express a concern for the future (e.g. *arrange, expect, hope, intend, plan*).

C Verbs followed by *-ing* OR *to*-infinitive

1 Verbs with a small or no change in meaning:
   - *begin, can't bear, bother, can't stand, continue, hate, intend, like, love, prefer, propose, start*:
     I **started watching/to watch** *television.* (no difference in meaning)
     Don't **bother washing/to wash** *the floor.*
   - *-ing* sometimes suggests a general statement (and acts like a noun) and the *to*-infinitive suggests a specific action in the future:
     I **prefer cycling** *to swimming.*
     (general activity NOT ~~I'd prefer to cycle to to swim~~)
     I **prefer to go** *by bike but you can walk.* (specific action)
     I'**d love to come** *to the cinema with you.* (specific activity after *would*)

2 Verbs with a change in meaning:
   forget, go on, mean, need, regret, remember, stop, try:
   - *I'll never* **forget seeing** *you looking so miserable.* (a past event)
     Don't **forget to post** *the letter!* (in the future)
   - I **remember locking** *the door.* (in the past)
     Please **remember to write** *to me.* (in the future)
   - *He* **went on talking** *and talking.* (continued)
     He **went on to ask** *me how old I was.* (changed the activity/subject)
   - *Being a good piano player* **means doing** *a lot of practice.* (involves)
     Did you **mean to leave** *the house unlocked?* (intend)
   - I **need to have** *a bath.* (I must – it's important)
     This room **needs painting**. (somebody needs to do it – passive meaning)
   - I **regret telling** *you my secrets.* (in the past)
     I **regret to have to tell** *you that I no longer love you.* (I'm telling you now)
   - **Stop worrying!** (no longer do something)
     She **stopped to talk** *to me.* (stopped and changed activity)
   - **Try changing** *the bulb.* (to see what happens – experiment)
     I **tried to phone** *you last night.* (made an effort)

D Verbs followed by infinitive

1 modal verb + infinitive
   I **might go** *to the meeting, but I* **can't stay** *long.*
   Note: the exception is *ought*:
   You **ought to tell** *him the truth.*

2 *make/let* + object + infinitive
   The teacher **made us do** *the exercise again.*
   My boss **let me go** *home early, because I wasn't feeling well.*
   Note: the passive form of this structure is:
   We **were made to** *do the exercise again.* (passive + *to*-infinitive)
   (▶ See also pages 190–191 for *make* and *let*.)

3 Certain expressions (e.g. *I'd rather, You'd better*) are followed by the infinitive (without *to*):
   I'**d better go** *now, or I'll be late.*

E Verbs followed by *-ing*/infinitive

Some verbs of the senses (e.g. *see, hear, feel*) can be followed by either *-ing* or an infinitive:
- I **heard** *her* **sing** *a lovely song.* (I heard the whole song)
  I **heard** *her* **singing** *a lovely song.* (I heard part of it)
- *He* **saw** *the book* **fall off** *the shelf. Then he picked it up.*
  He **saw** *the book* **falling off** *the shelf and caught it.*

17 *wish*

A Regret (present situation)

wish + past
(when we are sorry about a present situation and want it to be different):
I **wish** *we* **had** *a lot more money.* (but we haven't)
I **wish** *I* **was** *a bit slimmer.* (OR *I wish I* **were** … in formal style)
I **wish** *we* **weren't sitting** *in a classroom right now.*
I **wish** *I* **could** *swim.* (but I can't)

B Imaginary situations/events in the future

1 *wish* + *could*
   (when we wish for a change in the future that will probably not happen):
   I **wish** *I* **could** *see her.* (I want it to happen but it won't)
   Note: *hope* + present:
   I **hope** *I* **pass** *my driving test.* (this future event IS possible)

2 *wish* + other person/thing + *would*
   (often when we are annoyed with something):
   I **wish** *you* **would stop** *biting your nails.* (I want you to stop)
   I **wish** *it* **would** *stop raining.* (I want it to happen)

C Regret (past situation)

wish + past perfect
(when we are sorry about a past situation, but it is impossible to change it now):
I **wish** *I* **had worked** *harder at school.* (but I didn't work hard)
▶ pages 191–192 for Conditionals.

Writing reference

Contents

Introduction

This Writing reference is here to help you with your writing in preparation for Paper 2 of the FCE exam.

First, there is a checklist, which you should use every time you complete a piece of writing.

Then, for each type of writing that might come up in the exam, there is an example question (Question 1), a 'model answer' to that question, with notes to help you see the important points, and another exam question (Question 2).

If you are working on your own with this Writing reference, read Question 1 and the model answer carefully. Refer back to the pages in the main units for more information and help. Then answer Question 2, following the guidelines here and in the main units.

If you are working with a teacher, he/she will tell you when and how to use the Writing reference.

Writing checklist

Content and style

- Is your answer the right length? You will lose marks if it is under 120 words, and the examiner may not read more than 150 (Part 1) or 180 (Part 2) words.
- Have you answered all parts of the question? You will lose marks if you don't include all the required content points.
- Is your answer interesting to read?
- Have you communicated clearly?
- Is your style appropriate for the question (e.g. a formal or informal letter, a lively article)?
- Is your style consistent (e.g. no informal words in a formal letter)?
- Will your writing have the effect you want on your reader?

Organisation

- Have you divided your answer into paragraphs?
- Does each paragraph have ONE main idea, which is appropriate to what you are writing?
- Are the paragraphs in a logical order?
- Have you used linking expressions to connect ideas between paragraphs (e.g. *However, On the other hand*)?

Language

- Have you included a range of grammatical structures (e.g. in a story: past simple, past continuous, past perfect)?
- Is there a good range of vocabulary (e.g. in a story, adverbs to bring it to life: *He stopped suddenly, absolutely horrified.*)?
- Is your vocabulary specific, not general (e.g. *a hot, sunny day* not *a nice day, an enjoyable meal* not *a good meal*)?
- Have you used a range of appropriate linking expressions (e.g. *but, so, after, because* within a sentence, and *Finally, What's more,* to connect ideas in two sentences)?
- Have you used time expressions appropriately (e.g. *when, after, as soon as*)?
- Is your handwriting easy to read?
- Are your spelling and punctuation correct? You will not automatically lose marks for poor spelling, punctuation and handwriting, but it will affect the examiner's general impression mark.
- Have you checked for grammar mistakes, in particular the ones you know you often make?

Part 1: Email or letter

▶ See pages 42–43 for work on emails and letters.

Question 1

You want to visit the Paris Fashion Show and your pen friend Danielle, who lives in Paris, has agreed to put you up in her flat. Read the information about the show and the train timetable she has sent you. You need some more information. Using the notes below that you have made, write an email to Danielle.

PARIS FASHION SHOW

Spring collection

Saturday 4 May 09:30–18:30

London–Paris

FRIDAY
Depart London
14:00
16:00
18:00
Journey time approx. 3 hrs.

NOTES
Prefer last train Fri. – OK/too late?
Show – first time – what clothes to wear?
Weather/clothes?
Sun. – park? River cruise? Or...?

Write an **email** of between **120** and **150** words in an appropriate style.

Question 2

You would like to learn Russian and you see this advertisement in a newspaper. You would like to know more. Read the advertisement and the notes you have made. Write an email to the school asking for more information.

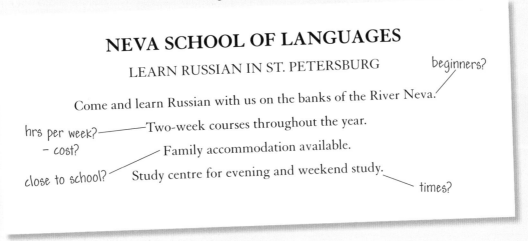

NEVA SCHOOL OF LANGUAGES

LEARN RUSSIAN IN ST. PETERSBURG   beginners?

Come and learn Russian with us on the banks of the River Neva.

hrs per week?——Two-week courses throughout the year.
 – cost?

Family accommodation available.

close to school?   Study centre for evening and weekend study.

times?

Write an **email** of between **120** and **150** words in an appropriate style.

Model answer (Question 1)

Set the context (mention something the other person has sent you, or give a reason for writing.)

Start a new paragraph for different subject matter.

Make sure the ending is in the same style.

Only include necessary information – but ALL the information necessary to answer the question. Don't repeat whole phrases from the input.

Keep the style consistent (informal).

Finish by referring to what will happen next.

New Message

To:

Cc:

Subject:

Dear Danielle,

Thanks for the information you sent me about the Fashion Show. It should be a great event.

I'm trying to decide which train to get. Personally, I'd prefer to get the last one from London but it doesn't get to Paris until about nine o'clock. Will that be OK, or is it too late for you?

I've never been to a fashion show before. What kind of clothes do you think I should wear? And what's the weather like at the moment? Will I need to bring some warm clothes?

By the way, what shall we do on Sunday? How about going for a walk in the park, or going on a river cruise? Or maybe you've got some other ideas.

Anyway, I can't wait! Looking forward to hearing from you. See you soon.

Love,

Ivana

(146 words)

Part 2: Informal letter or email

▶ See pages 14–15 for work on informal letters and emails.

Question 1

Last week, you organised a surprise birthday party for someone in your family, and your pen friend wants to hear about it. Write a letter to your pen friend, describing what kind of party you organised, who you invited and how it went.

Write your **letter**. Do not write any postal addresses. (Write your answer in **120–180** words in an appropriate style.)

Model answer

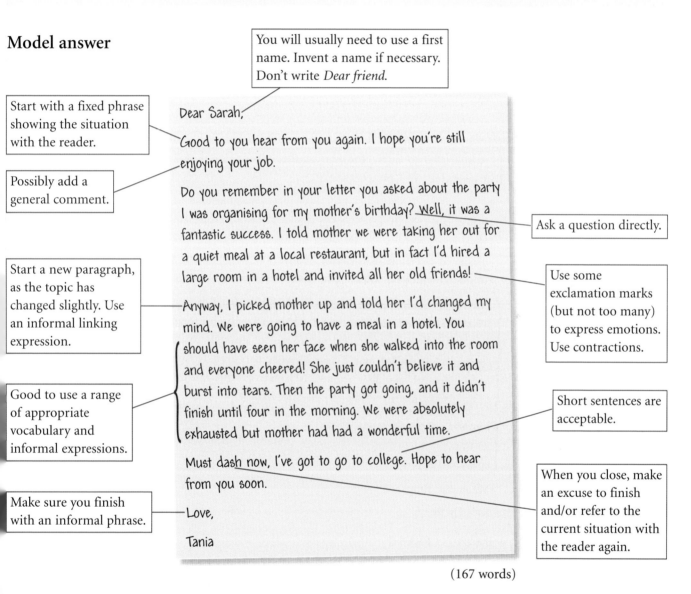

You will usually need to use a first name. Invent a name if necessary. Don't write *Dear friend*.

Start with a fixed phrase showing the situation with the reader.

Possibly add a general comment.

Start a new paragraph, as the topic has changed slightly. Use an informal linking expression.

Good to use a range of appropriate vocabulary and informal expressions.

Make sure you finish with an informal phrase.

Ask a question directly.

Use some exclamation marks (but not too many) to express emotions. Use contractions.

Short sentences are acceptable.

When you close, make an excuse to finish and/or refer to the current situation with the reader again.

Dear Sarah,

Good to you hear from you again. I hope you're still enjoying your job.

Do you remember in your letter you asked about the party I was organising for my mother's birthday? Well, it was a fantastic success. I told mother we were taking her out for a quiet meal at a local restaurant, but in fact I'd hired a large room in a hotel and invited all her old friends!

Anyway, I picked mother up and told her I'd changed my mind. We were going to have a meal in a hotel. You should have seen her face when she walked into the room and everyone cheered! She just couldn't believe it and burst into tears. Then the party got going, and it didn't finish until four in the morning. We were absolutely exhausted but mother had had a wonderful time.

Must dash now, I've got to go to college. Hope to hear from you soon.

Love,

Tania

(167 words)

Question 2

You have decided to go on holiday in the country where your English friend lives. Write aa email to your friend, explaining why you have not written for a while, and asking for advice on where to visit, what to see and the best way of travelling round the country.

Write your **email**. (Write your answer in **120–180** words in an appropriate style.)

Part 2: Formal letter

▶ See pages 28–29 for work on formal letters.

Question 1

You want to attend a course in English and American Studies in an English-speaking country and you see this section in a college prospectus:

> ## SCHOLARSHIPS
>
> Every year, two scholarships are offered to candidates from overseas who can show how our one-year course would help their career. Scholarships cover fees, accommodation and food, but not transport or personal spending money.
> Apply in writing, explaining why you think you deserve a scholarship.

Write your **letter**. Do not include any postal addresses. (Write your answer in **120–180** words in an appropriate style.)

Model answer

Say why you are writing and what you are responding to (e.g. an advert, a prospectus).

Use a formal, neutral style. (Remember: no contractions, no colloquial language, no direct questions, no informal punctuation such as exclamation marks.)

Be polite and positive, but not too much!

Use a formal ending.

Sign your name and then print your name clearly underneath.

Dear Sir/Madam,

I would like to apply for one of the scholarships I saw advertised in your prospectus.

At present I am training to be a secondary school teacher of English and I finish my course at the end of June. However, I feel I still have a lot to learn about the language and culture of the English-speaking world and would benefit considerably from a course in an English-speaking country.

The reason I am applying for a scholarship is that I cannot afford the cost of studying abroad. I have no income except for my student grant, so if I am fortunate enough to be given a scholarship, I would have to work part-time to save some personal spending money. My parents will borrow some money for my airfare if I am successful.

I would appreciate being given the opportunity to study at your college and would be very grateful if you would consider my application.

Yours faithfully,

Marco Prodi

MARCO PRODI

If you know the name of the person, begin *Dear Mr Smith/Dear Ms Jones*, etc.

In one paragraph, briefly describe you/your situation.

In the next paragraph, make it clear why you are applying for a scholarship and why you would be a suitable candidate. Make sure you cover all the points in the question.

If you have used the person's name, end *Yours sincerely,*

(162 words)

Question 2

You see this advertisement in an international newspaper. You are interested in applying for the job.

> ## WINTER IN THE ROCKIES?
>
> We are looking for young people to work in our ski shop this winter. If you are interested, write to us saying why you might be a good person. Reasonable salary, and we provide help with accommodation. Free ski pass included. Flexible hours. Apply in writing.

Write your **letter**. Do not include any postal addresses. (Write your answer in **120–180** words in an appropriate style.)

Part 2: Story

▶ See pages 56–57 for work on stories.

Question 1

You have decided to enter a short story competition in a student magazine. The story must **end** with these words:

'I'm very glad that's over!' said Katie as we made the long drive back home.

Write your **story**. (Write your answer in **120–180** words in an appropriate style.)

Model answer

If you have to invent an opening line, make sure it is dramatic enough to attract the readers' interest and stimulate their imagination.

Use adverbs to make the action more vivid.

You can create suspense and excitement by writing short sentences.

Remember to convey the feelings of the characters.

The city was deserted that night, as Katie and I wandered through the narrow streets. It had been raining earlier and the full moon shone brightly on the wet stones.

Suddenly we heard the sound of running footsteps. Then there was a cry and the footsteps stopped. Nervously, we walked back. Perhaps someone had been killed, or kidnapped in the street.

As we were turning the corner, we saw a crazy-looking man lying in the street, holding his ankle. He had obviously slipped on the wet stones and he was screaming at us to stay away.

To our relief, at that moment the police appeared. The man was in too much pain to move and they were easily able to force him into their car. They told us he was an extremely dangerous criminal and we had had a lucky escape. 'I'm very glad that's over!' said Katie as we made the long drive back home.

Create atmosphere when setting the scene. You might need to use the past continuous or past perfect continuous.

Make sure you make the sequence of actions clear.

Use vivid adjectives to bring what you are describing to life.

Use the words given in the question, without changing anything. Notice that direct speech can be used in a story for variety and interest.

(168 words)

Question 2

You have been invited to write a short story for a young person's magazine. The story must **begin** with these words:

Jack was asleep in the chair, dreaming, when the phone rang.

Write your **story**. (Write your answer in **120–180** words in an appropriate style.)

Part 2: Article

Question 1

You see this competition in an international magazine.

COMPETITION

Imagine you were on a desert island. What would you miss most?
Write an article briefly describing an important object, person or
place in your life and give reasons for your choice. The best article
will be published and the writer will receive £500.

Write your **article**. (Write your answer in **120–180** words in an appropriate style.)

Model answer

Introduce the topic.
Although you don't
know your readers
personally, you can
address them directly
and ask them a question.

Note the question
says the description
should be 'brief'.

Your style will not be
formal. This article
has a personal style;
others might have a
more neutral style.

Think of a title
that will catch the
reader's attention.

Give specific
examples to bring
your article to life.

Finish with a
sentence which
summarises what
you have said.

Life away from home

How would you feel about living on a desert island? I can't imagine anything worse. I would miss a lot of things, but most of all I would miss my home.

My home is a small house on the outskirts of a city. It was built about fifty years ago and has a small garden. In the summer our country gets very hot but our house is always cool.

You would probably think our house is nothing special, but I have lived there all my life and all my friends live nearby. It is a happy place, where I feel completely safe. Whenever I go away, I look forward to coming back, lying on my bed, reading a book and listening to my brother and sister arguing downstairs!

I love travelling and meeting new people, but if I were on a desert island I would be away from the place I love most – my home – and I would hate that.

(164 words)

Question 2

You see this advertisement in an international youth magazine.

Technology – how do you get on with it?

We are looking for short articles describing people's experiences –
good or bad – of technology. Write and tell us how you have used
technology and whether you have got on well with it.
We will publish the best articles in this magazine.

Write your **article**. (Write your answer in **120–180** words in an appropriate style.)

Part 2: Essay

▶ See pages 112–113 for work on essays.

Question 1

You have recently had a class project on animal welfare and vegetarianism. Now your teacher has asked you to write an essay, giving your opinions on the following statement.

Some people believe that humans should not eat meat. Do you agree?

Write your **essay**. (Write your answer in **120–180** words in an appropriate style.)

Model answer

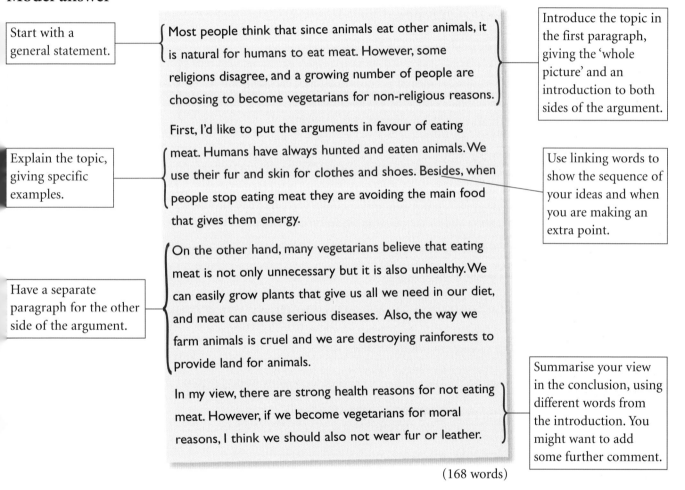

Start with a general statement.

Most people think that since animals eat other animals, it is natural for humans to eat meat. However, some religions disagree, and a growing number of people are choosing to become vegetarians for non-religious reasons.

Introduce the topic in the first paragraph, giving the 'whole picture' and an introduction to both sides of the argument.

Explain the topic, giving specific examples.

First, I'd like to put the arguments in favour of eating meat. Humans have always hunted and eaten animals. We use their fur and skin for clothes and shoes. Besides, when people stop eating meat they are avoiding the main food that gives them energy.

Use linking words to show the sequence of your ideas and when you are making an extra point.

Have a separate paragraph for the other side of the argument.

On the other hand, many vegetarians believe that eating meat is not only unnecessary but it is also unhealthy. We can easily grow plants that give us all we need in our diet, and meat can cause serious diseases. Also, the way we farm animals is cruel and we are destroying rainforests to provide land for animals.

In my view, there are strong health reasons for not eating meat. However, if we become vegetarians for moral reasons, I think we should also not wear fur or leather.

Summarise your view in the conclusion, using different words from the introduction. You might want to add some further comment.

(168 words)

Question 2

You recently had a class discussion about television. Now your teacher has asked you to write an essay.

Young children watch too much television. Do you agree?

Write your **essay**. (Write your answer in **120–180** words in an appropriate style.)

Part 2: Report

▶ See pages 140–141 for work on reports.

Question 1

Your college has been asked to accept a group of 50 students from another country for two weeks. You have been asked by your principal to find out what the advantages and disadvantages would be of accepting this group. Is it a good idea?

Write your **report** to the principal. (Write your answer in **120–180** words in an appropriate style.)

Model answer

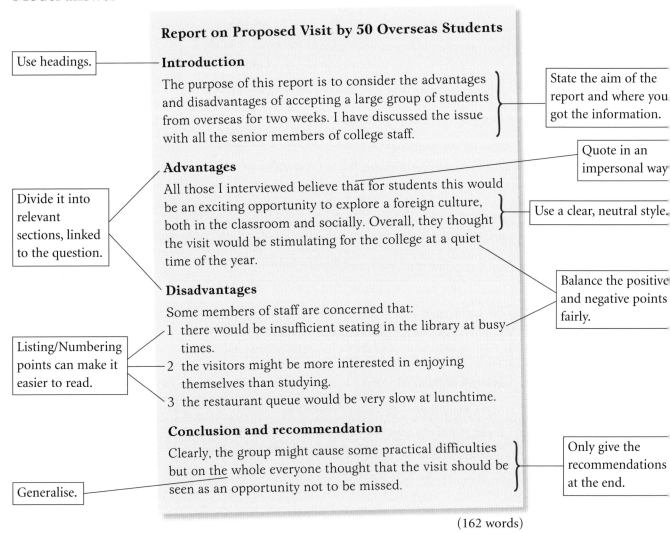

Report on Proposed Visit by 50 Overseas Students

Use headings.

Introduction

The purpose of this report is to consider the advantages and disadvantages of accepting a large group of students from overseas for two weeks. I have discussed the issue with all the senior members of college staff.

State the aim of the report and where you got the information.

Advantages

Divide it into relevant sections, linked to the question.

All those I interviewed believe that for students this would be an exciting opportunity to explore a foreign culture, both in the classroom and socially. Overall, they thought the visit would be stimulating for the college at a quiet time of the year.

Quote in an impersonal way

Use a clear, neutral style.

Disadvantages

Some members of staff are concerned that:

Listing/Numbering points can make it easier to read.

1 there would be insufficient seating in the library at busy times.
2 the visitors might be more interested in enjoying themselves than studying.
3 the restaurant queue would be very slow at lunchtime.

Balance the positive and negative points fairly.

Conclusion and recommendation

Clearly, the group might cause some practical difficulties but on the whole everyone thought that the visit should be seen as an opportunity not to be missed.

Generalise.

Only give the recommendations at the end.

(162 words)

Question 2

You work for a travel agent in an English-speaking country. You have been asked to write a report for your boss, recommending the best time of year to arrange leisure tours to your country. You have been asked to comment on such things as the weather, special attractions and festivities.

Write your **report**. (Write your answer in **120–180** words in an appropriate style.)

Part 2: Review

▶ See pages 84–85 for work on reviews.

Question 1

You recently saw this notice in an English-language magazine.

Reviews needed!
We are hoping to add a travel section to our college magazine, designed by the students. We would like you to write a review about a town or a city anywhere in the world that you have recently visited. The best review will win a mini-break in London! Describe the place you visited, and say why you liked it.

Write your **review**. (Write your answer in **120–180** words in an appropriate style.)

Model answer

Say what you are reviewing and try to catch the readers' interest.

Give a few details of what you are reviewing linked to the question but only focus on those that you think are most important.

Give your opinion of what you are reviewing linked to the question. Remember a review is not just a list of facts – it's largely your opinion.

Summarise your view, using different words from the introduction, and include a recommendation.

Seville, a wonderful city!

What a place! I recently spent a long weekend in Seville in the south of Spain. It was the best mini-break I've ever had!

The best thing about Seville is that it's compact so many of its main tourist attractions are close to the city centre. I headed straight to the world-famous cathedral and then on to one of the many art galleries. I discovered so many famous monuments and museums as I walked around in the glorious sunshine.

I loved Seville because it was very relaxing and there was plenty to do for free. When I was hungry I had a choice from hundreds of cafés or restaurants, all at good prices, serving delicious Spanish food. On my second evening there, I went to a fantastic flamenco dancing show.

So, with all its attractions I recommend that you go to Seville! In the end, it's the people who make a place, and the locals certainly made me feel welcome!

(161 words)

Question 2

You recently saw this notice in an English-language magazine.

Reviews needed!
We are hoping to create new section in our newspaper about dining out. To help give us some ideas for this, can you write a review of a restaurant you have visited recently? Describe the type of restaurant and the food you tried, and say if you would recommend it to others.

Write your **review**. (Write your answer in **120–180** words in an appropriate style.)

Part 2: Essay (set book)

▶ See pages 168–169 for work on set book essays.

Question 1

Animal Farm by George Orwell

Which is the most memorable character in *Animal Farm* Write an essay for your teacher describing what part the character plays in the story, and why the character is so memorable. Give reasons for your choice.

Write your **essay**. (Write your answer in **120–180** words in an appropriate style.)

Model answer

One of the central characters in Animal Farm is Napoleon. After the animals on Mr Jones' farm revolt against their masters, the pigs become their leaders and Napoleon is their chief.

> In the question, you are asked to describe the character's part in the story.

At first, Napoleon seems to be a good leader of the revolution. He and Snowball (another pig) organise the animals and introduce them to the Seven Commandments, which aim to make everyone equal. However, we see that Napoleon might be dishonest when he tells the other animals there are more important things to worry about than milk, and then the milk disappears. I think he takes it for himself.

> Give specific examples.

Napoleon and Snowball argue a lot and eventually Napoleon gets the dogs to drive Snowball off the farm. One by one the commandments are broken, and Napoleon becomes a cruel dictator. He kills many of the animals for plotting against him and he even hires a pig to taste his food in case someone tries to poison him.

> Show the character at a different stage of the novel and link your answer to the question.

I believe Napoleon is memorable because he is a very good example of how easily power corrupts.

> Summarise your opinion in a simple conclusion.

(176 words)

Question 2

Wuthering Heights by Emile Brontë

Which do you think is the most dramatic scene in *Wuthering Heights*? Write an essay for your teacher briefly describing the scene you have chosen, and how it fits in with the rest of the story. Give your reasons.

Write your **essay**. (Write your answer in **120–180** words in an appropriate style.)

Punctuation

Name		Uses	Examples
Apostrophe	'	To show someone owns something.	*Tom's car*
		To indicate a contraction.	*He isn't here.*
Capital letter	B	To begin sentences, for the pronoun *I*, names, countries, cities, days of the week and months (not seasons) of the year.	*Graham and **I** play tennis on **S**aturdays in **J**une.*
Colon	:	To introduce a list.	*There are three possibilities: first we could …*
		In formal writing, before a phrase that gives more information about the main clause.	*The house was small: it had a kitchen and one bedroom.*
Comma	,	To divide a sentence into sections to make it easier to understand:	
		Before and after a non-defining relative clause.	*Another man, who looked a lot younger, was drinking coffee.*
		To separate items in a list.	*The man was wearing black trousers, a white shirt and a blue tie.*
		To separate a tag question from the sentence.	*It's hot, isn't it?*
		To separate an introductory word or phrase from the rest of the sentence.	*By the way, how are you?*
		Before or after 'he said' (when writing conversation).	*'I'm tired,' she said.*
Dash	–	To separate a statement that is extra to the main idea.	*I love pasta – particularly spaghetti – and other Italian food.*
Exclamation mark	!	To express emotional emphasis in informal writing.	*What a lovely day!*
Full stop/point/ period	.	To show the end of a sentence.	*That's very clear.*
		In abbreviations.	*e.g. etc.*
Question mark	?	At the end of a direct question.	*Are you tired?*
Semi-colon	;	To separate two main clauses that have a link in meaning.	*It was late; it was getting dark.*
Speech marks (quotation marks/inverted commas)	"…" '…'	When we write down the exact words someone says. (They can be double or single.)	*"I'll help you," she said.* *'I'll help you,' she said.*

ing

1 Words ending in one -e

- Remove e before -ing:
  love ▶ loving
  (but **not** words with -ee: agree ▶ agreeing)
- Keep e before -ly:
  fortunate ▶ fortunately
  (but **not** -le adjectives: probable ▶ probably)
- Keep e before -ment:
  advertise ▶ advertisement

2 Verbs ending in -ie

Change -ie to -y:
lie ▶ lying

3 Words ending in consonant + -y

Change -y to -ie:
try ▶ tries, tried
baby ▶ babies
happy ▶ happier, happiest

4 Words ending in vowel +-y

Keep y:
play ▶ plays, played.
But note:
day ▶ daily
lay ▶ laid; say ▶ said; pay ▶ paid

5 Words ending in -c before -ed/-ing

Change -c to -ck before -ed/-ing:
picnic ▶ picnicking
panic ▶ panicked

6 Words ending in one consonant

Double the final consonant before -ing, -ed, -er, -est for:

- one-syllable words with 1 vowel + 1 consonant:
  stop ▶ stopping, stopped
  hot ▶ hotter, hottest
- two- or three-syllable words with the final syllable stressed:
  be'gin ▶ be'ginning

Do not double the final consonant of:

- words with 2 vowels before the final consonant:
  rain ▶ raining
  look ▶ looked
  cheap ▶ cheaper
- words with 2 final consonants:
  start ▶ started
  rich ▶ richer

- two- or three-syllable words with the final syllable **not** stressed:
  ' enter ▶' entering
  But note in British English: double final -l after one vowel:
  ' travel ▶' travelling
- words ending in -y or -w:
  stay ▶ stayed
  slow ▶ slower

7 Nouns ending in -o

Add -es in the plural:
potato ▶ potatoes
tomato ▶ tomatoes

8 Nouns ending in -our

Remove u in the adjective:
humour ▶ humorous

9 Endings often misspelt:

- Adjectives (see also Unit 4):
  -ible/-able: sensible, responsible; comfortable, suitable
  -ful: beautiful, hopeful
  -ent: independent, convenient, excellent
  -ous: anxious, conscious, delicious, famous, various
- Nouns (see also Unit 10):
  -al/-le: arrival, refusal, principal / principle
  -er/-or: actor, operator, visitor but driver, employer, writer
  -ent/-ant: excitement, employment but assistant, servant
  -ness: happiness, weakness
- Verbs (see also Unit 18):
  -ise/-ize: surprise, exercise
  British English usually: realise, modernise, recognise
  American English: realize, modernize, recognize

10 Some useful rules

- -ise (verb)/-ice (noun):
  advise/advice, practise/practice
- i before e except after c:
  niece/relieve; deceive/ceiling
  (Exception: foreign)

Some commonly misspelt words:

accommodation address affect (v.)/effect (n.) bicycle
business busy committee disappoint embarrass
Europe familiar guilty heard heart immediate
juice loose /luːs/ (adj.)/lose /luːz/(v.) medicine
necessary pronunciation recommend separate
similar until

Module 3B: Speaking
(Paper 5 Part 2) (p.45)

Individual long turn: Exercise 9

STUDENT B:

Module 3B: Use of English 1 (p.47)
Answer key: Lead-in: Exercise 1a

1 True. (Although cats distinguish some colours better than others, they don't generally distinguish colours very well.)
2 True. (It is estimated to be anywhere between 100 and a million times better.)
3 True. (They have a very large brain and live for a long time. They particularly remember extremes of kindness and cruelty on the part of humans.)
4 True. (The snowy tree cricket (*Oecanthus fultoni*) is popularly known as the 'thermometer cricket' because the approximate temperature (Fahrenheit) can be estimated by counting the number of chirps in 15 seconds and adding 40.)
5 True. (It is believed they sense changes of air pressure in their digestive system.)

Module 4B: Speaking
(Paper 5 Part 3) (p.59)

Collaborative task: Exercise 6

STUDENT 1: **You are the examiner. Read the instructions below to Candidates A and B. Stop the discussion after three minutes.**

Instructions:
Now, I'd like you to talk about something together for about three minutes. I'm just going to listen. Here are some pictures which show people doing different sports. (*Point to the photos on pages 58–59.*)
First, talk to each other about the advantages and disadvantages of taking up each of these sports. Then decide which one is most suitable for someone who doesn't have much spare time.
You have only about three minutes for this, so don't worry if I stop you. Please speak so that we can hear you. All right?

Module 6B: Speaking

(Paper 5 Part 2) (p.87)

Individual long turn: Exercise 8a, Task 2

STUDENT B: Compare and contrast the photographs, and say why you think people enjoy concerts like this.

STUDENT A: Listen to student B without interrupting. Stop him/her after one minute, and say briefly which concert you would prefer to go to.

Module 7B: Speaking

(Paper 5 Part 3) (p.101)

Collaborative task: Exercise 5a

STUDENT 1: You are the examiner. Read the instructions below to students 2 and 3. Stop the discussion after three minutes.

Instructions:
Now, I'd like you to talk about something together for about three minutes. I'm just going to listen.
Here are some pictures which show different styles of clothes. (*Point to the pictures on page 101.*)
First, talk to each other about which of the clothes you would wear and which you would not wear. Then decide which would be best to wear at a friend's birthday party. You have only about three minutes for this, so don't worry if I stop you. Please speak so that we can hear you. All right?

Module 8B: Speaking

(Paper 5 Part 1) (p.114)

Vocabulary: Exercise 1

Russell Crowe knits; Kylie Minogue plays Scrabble; Jodie Kidd does archery, George Foreman keeps pigeons; Geena Davis goes car racing; Clint Eastwood plays jazz piano.

Module 9B: Speaking

(Paper 5 Part 2) (p.129)

Individual long turn: Exercise 7a, Task 1

STUDENT 1: You are the examiner. Read out the instructions below to Candidates A and B and point to the photos on page 129 (Module 9A, Speaking). Stop Candidate A after one minute.

Instructions:

To Candidate A: [Name], here are your two photographs. They show two different ways of shopping. *(Point to the photos on page 129.)* I'd like you to compare and contrast these photographs, saying which you think is a better way to shop. You only have about a minute for this, so don't worry if I interrupt you. All right? *(Stop Candidate A after one minute.)*

To Candidate B: [Name], which way do you prefer to shop?

Module 10B: Speaking

(Paper 5 Part 2) (p.143)

Individual long turn: Exercise 5b, Task 2

STUDENT 2: You are the examiner. Read out the instructions below to Candidates A and B and point to the photos on page 212. Stop Candidate A after one minute.

Instructions:

To Candidates A and B: I'm going to give each of you two different photographs and I'd like you to talk about them.
To Candidate A: [Name], here are your two photographs. They show two different types of dancing. *(Point to the two photos on page 212.)* I'd like you to compare and contrast these photographs, and say which one you think is more popular. You only have about a minute for this, so don't worry if I interrupt you. All right? *(Stop Candidate A after one minute.)*

To Candidate B: [Name], do you like dancing?

Module 10B: Speaking

(Paper 5 Part 2) (p.143)

Individual long turn: Exercise 5a, Task 1

STUDENT 1: You are the examiner. Read out the instructions below to Candidates A and B and point to the photos on page 143 (Module 10A, Speaking). Stop Candidate A after one minute.

Instructions:

To Candidates A and B: I'm going to give each of you two different photographs and I'd like you to talk about them. *To Candidate A:* [Name], here are your two photographs. They show two different ways of spending an evening. *(Point to the photos on page 143.)* I'd like you to compare and contrast these photographs, and say which people you think are enjoying themselves more. You only have about a minute for this, so don't worry if I interrupt you. All right? *(Stop Candidate A after one minute.)*
To Candidate B: [Name], what kind of films do you like watching?

Module 9B: Speaking

(Paper 5 Part 2) (p.129)

Individual long turn: Exercise 7b, Task 2

STUDENT 2: You are the examiner. Read out the instructions below to Candidates A and B and point to the photos on page 211. Stop Candidate A after one minute.

Instructions:

To Candidate A: [Name], here are your two photographs. They show different places to buy food. *(Point to the two photos on page 211.)* I'd like you to compare and contrast these photographs, saying which you think is a better place to buy food. You only have about a minute for this, so don't worry if I interrupt you. All right? *(Stop Candidate A after one minute.)*
To Candidate B: [Name], do you like shopping for food?

Module 12B: Speaking
(Paper 5 Part 2) (p.171)
Individual long turn: Exercise 5b

Module 12B: Speaking
(Paper 5 Part 3) (p.171)
Collaborative task: Exercise 6b

Module 11B: Speaking

(Paper 5 Part 3) (p.158)

Collaborative task: Exercise 2

STUDENT 1: **You are the examiner. Read out the instructions below to Candidates A and B and point to the pictures on page 157 (Module 11B, Listening). Stop the discussion after three minutes.**

Instructions:

Now, I'd like you to talk about something together for about three minutes. I'm just going to listen.

Here are some pictures which show ways of keeping healthy. *(Point to the pictures on page 157.)* First, talk to each other about how each of these things can help. Then decide which you would recommend to somebody who wanted to get healthy quickly.

You have only about three minutes for this, so don't worry if I stop you. Please speak so that we can hear you. All right?

Module 12B: Speaking

(Paper 5 Part 1) (p.171)

Interview: Exercise 4

Home town

Where are you from?

How long have you lived there?

What do you like about living there?

Family and home

Could you tell us something about your family?

And what about your home? What's it like?

Work/Education

Do you work or study?

(if working):

What does your work involve?

What do you enjoy most about your job?

(if studying):

What are you studying at the moment?

Why did you decide to study *(candidate's subject)*?

What sort of job are you hoping to do in the future?

Free time/Leisure

What do you like doing in your free time?

What do you enjoy most about *(what candidate does in his/her free time)*?

Likes and dislikes

Music

What sort of music do you like?

Do you like going to concerts or listening to music at home? Why?

Films

How often do you go to the cinema?

What sort of films do you enjoy?

Sport

Are there any sports you enjoy doing? *(if yes):* What do you like about it/them?

What sports do you enjoy watching on television?

Functions reference

1 Adding information

Yes, and as well as that … .
Apart from that … .
Not only that … .
And there's another thing … .
I hadn't thought of that. We could also … .

2 Agreeing and disagreeing

Yes, that's true.
So do I.
Neither do I.
I couldn't agree more.
I suppose so.
I agree up to a point, but … .
Yes, but (what about) … ?
Do you think so?
But don't you think that … ?
Actually, I think it's more important … .

3 Checking you understand

I'm not quite sure what we have to do first.
So you want me to … ?
Sorry, do you mean we have to … ?

4 Comparing and contrasting

They both show … .
They both seem to be … .
Both of … are … .
Both of these people look as if … .
There are … in both photos.
In this one … and this one … .
Neither of them … .
The one on the right shows … while/whereas in the
other one there's … .
One thing which is different (in this one) is … .
The main difference is that the top one seems to be …
while the bottom one … .
The main difference between … and … is … .
This one is … whereas … is … .

5 Correcting yourself

What I meant was … .
Sorry, I meant to say … .
I mean … .

6 Expressing advantages and disadvantages

The good thing about … is … . On the other hand … .
One disadvantage about … is … . Having said that, … .

7 Expressing likes, dislikes and preferences

I would like … but … .
I wouldn't mind … but on the other hand … .
Although … I'd like … because … .
I think I'd prefer … as … .
I'm not really very interested in … .
If I had to choose … .
I prefer … .
I think I would say … .
To be honest, I haven't thought much about it.

8 Expressing opinions

I think … .
For me, one of the most important … is … .
I don't think it matters … .
I just don't think it's … .
Personally, I … .
It's very hard to say, but … .

9 Giving and asking for suggestions

Why don't we start by … ?
Shall we … first?
Let's begin with … .
We could start by talking about … .
Let's decide which … .
Shall we make a decision?
Do you agree?
What would you say?
Do you think we should … ?

10 Interrupting

Can I just say … ?
Sorry to interrupt, but … .

11 Paraphrasing

It's something you need when … .
It's when you … .
You use it to … .
It's like a … .
It's a … where/that/who … you (+ verb).
It's a kind of … .

12 Speculating

It could be/could have been … .
It can't be/can't have been … .
It might be/might have been … .
It must have/must have had … .
I get the impression that … .

Exam Practice: Reading (Paper 1)

Part 1

You are going to read a magazine article about the author Dick Francis. For Questions **1–8**, choose the correct answer **A, B, C** or **D**.

STRAIGHT FROM THE HORSE'S MOUTH

Dick Francis, the novelist, has written over 40 thrillers based on the world of horse racing.

Dick Francis has written his last book. Actually, he's said that four times before, but every time he decides to stop writing, he meets someone interesting or something unusual happens to him, and he gets the idea for a story which he feels he really must write. This must delight his publishers, for whom he has been turning out best-selling novels at the rate of one a year for the last 40 years. But now, at the age of 80, he may actually mean it about not writing any more. Until something else fires his imagination, of course!

It is hard to see what else Francis could aim for apart from a pleasant retirement. Since 1991, he has lived in the Cayman Islands with his wife, Mary. Both have medical conditions which get worse in the cold, damp weather of their native Britain, so for five months a year Francis works at his desk overlooking the sea. He writes by hand, only transferring his novel to the computer once it is complete. The other seven months, he takes holidays and does research for his books.

Francis' first career was in horse racing, where he trained as a jockey. He rode 74 winning horses and became national champion before being persuaded to take early retirement after suffering a number of terrible injuries. It was at this point that he wrote his first book – his autobiography. But another 16 years, during which he worked as a racing writer for a national newspaper, passed before he attempted another. His first novel was published in 1962 to great acclaim, after which he never looked back. Although his novels, mostly thrillers based on the world of horse racing, are unfairly looked down on by some educated readers of literature, all sorts of people around the world buy and enjoy them in their millions. Francis provides thrilling stories in which criminals drink champagne while the hero battles against all odds to bring them to justice. Good always wins, although you never know how it will happen until the last couple of pages.

However, Francis' achievements were once called into question recently when a rather critical biography suggested that his books were partly the work of his highly intelligent wife, Mary. Francis denies this, but it is undoubtedly true that once he has **come up with** the idea for a book, researching *line* the locations and details of a new story is something they do together as a team. To help him in **this**, Mary, *line* amongst other things, qualified as a pilot and learned photography.

So why does he find it so difficult to give up writing? Up to a point, it's helped to make up for having to give up his first career. The loss of his old life left a huge hole which has never, despite the fame and the great wealth, quite been filled. 'I started writing stories about it, which helped to compensate,' he concludes. But one doesn't feel that he's been so dissatisfied with the result. 40 years of compensation, after all, is not so bad.

1 What do we learn about Dick Francis in the first paragraph?
   A He denies that his writing career is over.
   B Not all of his books have been equally successful.
   C His books are partly based on his own experiences.
   D His publishers have asked him to write another book.

2 Why does Dick Francis choose to live in the Cayman Islands?
   A It's a good place to do his research.
   B Most of his novels are based there.
   C His wife comes from that area.
   D The climate is good for his health.

3 Why did Dick Francis give up horse racing?
   A He was offered a job working for a newspaper.
   B He was advised to do so for medical reasons.
   C He wanted to concentrate on writing a book.
   D He had reached the retirement age for jockeys.

4 What do we learn about Dick Francis' novels in the fourth paragraph?
   A They have won literary prizes.
   B They do not all have happy endings.
   C They appeal to a wide range of people.
   D They deal with all sorts of different subjects.

5 What do we learn about Francis' wife?
   A She has co-written some of his books.
   B She takes the photos for his books.
   C She works out the plots for the books.
   D She assists with the preparation of the books.

6 What does *come up with* (line 39) mean?
   A He's suggested something.
   B He's agreed to something.
   C He's invented something.
   D He's accepted something.

7 What does the word *this* in line 41 refer to?
   A doing the research
   B qualifying as a pilot
   C being a photographer
   D having a good idea

8 What impression of Dick Francis' life do we get from the last paragraph?
   A He is happier now than he's ever been.
   B He wishes that he had started writing earlier.
   C Horse racing was the thing he always loved best.
   D He has no regrets about changing career.

Turn Over ➤

Part 2

You are going to read a newspaper article about exploring the oceans. Seven sentences have been removed from the article. Choose from sentences **A–H** the one which fits each gap (**9–15**). There is one extra sentence which you do not need to use.

Filming the mysteries of the deep

More people have travelled into space than have dared venture into the deep ocean. The oceans cover 70 per cent of our planet. However, 60 per cent of their area is more than 1,000 metres below the surface, a depth at which very little has been explored. Below 200 metres there is a strange and gloomy world where very little life survives. **9** [ ] This vast black world is a desert, a bottomless hole. We know almost nothing about it.

Alistair Fothergill has just been down there to make *The Blue Planet*. This natural history documentary cost more, and took longer to make, than any other television series before it. **10** [ ] What is more, at least ten of these strange, wonderful and sometimes horrific groups of creatures were completely new to science.

Among the fish filmed for the first time was the Deep Sea Angler, which illuminates itself by bacteria in its body, and the Fangtooth, which has teeth so large that it can never close its mouth. Their most exciting discovery, however, was one which had never been heard of before, which they called the Hairy Angler fish. **11** [ ] And with its huge mouth, full of sharp teeth, it is therefore able to kill passing fish – even those far larger than itself – and put them into its expandable stomach. In the deep ocean, where there is very little food, it's important to eat whatever is available.

While Fothergill went to a depth of 'only 1,000 metres' to film these creatures, some specially trained members of his team descended a further 3,000 to visit the so-called 'black smokers' in the middle of the ocean. **12** [ ]

Until about 20 years ago, when these areas were found, all life on our planet was thought to be dependent on the sun's energy. The discovery of the smokers disproved that theory. 'We now realise that even right down at the very bottom of the deep ocean there are extraordinary pockets of life.' explains Fothergill. 'The energy comes from bacteria, that feed on salt from a rock. **13** [ ] The most amazing of these creatures are the tube worms, which are about two metres long, as thick as your arm, with bright red feathers. They have no stomach or mouth, but are completely packed full of bacteria.'

14 [ ] 'But we'll be back,' he insists. 'The deepest point in the ocean, at more than 12,000 metres, is the Marianas Trench in the Pacific. There is still so much to discover down there in the depths of the sea. The giant squid, for instance, is the size of a London bus, and has never been seen alive.' What he would find even more thrilling, however, would be to discover the secrets of an even larger ocean creature.

15 [ ] He explains that scientists are studying a big population which goes up and down the coast of California at an incredible speed of over 30 kilometres an hour, and then disappears under the surface for long periods at a time. However, American biologists have finally succeeded in attaching satellite tags to a few individuals. 'We're now getting some exciting information back to suggest that they're heading for a place off Costa Rica,' says Fothergill. 'That's where I want to go looking for them.'

A The features from which it gets its name are actually sensors that can detect the slightest vibration made by other marine life nearby.

B These are openings created when water flows through cracks in the sea bed, hits very hot volcanic rock and comes shooting out again.

C Fothergill's most passionate ambition is to discover where the blue whale goes to have its young.

D These tiny life forms, in turn, provide food for a whole range of 'new' animals.

E At 1,000 metres there is permanent darkness, where the only light is created by the animals that live there.

F Excited by these discoveries, Fothergill would have sent a camera down even further, but this proved impossible.

G For a long time scientists thought they must be a completely different species of fish.

H And in filming natural history, he made real history too, because his team found 50 species that had never been filmed before.

Turn Over ➤

Part 3

You are going to read an article about five young people who have each made a lot
of money by setting up a business. For Questions 16–30 choose from the people
(A–E). The people may be chosen more than once. When more than one answer is
required, these may be given in any order.

Which young person:

found one part of the work hard at the beginning?	16
says that he/she prefers to be his/her own boss?	17
is careful with money?	18 19
got financial help from an organisation?	20
says he/she does the work mostly for the money?	21 22
feels that further education would be a waste of time?	23
ignored advice that he/she was given?	24
says he/she finds the work itself the main motivation?	25
has turned an initial disappointment to his/her advantage?	26 27
says he/she enjoys the creative side of the business most?	28
is willing to give up aspects of his/her social life for the business?	29
has received a prize in recognition of what he/she has achieved?	30

How to get rich young

*We asked five young people who have already made their fortunes in business
to tell us the secret of their success.*

A Justin Etzin (29)

It all began when Justin, then aged 16, tried to get into a nightclub and was turned away for being too young. 'After that, I kept on at them until they let me organise an under-20s party,' he recalls. 'They were expecting about 50 teenagers to turn up, but I'd found them 2000!' Justin continued organising parties during his school holidays and had made enough money by the age of 18 to buy himself a speedboat. Today, at 24, he has other business interests and a fortune of £2 million. But Justin's not just in it for the financial rewards. 'What gets me excited is coming up with new ideas,' he insists, 'and at the end of the day, I'd rather be healthy than wealthy.'

B Lee Allen (25)

Lee set up a sports-coaching business when he was just 18. 'Everyone warned me that it was a tough world and I wasn't experienced enough to take the disappointments that lay ahead. But I felt confident in what I was doing, so I took no notice of them. My idea was to coach children with special needs and because nobody else was doing that, I got a grant and an office from Mencap, a charity which helps the mentally disabled. At first, the administrative side was a real struggle, but I managed it somehow. Last year, the company I set up won an award for being the most innovative new business in the country. That means more to me than any money I've made out of it.'

C Charlotte Crossley (23)

Charlotte first started up in business when she was 12 years old, making and selling things called 'friendship bracelets.' She paid friends to make them, using her materials and designs. Since then, she's expanded into make-up and hair accessories and was able to buy herself a brand new car last year. 'My father and grandfather were both successful businessmen, so making money seemed natural to me. I am studying for A levels, but I have decided not to go to university because I don't feel it has anything more to offer me. Work excites me more. I can work all day every day without a break and never get bored. I lead a hectic life – socialising, schoolwork and working. But why not? I feel like I can have it all.'

D Thomas Jones (21)

Tom started playing with computers when he was five. By the time he was 12, he'd set up his own web page on the Internet and was selling advertising space. He now runs a profitable business from his bedroom at home, offering a complete Internet and technical support service. 'I have always been fascinated by computers. I'm proud of what I've achieved. But what really keeps me going is the thought of all the cash I'm making. I think it's worth giving up a few nights out in case there aren't the same opportunities later. Our projected turnover for next year is £160,000, so the business is a huge investment.' Apart from buying himself a few treats, Tom mainly reinvests his money. 'But I still intend to go to university, no matter how much I make, because in any business you need to keep up with new developments.'

E Louise Bagshawe (30)

Things haven't always gone well for Louise. After she'd written her first book at the age of 23, a publisher took one look at it and advised her to tear it up and start again. 'I was so upset by their reaction,' said Louise. 'that I bought a pile of very successful novels and read them from cover to cover to remind myself of my business aim. This was to write 'popular' books that would earn me a fortune by working for myself, rather than earning peanuts working for someone else.' The rewritten novel became the first of four 'blockbusters' which have made Louise a millionaire. However, she does not splash her money around. 'I'm saving up for a rainy day. Who knows what will happen in the future.'

Exam Practice: Speaking (Paper 5)

Part 1 The Interview

(This part takes about three minutes in the exam.)

In pairs, take it turn to answer these questions.

- How long have you been studying English?
- Do you work or are you a full-time student? Where do you work/study?
- What are/were your best worst subjects at school?
- What would you like to do in the future?

Part 2 The individual long turn

(This part takes about four minutes if there are two candidates in the exam.)

In pairs, look at the pictures 1 and 2 on page 223.

They show different people practising a hobby.

| Student A | Compare and contrast these pictures and say which hobby would be more difficult to learn. |
| Student B | Which of these hobbies do you prefer? |

In pairs, look at the pictures 3 and 4 on page 223. They show different types of holiday.

| Student B | Compare and contrast these pictures and say what are the good and bad points of each type of holiday. |
| Student A | Which of these holidays would you prefer to go on? |

Part 3 The two-way collaborative task

(This part takes about three minutes in the exam.)

In pairs, look at the pictures on page 224 and do the task below together. For each of these pictures, say which of the crimes are the most and least serious.

Part 4 The three-way discussion

(This part takes about four minutes in the exam.)

- Are you annoyed or bothered by any of the issues you talked about in Part 3?
- What do you think is a suitable punishment for these crimes?
- What is the punishment for this in your country?
- Are any of the issues you discussed a problem in your country?

Which hobby would be more difficult to learn?

What are the good and bad points of each type of holiday?